TIME, ROLES, AND SELF IN OLD AGE

Gerontology Series

Research Planning and Action for the Elderly
D.P. Kent, Ph.D., et al

Retirement
F.M. Carp, Ph.D.

Sound Sex and the Aging Heart
L.D. Scheingold, M.A. and N. Wagner, Ph.D.

Time, Roles, and Self in Old Age
J.F. Gubrium, Ph.D.

A Guide to Long-Term Care Facilities
E. Brody, M.S.W.

Toward a Theology of Aging
S. Hiltner, Th.D.

TIME, ROLES, AND SELF
IN OLD AGE

Edited by

8

Jaber F. Gubrium

Marquette University

HUMAN SCIENCES PRESS
SUBSIDIARY OF BEHAVIORAL PUBLICATIONS INC.
72 FIFTH AVENUE, NEW YORK, N.Y. 10011

Library of Congress Catalog Number 74-12131

ISBN: 0-87705-230-1

Copyright © 1976 by Human Sciences Press, a division of Behavioral Publications, Inc., 72 Fifth Avenue, New York, New York 10011

Printed in the United States of America

56789 987654321

Library of Congress Cataloging in Publication Data

Gubrium, Jaber F
    Time, roles & self in old age.

    1. Old age—Addresses, essays, lectures. 2. Social role—Addresses, essays, lectures. 3. Retirement—Addresses, essays, lectures. I. Title.
HQ1061.G85   301.43'5   74-12131

CONTENTS

iii

PREFACE

It is commonly assumed by social scientists that social life has a deep and persistent impact on people's selves, their feelings, and their troubles. This impact is a product of such social factors as societal change, community conflict, and role discontinuity. In this book, roles and variations in them over time are considered in relation to persons in or near the later stages of life.

Roles may be considered from a variety of viewpoints. For instance, the continuity of any specific role over the life cycle is of interest to sociologists, since this continuity or lack of it affects the stability of the self, and of self-definition. Other social scientists explore the personal impact of highly institutionalized changes of role, such as mandatory work retirement. Still others examine cultural variations in role relationships, in order to reach general conclusions, free of societal specificity, about these relationships. Each of these viewpoints is taken by some paper in this collection.

One question that underlies all the papers is what place elders hold in various social orders, both large and small. How general is the phenomenon of disengagement? Does widowhood have any universal meaning to those who have experienced the loss of a spouse? Is there any common cross-cultural relationship between people who occupy different generational roles? These are all part of the gerontologist's search for patterns and variations in aging.

This book is a timely one. The role issues that it deals with are among the public issues of the seventies.

Some of the papers concern the behavior of aging women. How do women, rather than men, adjust to retirement? This question is increasingly important, since women are entering the labor force in ever higher numbers. Because of the lengthening life span, widowhood is also becoming quite prevalent in industrial societies. This role tends to be most often occupied by women. The study of old age itself comes close to being the study of the personal and social life of older women.

The ratio of elders to other age groups in the population is growing. This, in turn, is likely to make the influence of the aged in the economics and politics of industrial societies progressively more visible. The aged are prominent dependents of the welfare state. They are also a potentially effective group in elections and public referenda. The impact of status patternings on political action in old age is considered here.

This collection also deals with a question that has been prominent in public debate since the sixties: Is there such a thing as the generation gap? In this book, a conceptual model of the nature of the gap within families is constructed. Also, the generation gap in a non-Western society is discussed.

The book is divided into five sections. Parts I and II are general, in the sense that they do not focus on specific aspects of the roles of elders. Parts III, IV, and V, on the other hand, are concerned with particular problems of time, roles, and the self in old age.

Chapter 1, a paper by the Hendricks, is a methodological commentary on the measurement of the societal and role "worlds" of the elderly. They ask whether the traditional conceptions of time, which have underpinned much research on aging, have become too confining to analysis. They suggest that a more phenomenological consideration of time would open a new panorama of understanding on elders and the aging process.

Chapters 2 and 3 reconsider the relatively old issue of what role disengagement means in old age. Hochschild's paper examines the logic of disengagement theory from the viewpoint of a social phenomenologist. Her assessment and criticism of the theory have affinities with the Hendricks' criticism of the use of conventional concepts of time in social research. Gutmann's paper delineates, through argument and with evidence, what he describes as an alternative to disengagement, found among the Highland Druze in the Middle East.

Part III deals with the impact of role consistency on the aged. Seltzer's chapter is analytical. Using a model developed by Merton (1938), she describes various types of response to the time-disordered relationships between a person's roles. Trela develops a framework through which we can view the political behavior of the aged in terms of status consistency theory. In Chapter 6, Bell considers the continuity theory of roles in old age, and tests the theory's predictions on retirement and life satisfaction. Bultena and Powers explore the effects of age-grade comparisons on adjustment in later life. They hypothesize that favorable comparisons made by elders of their own life situations with those of other older people are associated with high levels of life satisfaction. Finally, Gubrium explores the personal meaning of lifelong continuity in a marital role by focusing on single elders. He suggests that some common problems of aging, such as loneliness and growing dependency, may be meaningless to the single elder; thus these are not general problems of growing old, but rather of having grown old with a spouse and family.

Part IV contains three chapters on retirement roles. Atchley tests two hypotheses on the causes and consequences of having had a positive orientation toward the job role for women in retirement. He hypothesizes that positive work orientation is related to both the extent and the length of women's retirement. In Chapter 10, Rowe gives evidence that the stereotyped image of the withdrawn and inactive retiree is not generally true of the aged, and may be limited to persons who retire from specific types of occupation. Strauss, Aldrich, and Lipman close this section with an analysis which suggests that we should reevaluate the popular notion that loss of status and a lessened sense of worth are inevitable concomitants of male retirement.

Part V is concerned with intergenerational roles. It opens with an outline by Bengtson, Olander, and Haddad of a conceptual model of intrafamilial generational relations. Hamer describes the generation gap among the Sidamo, a south Ethiopian people. Wood and Robertson review various studies of grandparenthood, and then describe a study of the meaning of grandparenthood to middle-aged and older working-class adults. The last chapter, by Chevan and Korson, is a study of the residential consequences of widowhood in families at different levels of modernization in Israel.

The papers in this book are the products of two kinds of effort. First, the subjects of its discussions and researches are older men and women and their social roles. Their efforts to make life reasonable for themselves (and indirectly for us, as social scientists) make gerontologic research possible. Second, it is the effort of various social scientists who have tried to understand roles in old age. I am grateful to both of these groups for bringing this volume to completion.

Any collection of papers that is compiled into a book requires a good share of secretarial assistance. For their faithful service and skilled work, I wish to thank Mrs. Sharron Johns and Mrs. Diane Willette.

CONTRIBUTORS

Bruce W. Aldrich, Department of Sociology, University of Miami, Coral Gables, Florida.

Robert C. Atchley, Scripps Foundation Gerontology Center, Miami University, Oxford, Ohio.

Bill D. Bell, Department of Sociology and Anthropology, University of Arkansas, Little Rock, Arkansas.

Vern Bengtson, Andrus Gerontology Center, University of Southern California, Los Angeles, California.

Gordon L. Bultena, Department of Sociology, Iowa State University, Ames, Iowa.

Albert Chevan, Department of Sociology, University of Massachusetts, Amherst, Massachusetts.

Jaber F. Gubrium, Department of Sociology and Anthropology, Marquette University, Milwaukee, Wisconsin.

David Gutmann, Department of Psychology, University of Michigan, Ann Arbor, Michigan.

Anees A. Haddad, Loma Linda University, Loma Linda, California.

C. Davis Hendricks, Department of Sociology, Georgetown College, Georgetown, Kentucky.

Jon Hendricks, Department of Sociology, University of Kentucky, Lexington, Kentucky.

Arlie Russell Hochschild, Department of Sociology, University of California, Berkeley, California.

J. Henry Korson, Department of Sociology, University of Massachusetts, Amherst, Massachusetts.

Aaron Lipman, Department of Sociology, University of Miami, Coral Gables, Florida.

Edward B. Olander, Olander, Caddell & Associates, Los Angeles, California.

Edward Powers, Department of Sociology, Iowa State University, Ames, Iowa.

Joan F. Robertson, School of Social Work, University of Wisconsin, Madison, Wisconsin.

Alan R. Rowe, Department of Sociology, Florida Atlantic University, Boca Raton, Florida.

Mildred M. Seltzer, Scripps Foundation Gerontology Center, Miami University, Oxford, Ohio.

Harold Strauss, Department of Management, University of Miami, Coral Gables, Florida.

James E. Trela, Department of Sociology, University of Maryland-Baltimore County, Baltimore, Maryland.

Vivian Wood, School of Social Work, University of Wisconsin, Madison, Wisconsin.

John H. Hamer, Department of Sociology and Anthropology, Brandon University, Brandon, Manitoba, Canada.

Part I

TIME WORLDS

Introduction

The analysis and measurement of time as a variable that affects behavior has been of prime interest to social scientists concerned with human growth and aging. Even when they have not regarded it as of prime interest, it has cut across a wide range of other variables that are part of the process of growing old. Whether the research focus is typically sociological, as in the analysis of roles, or more sociopsychological, as in the study of the self and its varied aspects, time is taken into consideration.

The first part of this book is concerned with time in a general sense. It does not consider it in any specific research context, but rather deals with how time has been treated in social thought.

Two streams of thought on time are identified. One of these, a highly mechanistic conception of time, has its roots in the writings of Aristotle. With the growth of science, this idea of time became "objective." Time is considered and treated as separate from our consciousness of it; its main features are its quantity and its progress. A second stream of thought on time stems from Augustine. This is a highly subjective, existential conception, which developed significantly with the growth of philosophical and social phenomenology. Its principle feature is that time has many qualities, separate and not reducible to each other. Time is the meaning it has for the people who keep it.

The importance of making alternate conceptions of time visible to those concerned with the study of old age is that it shows us how to expand our research horizons. For one thing, it suggests that we look to our subjects and ask them what time means to them. It has been traditional in gerontological research to examine their behavior within a world of time as defined by us. Can we assume that our time, as researchers, is the same as the time of our subjects? Is it possible that much of what we know about roles and the self in old age is "true," but for the wrong reasons? These questions are not answered here, but they serve as ways to think about the ideas and findings in this book.

12

Concepts of Time and Temporal Construction among the Aged, with Implications for Research

C. DAVIS HENDRICKS
JON HENDRICKS

Although time is a basic component of man's existence and an essential concept in scientific constructions, it is ambiguously defined, and in the social sciences it is generally cast in an implicit role. The definition of time depends in large measure on the differential emphasis that is characteristic of each discipline. Time has many faces, be they biological, physical, or psychological. For instance, a temporal model may be linear and nonrepetitive or cyclical and recurrent. The major point of contention in the available literature however, is the determination of the source of time.

Is time merely a human construct, measured at will, or is our perception of it founded on a categorical reality, external to human consciousness, yet appropriated by it? Too often in scientific research the nature of time is presumed to be known and understood without examination. This is particularly true in the field of gerontology, in which the central variable, age, is predicated on the concept of temporal flow.

Among the norms that govern scientific research is the need for the clear, cogent, and precise definition of concepts. This becomes especially crucial in the empirical verification of theoretical propositions. Concepts represent reality, abstractions intended to convey the same idea to a number of people. The concepts that comprise man's thoughts are both predictive and prescriptive. In everyday use, a concept delimits the present and any possible future cognitions. It constructs the boundaries of reality, determining what is experientially possible; it delineates the essential characteristics that must be perceived in any entity before that entity can enter our experience.

Conceptions of time clearly illustrate this position. The model of time most often utilized in the sciences, including gerontology, is chronological, physical, and "objective." Time is often equated with its measure. This lends itself to easy operationalization, as time then becomes simply a mechanical construction. The problems arising from this singular definition of time become apparent in gerontology. If time exists external to human existence, independent of human intervention, then man's perception of time —a subjective action— is potentially distorted. The emphasis on the "objective," quantitative nature of time presupposes that it represents externally real facts, separate from the consciousness of the observer. The processes of aging, which encompass individual requirements and interpretations, are conditioned by a reified view of time. Time has become an object, not a process; it can be accumulated, wasted, invested. Since all conceptualizations are normative, particular patterns are imposed on our study of old age. Our questions revolve around the disposition of time (an object), perceptions of its speed, and reactions to its passage. As a consequence, time has become a coercive concept.

It is the thesis of this paper that such a stance significantly affects the future of, and obscures, potentially rewarding theoretical contributions to gerontology. The
historical dichotomy of a mechanistic, "objective" model of
time based on quantitative measurement, reflected in the
writings of Aristotle and Newton, and a qualitative, multiple, subjective view of time, defined by Augustine, Bergson, Husserl, Mannheim, Sorokin, and Gurvitch, clouds the
issue. Yet both views of time can be seen as components of
a larger sphere of temporality, which is constituted by the
consciousness of the actor. As with previous considerations
of time, the image of temporality and the nature of man
involve *a priori* assumptions that condition the investigative
process and the subsequent conclusions. This position is
itself an expression of the assumption that science by its
nature provides us with a world perspective.

Schutz, Berger and Luckmann, Blumer, and others
maintain that the sociologist or social scientist interferes
with existing patterns of relations and interactions wherever he operates. The scientist actively creates knowledge
in his identification of symbols, his choice of a topic and his
research instruments, and his interpretation of data. Thus
objectivity is associated with a particular paradigm, which
depicts a specific world view (Kuhn, 1962; Hutcheon,
1970). Each paradigm structures the area of reality on
which it concentrates, narrowing the focus of its concepts
and limiting the questions that can be asked (Friedrichs,
1970, p. 143). Thus the model of time utilized by the scientist reflects his perception of reality. It follows that social
scientists, and gerontologists in particular, should be aware
of the implications of those models of time that characterize their disciplines. In addressing ourselves to the role of
time in gerontology and the tacit assumptions involved, we
must consider the historical development of concepts of
time. If we assume that there has been a progressive evolu-

tion within the scientific enterprise, the question becomes: how did we achieve our present status?

HISTORICAL DEVELOPMENT OF CONCEPTIONS OF TIME

Any outline of the history of the concept of time must deal with Plato, Aristotle, and Augustine. They provide a basis for the subsequent treatment of time, which was altered only by the Copernican revolution and Einstein's theory of relativity. It is possible to identify two streams of thought, which trace their origins to the writings of Aristotle and Augustine respectively; however, it was not until the growth of science and the vast changes accompanying Einstein's theories that the bifurcation of these trends became evident.

The Aristotelian tradition viewed the concept of time as closely related to that of motion, if not based upon it. Time came to be an objective variable, which ontologically preceded any consciousness of it; although measures might vary, its ultimate quantifiability was seen as absolute. In the Aristotelian model, subjective perceptions were deemed irrelevant to the existence of time.

The second view flows from Augustine to Bergson and Husserl. It received support from Einstein's theory of relativity, and it is represented today in the writings of phenomenologists and of sociologists such as Mannheim, Sorokin, and Georges Gurvitch. This orientation considers time as a multifaceted, qualitative variable based on subjective perception; quantification thereby assumes a secondary role. Just as Einstein theorized that the number of times corresponds to the number of frames of reference, and different times apply to different levels of analysis, these writers developed particular definitions of time, applicable to the social sciences, which differ from the dominant physical model of time.

Classical Perspectives on Time

Prior to the descriptions of Plato and Aristotle, several writers including Democritus, Pythagoras, and Zeno attempted to isolate the nature of time by formulating links between it and its measure. The problems they highlighted are recurrent: namely, the interaction of time with its measure, and the nature of reality as eternal and unchanging, and thus nontemporal.

Plato was the first to offer an extensive explication of the nature of time. In *Timaeus* he contrasts time with eternity, illustrating the changing character of time (1937, 370E). In his view God took unchanging eternity as his model to bring order out of disorder and create the universe. Plato's interest in time is focused on the manner in which it reflects eternity; it is an imperfect image, as is man, yet only through the analysis of images is one able to approach the truth that resides in eternity. Time is thus an image that proceeds according to number and must be measurable (1937, 37D, 1–5).

Aristotle's definition of time differs from Plato's, as do his orienting questions. Aristotle does not address himself to the origin of the universe; rather he considers the principles of nature, which include motion and change. Time is "the number of motion according to the before and after [1961, iv. 11. 220a, 26–28]." To recognize time we must perceive not only motion, but motion with a before and after, on which a numbering process is based. Time becomes objectively real, a matter of the inherent motion of the universe; time remains unaffected by the choice of measure (Aristotle, 1961, iv. 12. 220b, 10–15).

Several centuries later, in *Confessions,* Augustine alters the neo-Platonic model in his discussions of time (1953, xi. 10–31). He begins with a clear statement: "What, then, is time? If no one asks me, I know; but if I want to explain to him who asks, I know not [xi. 14]." Augustine asserts that time is inferior to eternity; eternity, wherein God resides, is changeless, while time is dependent on motion or change. Time is not a part of God's nature; therefore the world and change must exist if time is to exist. Augustine echoed Plato when he stated the world and time came into being simultaneously. Time is not the motion of anything; it is that by which we measure the motion of a body.

For Augustine the present is without extension; otherwise it could be divided into past and future. By definition, the past and future do not exist and cannot be measured; neither can the present, as it has no extension. Yet it is common to think of long and short periods of time (xi. 11.15). With this introduction Augustine presents his case for the most subjectively oriented view of time up to that point in history.

Past and future, in Augustine's view, must exist as present, or else they do not and cannot exist. Thus whatever exists is present, and if it appears to be past, it is not the event itself that exists, but the image of the event, in the memory of what he terms the soul. When we predict the future we perceive not the future events, but their foreshadowings in the present. He maintains that nothing is perceived unless it is present in the soul. Thus in the soul there are a present memory of past events, a present attention to present events, and a present anticipation of future events (xi. 20.26).

The soul of man measures intervals of time, and measures motion by means of time. For Augustine the soul was of primary importance in any consideration of it. For Aristotle time is an aspect of motion; it exists insofar as it is perceived by the mind, but it can be considered in relation to motion without explicit reference to the perceiving mind. For Augustine the mind is independent of external motions; time is present in the mind, where it is an absolute in relation to which motions proceed (xi. 24). The soul is not in time, since its attention never becomes memory.

Time is in the soul, yet the universe of changing things is in time. Time demands a universe in succession and a mind apart from the universe, able to grasp phases of this motion and measure its duration.

Even though he clearly specified the relation of time to mind, the measurement of time presents a difficult problem for Augustine. The soul is an absolute, the standard by which motions are measured. "We cannot measure past and future time, because they do not exist; present time, because it is indivisible; passing time, because it is not complete [xi. 21.8–10]." To resolve this dilemma, he states that we do not measure things themselves, but something that remains fixed in our memory (xi. 27.35). Thus we measure the present impression that passing events leave in the soul. One measures a distension of the soul itself.

Augustine represents a new departure in the conceptualization of time. For him time is a matter of the soul and consciousness; it is an activity of the soul, by which man measures motion. Outside the soul only the present phase of time exists, but in consciousness there is memory, attention, and anticipation. Time is that which in passing characterizes consciousness. Physical motion might cease, but the three acts of consciousness would still remain, and so would time.

These two streams of thought set the stage for subsequent considerations of the nature of time. It is a variable that permeates man's existence and influences his every realm, not merely the limited one of scientific inquiry. New factors came into play with the rise of science and the mechanization of man and the universe, which altered the basic conceptions of time. The earlier definitions were not eclipsed, however; the Platonic model was expanded as physical science sought to explain the universe, and the Augustinian model was refined as the subjective came to the fore in the phenomenological school of inquiry.

The Rise of Science

With the Copernican revolution and the development of theories on the relativity of motion, there came new conceptions of time. If there is no absolutely regular motion, and if time is dependent on motion, then there can be no absolute measure of time. Kepler demonstrated that for any scientific knowledge of the world there must be a recognition of quantitative relations. Galileo recognized the existence of quantitative relations in nature; he and Newton reduced reality to an external, objective mechanism wherein number, magnitude, and motion were real, and qualities usually associated with the self or subjectivity were of a lower order of reality, if not illusionary. Objective reality was external to man, and existed apart from his consciousness.

Newton's theories proposed both an absolute and a relative space and time. Absolute time flows without regard for external events, being continuous and subjective. Relative time is the commonly used measure of duration by motion (Heath, 1936). Duration as used by Newton differs from the later definition by Bergson in its lack of reference to its direction or its cumulative effect in passing. In his view these latter aspects would apply to specific events in time, rather than to time itself. In Newton's model events are dependent on time, and simultaneity is determined by existence in the same moment of time. In the relative view developed by Einstein, however, time is derived from events whose simultaneity does not require the presence of an entity of time.

The conception of time introduced by Newton was vastly altered by the theories of Einstein. He departed from the purely mechanical model of Newton by locating the basic data of physical science in energy rather than matter. With the emergence of relativity theories, concepts of space and time lose their stability. As a consequence, time corresponds to its frame of reference, and hence may take many forms. Similarly, the speed of movement is relative to the point of view of the observer. Space and time lose their objective status, and have no existence apart from the events through which the actor perceives and measures them. Einstein clearly realized that time in macrophysics is not the same as time in microphysics. Thus the multifaceted nature of time must lead to a plurality of measures.

Writers in fields other than physics have also addressed themselves to the problem of time. Descartes, couching his discussion in philosophical terms, made this distinction between time and duration: duration is a mode of extension, and time is a mode of thought about extension. Substance can be conceived without time, but time cannot be conceived without substance (1956: I). In contrast to Descartes' formulation of time, Kant (1956) sees time as a pure form of sensible intuition, a universal precondition for any possible knowledge. Intuition is that through which knowledge is related to objects, and time is a subjective condition under which intuition occurs. It has objective validity with respect to appearances, the objects of our senses. All things are in time, including change and motion. Thus there would be no empirical world without forms of sensibility. Substance is permanent and objectivity rests on permanence, which in turn is found in the order of events in time (p. 209).

For Kant, time is a function of the mind, which makes perception possible; we do not reflect on it, as it is an *a priori* condition for all experience (p. 74). It has empirical reality because all things, as objects of sensible intuition, are in time (p. 79). Time does not inhere in objects, merely in the intuiting subject (p. 81). Time is a condition for perception.

Throughout the nineteenth century, the spirit of Newtonian physics imbued nearly all spheres of intellectual endeavor. Neutral objectivity and analytical reduction, two aspects of the scientific process espoused by Newton, became fundamental elements in the mechanistic model of the universe (Matson, 1964). In addition there was a popular tendency to define a single principle as underlying all reality; this was often assumed to be an objective, impersonal reason, superior to individual men. Darwin and organic evolution fell naturally into the scheme of reality that flowered from Newton's model. The image of man as a creature of involuntary behavior was the basis not only of Darwin's theories, but also of other widely differing views of society. Many of the theories contained common elements that reflected the mechanistic model, in which man is a spectator and nature is perceived as rational.

Subsequent definitions of time were not exempt from the influence of Newton's physics; indeed they were more closely bound to it than many theories of the physical sciences. As was noted above, by the end of the classical period two major conceptions of time existed. The one flowing directly from Newtonian physics posits two senses of time: time as experienced, a product of consciousness; and time that is independent of consciousness, or objective time. In this view, time *per se* ontologically precedes consciousness. Time arises from physical processes that are not dependent upon the perceiving subject. According to this conception, mind-dependent time, or time as experienced, is a relatively unimportant facet of an indispensable variable (Reichenbach, 1958).

This accentuation of a unidirectional, objective, mechanistic model of time had its greatest impact during the industrialization of Western societies. Scientists often assumed that time was first defined by religious or philosophical men in their studies on the nature of humanity. Eventually time was pressed into the service of social institutions to demarcate religious, economic, or political activities. By the medieval era time had assumed a value as an objective entity, mainly in relation to God and man's purpose in worldly life. The final stage was set by the rise of the scientific perspective and industrialism in the sixteenth century. Time was secularized and accorded a commodity-like status, and gradually it gained ascendancy over man's affairs (Rezsohazy, 1972; Woodcock, 1944). Time was inextricably related to production and profit in the economic arena. Eventually this model became predominant in the social sciences; in sociology this is illustrated by the early evolutionists, such as Comte and Spencer (Durkheim, 1933). Much of the focus in gerontological research can be traced to this model. The implications of the view that time has one face, external to man, and that man is the subject rather than the author of his world will be explored at a later point.

The second stream flows in opposition to the objective and mechanical view of the world and time. It runs directly from Augustine through Einstein and Henri Bergson to the writers currently labeled phenomenologists. In general this view emphasizes the subjective basis of time, its multiple nature, and the special origin of objective time.

Phenomenological Conceptions of Time

Influenced by the second stream of concepts, many writers sought alternatives to the quantitative, physical model of time. The criticism was often voiced that objective clock time was a coercive factor in the study of men, and that since it was external, it was hardly the most relevant view of time for their lives.

Henri Bergson (1965) sought the reality of time in inner experience. For him real time was found in pure duration and experience; he represents a totally subjective view. He considered Kant's description of time as a homogeneous entity erroneous; real time is heterogeneous and indivisible, constantly unfolding. "Time is identical with the flow of the continuity of our inner life. ... [p. 44] Duration is continuation of what no longer exists into what does exist. This is a real time, perceived and lived [p. 49

Bergson also conceived of a form of time that is homogeneous or spatialized, time that is quantitative.

Pure duration flows, while measured time is composed of instants. Through the intermediary of motion, successive moments are marked off in duration to create the measure of time; hence it is only by conversion to spatial models that time can be quantified (p. 54). Bergson did not reconcile these opposing times; he presented a strong case for qualitative, experienced time, but did not base scientific and quantitative time on this inner experience, which he considered fundamental and real.

Husserl and Merleau-Ponty expanded the concept of time presented by Bergson: Husserl arrived at the inner constitution of objective time, and Merleau-Ponty at an emphasis on the subjectivity-in-the-world that constitutes time. For these writers the objective, physical model is only one of several types of time derived from the qualitative inner experience of time.

Husserl found the roots of knowledge in the consciousness of the knowing subject to whom things appear. In the study of any phenomenon, the subjective, intending (noetic) must be linked with the objective, intended (noematic); in fact, they are inseparable. All forms of objectivity have their origin in the subjective consciousness, and the essences are constituted by conscious intention based on the perception of particulars (Lauer, 1965).

The transcendental ego is the *a priori* source of objectivity insofar as experience is the source of subjectivity. An object becomes known only through knowledge of the subjective act that intends it. Likewise, the world becomes known when the individual begins to constitute it. The world is the totality of objectivity, but it is objective only as the subjectivity focuses on it. The transcendental ego constitutes time and other intentional objectivity; as with Kant, it is the temporality of consciousness that enables us to perceive. Objective time arises as we focus on the objects of consciousness that endure: the constancy becomes attached to the objects themselves, creating temporal accessibility (Husserl, 1966; pp. 85–89, 145). Memory, the possibility of returning to an object over and over again and comparing it temporally with others, is the source of objective time. It establishes the objective in the before-and-after relationship, and provides permanent identifiability.

Husserl traces the roots of the life world back to the subject, grounding all knowledge in the subjectivity, but Merleau-Ponty (1962) contends the following: "The world is there before any possible analysis. . . . The real has to be described, not constructed or formed. . . . Truth does not inhabit only the inner man . . . there is no inner man, man is in the world and only in the world does he know himself [x–xi]." For Merleau-Ponty the subjective and objective, the internal and external, are inseparable. All our experiences orient themselves in terms of before and after; the individual lives through time and is involved and permeated with it (p. 422). Man is a temporal being by virtue of inner necessity, and in analyzing time we gain access to the concrete structure of subjectivity (p. 410).

The past and future are dimensions of subjectivity that appear in the field of the present consciousness of time. What is past and future for an individual is present for the world. "Time is not a real process, not an actual succession which I record. It arises from *my* relation to things [p. 412]." Time is not a series of successive events, because events are shaped by an observer from the spatiotemporal totality of the objective world. "Change presupposes a certain position which I take up and from which I see things in procession before me: there are no events without someone to whom they happen and whose finite perspective is the basis of their individuality [p. 411]."

Time is always in the process of constituting itself

(from consciousness); hence true time is characterized by flux and transience, a synthetic relationship between before, present, and after that is a dimension of the being. The past and future exist only when a subjectivity is there to introduce a perspective (p. 421).

Merleau-Ponty emphasizes the role of the world over that of Husserl's subjectivity in the perception of time. Objects exist in the world in a present sense, and only as we introduce consciousness do succession and time appear. Both writers reject the foundation of time on motion, and focus instead on the perception of the actor and his role in creating his world.

Heidegger presents a similar analysis. He views temporality as basic to the structure of knowledge; time becomes the center of all cognitional syntheses. The temporality of consciousness is seen as unifying the thought processes and the objects of reflection. The consciousness of time arises from the temporal modes expressed in the synthetic process that is fundamental to any cognition. The modes involved in the synthesis and cognition are: what is as having been, what is as can be, and what is as presenting itself (Sherover, 1971). Clearly these elements are reminiscent of Augustine's formulation of the awareness of time. Time is not a thing, it cannot appear as the object of sensory perception; instead it permeates the knower, the knowing, and the known. It is indispensable to intelligibility. Man needs this presupposed temporal framework in order to know, act, think, and relate to the world. Temporality is a function; it is the human mode of constituting general experience. The human mind is in some senses a free causal agent which makes an essential contribution to its own knowledge.

Sociologists who have investigated the nature of time have drawn on the foregoing concepts when presenting their versions of both mechanical and qualitative orientations. Few sociologists have directed prolonged attention to the subject of time—perhaps this reflects the security of its implicit status. Mannheim, Sorokin, and Gurvitch have been among the first to propose a specific concept of time for sociology: they have objected to the ties to the mechanistic model, and have decried its assumed objectivity.

Sociological Conceptions of Time

Durkheim represents the first stream of thought on time; he viewed space and time neither as existing *a priori* nor as empirical in the traditional sense. Both concepts were provided by society or culture, taken from the "social life" to become the abstract and impersonal framework that surrounds all of personal life and humanity (1915, pp. 10–12). There is private experience in the flow of time, but it is by no means enough to constitute the category of time itself. For Durkheim, man is not primarily one who imposes his order on nature; he is to a greater degree produced by the cultural system. The individual's private experience of time is systematized and ordered by the culture, which also provides the abstract and universal nature of time. It is through the coercive power of the collective memory that the flow of an individual's past experience is stabilized. The function of time is pragmatic; it is determined by the rhythmic ordering of cultural life (Durkheim, 1915, p. 349).

More recently, Karl Mannheim searched for an alternative to the objective time posited by classical physics. He rejected the positivist formulations of historical development and the mechanical divisions of generational length and time, because they were based solely on the "biological law of limited life-span of man [1952, p. 278]." Mannheim, following Dilthey, postulated the generation as his unit over quantitative temporal units: the generation as determined not merely by chronological data, but by the experience of common influences. "The time interval separating generations becomes subjectively experienceable time; and contemporaneity becomes a subjective condition of having been submitted to the same determining influences [1952, p. 282]." He sees the generational style and rhythm as conditioned by the social and cultural processes, in a manner reminiscent of Durkheim.

Sorokin (1964) also distinguished a definite sociocultural time, which has characteristics different from those of physical, biological, or psychological times. The periodization and rhythms of social life are of purely social origin, and have little in common with natural phenomena as such (p. 182). Mathematical time becomes a subset of sociocultural time, made possible only under certain sociocultural circumstances. Sociocultural time, therefore, cannot be replaced by quantitative time without a loss of orientation in the time process, a homogenizing of time, the division of indivisible durations into identical units, or the equalizing of unequal phenomena (pp. 197–215).

The qualitative and discontinuous flow of sociocultural time specified by Sorokin is further explicated in the work of Georges Gurvitch. Gurvitch is one of several writers who offer a dialectical model of the world wherein man creates a social order which in turn acts upon him to alter his nature (Schutz, 1967; Berger, 1967; Gurvitch, 1964). Although the role of the actor in the formation of the social world is of prime importance, the reality that arises from his interaction is the usual subject of sociological study.

From this vantage point Gurvitch (1964) presented his theory of social time. Earlier writers had moved toward a view of the multiple nature of time, but until Einstein it had not been made explicit. For Gurvitch each social system, with its particular components, has its own time, which varies in duration, rhythm, and orientation. Time is conditioned by the social framework and reciprocally affects it. The multiple manifestations of time are not unified; any attempts to do so represent man's struggle to remaster his created world (p. 21).

Different times exist for physical and social life, besides the particular definitions used by scientific disciplines. Gurvitch refused to accept the subjective-objective dichotomy or the ontological status of time. He decided (1964) to cull relevant factors from the two streams of thought, thus: "From Aristotle I retain the idea that time is movement (rather a plurality of movements), and from his opponents the idea that time possesses a qualitative element, it is not always measurable and even more not always quantifiable [p. 19]." Gurvitch defined time as "convergent and divergent movements which persist in a discontinuous succession and change in a continuity of heterogeneous movements [p. 18]." The important aspect of time is its dialectical nature, which is the source of its multiplicity.

Gurvitch distinguished different times for different spheres of reality; for example, the micro- and macrophysical, astronomical, mechanical, chemical, geological, biological, psychological, historical, and social spheres. Social time marks the dialectical movement of the total social phenomena of whatever level is the subject of analysis. Social time is more complex than physical time, and is harder to unify; it takes one of eight possible forms, and exhibits more discontinuity than any other manifestation of time (1964, p. 31). The eight social times that Gurvitch constructed for sociological analysis are the Enduring (time of slowed-down, long duration), Deceptive, Erratic (time of irregular pulsation between the appearance and disappearance of rhythms), Cyclical, Retarded, Alternating, Time in Advance of Itself (time that pushes forward), and Explosive time (1964, pp. 31–33).

While sociologists have recognized the importance of time in the social world, they have not, for the most part, acknowledged the complexity specified by Gurvitch. Durkheim felt that conceptions of time were determined by societal conditions, Sorokin saw time as a social necessity, and

Gurvitch felt that time, a product of inner experience, had qualitatively distinct faces that corresponded to specific social contexts.

Is it possible to reconcile these divergent streams? Are there common themes to be found in the Greek conception of time as secondary to the eternal, or timeless, and that of time as a linear progression of instants, reflected in human existence by the meaning that man gives to each unit (clearly characterized by the ancient Hebrews)? Where do phenomenologists and others enter the scene, with their firm assertions of the temporality of human consciousness and the constitution of time by human action? Finally, what roles do these conceptions play in the study of aging?

TIME AND AGING

A number of contemporary views see the temporal flow as destructive; men focus on the world of external phenomena, which are continually passing away, so that what is momentarily present provides the basis for temporal reality in science. The objective character of time, measured by arbitrary devices, comes to overshadow the role of the actor, man, in the creation of this convention.

The unique problems associated with this orientation are apparent in analyses of human aging. Aging is predicated on the passage of time or awareness of change. The conception of time as unilinear, externalized, and beyond the control of the actor curtails his creative role in temporal experience. In technological societies life satisfaction is dependent in large measure upon social conditions that are defined by mechanistic models of causality, which establish norms for the judgment of the passage of time and for individual time perspective. On the one hand research in social gerontology focuses on the estimation of time intervals, measured by the clock or calendar, and on temporal perspective, the degree to which the elderly refer to past or future time. The model of time utilized is constructed from quantitative and linear dimensions, external to the subjective. Time is seen as being analogous to points on a line, in both direction and order; it is a unique standard by which everyone can be compared. In the same literature, gerontologists often assert that the perception and experience of the speed and duration of time vary greatly among individuals. Aging is thus a relative process, and the labels "aged," "elderly," or "old" are differentially applied to individuals of the same chronological age. The necessary groundwork has been laid, however, for a dynamic conception of the multiplicity of temporal coordinates that interact to position man in a distinctive temporal perspective, such a conception would give rise to the potential cognizance of his role as actor. In the interests of future research into temporal construction and experience, we present the following.

The difficulty of constructing adequate theories about the complex nature and measure of time is painfully clear in social gerontology, the interdisciplinary study of aging. "To each his own" might well apply to the various measures of time contributed by highly divergent disciplines, each of which represents a portion of reality characterized by a different level of analysis. Though it is commonly accepted that one standard, one measure of time equally applicable to the various components of man's existence, is beyond reach, the search continues for a theme that would enable researchers to begin to weave an integrated theoretical fabric from man's temporal experiences.

The need for distinct temporal measures that apply to the atomic, cellular, physiological, and psychological levels of man's existence follows from research into circadian rhythms, environmental modifiers, and biological rates of senescence (Pittendrigh, 1972; Strehler, 1962). Though the multiplicity of time is evident, most research on aging consistently identifies the aging processes with the linear flow of objective time. This tends to obscure the possibility that individuals may contribute to or modify the uniform temporal measure. Even a cursory review of the literature reveals the prevalence of this orientation. Birren (1959) stated that "chronological age is one of the most useful single items of information about an individual if not the *most* useful [p. 8]." Although aging has many definitions and modes of measurement, a crucial factor lies in the changes in the various properties of an organism over time (p. 6). Nonetheless, the very nature of science presupposes that there is a causal ordering of the processes of aging, such that time has a linear flow.

The concept of linear, unidirectional time that is basic to most analyses of aging serves to separate physical from psychological temporal experiences. Objective time is measured by physical properties (movement of the earth, a pendulum, atoms) whose relations are defined by an instrument (a calendar, a clock) dependent upon periodic rhythms among physical phenomena. There is thus an objective time that determines the objective criteria of aging (Reichenbach, 1958; Grünbaum, 1967). The subjective experience of time is thought to reflect the physical, objective properties of time. Reichenbach and Mathers (1959) put it thus: "It is not a human prerogative to reflect the flow of time. What we feel to be the direction of time, the direction of *becoming,* is a relation between a registering instrument and its environment [p. 74]." This assumption proves essential to most of the research on the temporal experiences associated with aging; man's mind is seen as a registering instrument, able to record the objective properties of time. Due to the nature of the physical universe, man experiences a temporal direction that reflects the increasing entropy of systems.

Researchers often give similar support, if only implicitly, to an endogenous-exogenous dichotomy of temporal experience. The endogenous perception of time emphasizes internal cues, biological clocks, alpha rhythms (the electroencephalograph) and body temperature (Pöppel, 1972, p. 220). On the other hand, exogenous explanations of the perception of time involve mechanisms of learning and processing information, environmental cues, and adaptation. The dichotomy presented neglects the interaction that takes place among these sources of temporal experience. The issue of the external objectivity of physical time and the resulting mind-dependency of perceptions of time permeates the research on physiological time associated with aging.

Physiological time does not flow at a constant rate as does physical time, yet if it is viewed in reference to physiological time, the rate of passage of physical time appears to change. To illustrate, though the measure of days remains constant, as the individual ages and certain physiological processes deteriorate, the speed of the passage of days begins to change; the two measures may at first have passed at identical rates, but changes in one cause apparent changes in the other when the first is used as a reference point. According to Carrell (1929), the major difference in the passage of physiological time as compared to physical time is that "the present of a living organism does not pass into nothingness. It never ceases to be, because it remains in the memory and is entered in the tissues [p. 620)."

Drawing from the lessons of physics on the existence of relative times, each of which has a unique measure (radioactive disintegration, movement of electrons, speed of light, earth's rotation, and so forth), a few researchers have proposed relative measures of age based on concepts other than the direct and uniform flow of physical time. In 1936 Lecomte du Noüy suggested that the measure of biological age might be the speed of cicatrization of a wound, which would vary inversely with the square root of chronological age (Wallis, 1966, p. 12). Benjamin (1947) searched for a diagnostic method of determining biological age that would take into account the entire human system, rather than just the isolated subsystems measured by du Noüy's cicatrization or Ruzicka's concentration of hydrogen ions in the tissues (p. 218). Citing the discrepancy between biological age (a physiological measure unmarred by pathology) and chronological age (the number of years lived), Benjamin concluded that biological indices provided a far more accurate measure of an individual's age. Biological age is dependent upon hereditary, general health, and the functioning capacity of the individual; hence it is difficult to determine it accurately, due to the variable rates of change in the organic systems of different individuals. An alternative was suggested by Murray (1951), who focused attention on physiological age as indicated by measures of hearing, vision, blood pressure, and muscle force.

In all the attempts to specify measures of aging by other than the passage of clock time, the external validity and operation of time remains an underlying assumption. This is not modified to any degree by consideration of the psychological perceptions of temporal experience among aging individuals. In an exchange of letters in *Science* in the early 1940s, several explanations of perceived time passage were suggested. Three interested observers voiced their opinions on the changing perceptions of physical time along the life course of the individual. Although he did not describe the process in any detail, Wilen (1943) contended that the rate of temporal passage appears to speed up as the individual ages, due to the fear of approaching death. Another view was offered by Nitardy (1943), who emphasized the logarithmic relationship of elapsed time to "total time experience." Ennis (1943) gave the alternative suggestion that the increasing contents and resources available to the adult mind prompt the apparent speedup in the passage of time during the adult years.

The commonsensical view that time appears to pass

more rapidly with advancing age implies the importance of subjective estimation of a uniform temporal flow. Closer examination reveals the crucial role played by consciousness in the development of conceptions of time. Physical events do not of themselves display before-and-after qualities; rather these determinations are made by the observer (Denbigh, 1972, p. 152). We cannot reverse time in experiential knowledge, because certain impressions cannot be received in a reverse direction (throwing a baseball or learning a concept). Yet all men have the advantage of accumulated experience, through which they may travel backward in time via their memories.

Fraser (1972) has made a distinction between two modes of dealing with time on the psychological level. The first, time preception, involves "judgments of sequence and duration as functions of experimental variables" or "studies in the behavioral function of man as a clock [p. 494]." The second, time sense, deals with expectation and memory, awareness of death, the consensual determination of time, and the temporal structuring of personality and language. Time perception is dependent upon time sense to the degree that any experiment involving a judgment of sequence and duration presupposes an awareness of the past and future. It is within a larger social and psychological framework that man makes his determinations of temporal experience with reference to clocks or other timepieces. Although man does not alter certain universal physical processes, he alone decides how to quantify time, how to spatialize it so that it may be divided into instants. This is not to say that it is unimportant to deal with the individual's perception and estimation of intervals of clock time, only that the results of such explorations should be couched within a discussion of the significance of the time measure to man's temporal experiences.

The research on the relationship of time estimation and age must be interpreted with caution, as the various methods used present results that cannot be compared without some translation. In the absence of a complete description of the experimental method, true replication or interpretation of the study is impossible. The methods of time estimation, production, and reproduction yield vastly different results, creating confusion over their comparability. Bindra and Waksberg (1956) said that "identical differences may signify faster internal clock in verbal estimation, slower internal clock in production, and slowing down of internal clock in reproduction [p. 159]." With this *caveat* in mind, certain themes emerge from investigations of age and of the estimation and perception of time.

Researchers in general have not found age to be the crucial variable that differentiates subjective estimations of a constant objective temporal interval. Subjective estimates may be differentiated by variables such as the activity level, socioeconomic status, intelligence quotient, education, and external dependencies. Wallach and Green (1961) reported that subjective judgments of the speed of time were directly related to the value ascribed to time by the judges. Thus the oldest members of their sample preferred dynamic, swift descriptions of time, while younger members selected static metaphors. Tejmar (1962), reporting on an elderly group, and Surwillo (1964), reporting on institutionalized older people, found older members of both groups showed a tendency to underestimate time intervals to a greater degree than their younger counterparts. Goldstone, Boardman, and Lhamon (1958) offered supporting evidence that individuals with median ages of 6 years and 69.5 years made significantly shorter estimations of seconds than did those at all other age levels.

The underestimation of temporal intervals by older adults is thought to be related to the quality of the experienced duration. Intervals filled with activity will appear to pass more rapidly than unfilled temporal intervals. Swift and McGeoch (1925) and Gulliksen (1927) found their participants consistently overestimated the length of empty or unfilled intervals. Objective time, as measured by the clock or calendar, has a profound influence over man's life, and is judged variably according to emotional experience and psychological attitudes. Since clock time appears to move rapidly when interesting events are occurring, Feifel (1957) expected that older persons would underestimate objective time, due to the prospect of a foreshortened future containing fewer events of interests. He did find that older persons underestimated time intervals significantly more often than younger persons. The relationship was modified by a positive outlook on the future, however; this was correlated with a more accurate judgment of a time standard than was a negative outlook. He concluded that the way in which time is filled, rather than age *per se,* has a great influence upon the perception of the rate at which time passes.

The relationship of activity to time perspective was explored by Fink (1957). Institutionalized older men over 50 were found in Thematic Apperception Tests and self-report of thoughts over the recent past to be more concerned with the past and less with the future than noninstitutionalized men (p. 414). Though older man were more occupied with the past than younger men, institutionalization was judged to have had a greater impact than age on time perspective. The possession of jobs or hobbies was associated with a higher degree of future orientation among the elderly. Again the quality of the filled time was an important determinant of temporal perspectives. The individual is able to construct an extended future if he has access to personally and socially significant types of activity.

Other researchers into time perspectives have attempted to isolate a perspective that indicates the personality of the aging individual. Again the evidence is contradictory, in spite of the comparable experimental methods employed. Eson and Greenfeld (1962) did not uncover great differences in temporal perspectives among their samples of adolescents, young adults, and adults in their sixties; the older adults could not be "differentiated from the other groups either in regard to greater emphasis on past, or certainly, with regard to a less hopeful expectancy of the future [p. 124]." All participants revealed a preference for the near-future over the other temporal perspectives.

Time perspective as defined above is affected by the motivational state of the individual, so that the desire that time should pass at a specified rate may affect the perception of its duration (Triplett, 1931). The more future-oriented an individual is, the more rapidly time seems to pass for him (Siegman, 1962). Time perspective as it relates to futurity may have two dimensions, the personal and the cognitive (Kastenbaum, 1966). Though the personal future, as measured by the life span, decreases as the individual ages, cognitive futurity remains open and viable as a tool in the abstract organizing and categorizing of experience. The individual is bound by these two senses of the future, though one or the other may predominate. In an earlier study (1963), Kastenbaum also found that individuals over 65 do not differ significantly from the young in their ability to use future time as a hypothetical, abstract concept.

Research has shown that language and cultural orientation do affect time perspective; indeed, in American society time is often portrayed as a commodity to be economically utilized. Zibbell (1971) noted that the future time perspective is defined by the expectations and activities with which one plans to fill that time; long-range planning and the time required for the completion of desired activities determine the extent of the future time perspective. In his sample of elderly Americans, he found that men had a greater degree of future time orientation than women, due in part to their previous work orientation, which had involved organizational planning, the establishment of goals, and satisfaction. Another study of the time perspectives of younger and older subjects from three separate cultures revealed that Anglo-Americans experienced decided changes in these perspectives over the life course, and had a greater degree of future time orientation than did either Mexican-Americans or American Indians. The differences between the perspectives of the young and old individuals from the latter two cultural backgrounds were much smaller than those among the Anglo-Americans. The oldest members of the three groups perceived filled time intervals as shorter than empty intervals, but for all three cultural groups the difference was significant only when the empty intervals were presented first (Bongers, 1971).

It is conceivable that an individual uses a variety of time perspectives, each applicable to different arenas in his life space. Phenomena must be considered on various temporal levels, each of which entails a distinct perspective, be it atomic, physiological, psychological, or cosmic (Frank, 1939, p. 294). As the individual ages he experiences transformations on each level; physiological processes undergo gradual alteration, while the social environment and psychological reinforcements provide ever-changing cues to the perceiving subject. We might reasonably expect concomitant changes to occur in his temporal perspectives. The multiple qualities of time in the structure of experience would lead us to assume that a number of temporal orientations would be possible for the aged individual.

We find instead an implicit denial of this expectation in the literature. The emphasis on the linear, irreversible, and uninterrupted flow of physical time supports the assumption that the normal human experiences a steady, even temporal flow and duration. A distorted time perspective is commonly identified only with mentally deranged, abnormal, or suicidal individuals (Binswanger, 1960). Unless a qualifying condition such as old age or emotional disturbance is present, individuals are presumed to undergo similar temporal experiences (Kastenbaum, 1966; Surwillo, 1964). Society enjoins its members to function within rather narrowly prescribed temporal boundaries, lest a label of abnormality be affixed. The categorization of unusual temporal experiences serves to maintain the proper boundaries: each of us realizes that certain sensations, such as excessive daydreaming, dwelling in past time, perception of the temporal flow as discontinuous, memories of greater impact and vividness than our present perceptions, or reified time as one's guiding life force, constitute abnormal temporal perceptions or perspectives.

Every individual comes by his temporal perspectives during the process of socialization, in which immediate events are cast in terms of future consequences. Frank (1939) put it thus: "A time perspective has been imposed upon events which thereby assume an altered meaning or value that is a function of that time perspective [p. 296]." As man ages, the extent of his experience grows, the events and emotions retained in his memory increase, and the quality of time, on any number of levels, is irrevocably altered. Both language and memory serve to influence the reception and retention of temporal experiences. If time becomes reified and coercive or runs out of control, man has lost the ability to command himself and his temporal experiences; consequently he becomes subject instead to external phenomena which are often given life through his very submission to them. At one extreme this has been seen as representative of certain mental disorders (El-Meligi, 1971, p. 234; Meerloo, 1970, p. 155). Man would seem to have the ability to transform temporal experience and perspective, so that there are interactions among physiological time, psychological temporal perception, and societal prescriptions on the nature of time. Definite societal differences in the roles attributed to time and the perception of time have been noted by writers such as Gurvitch (1964), Sorokin (1964), and Whorf (1956). Man is a temporal creature, who lives in time and is bound by external temporal referents; even so, Pollock (1971) notes that "certain temporal qualities such as duration, sequence, continuity, eternity, or progression toward death are subjectively and individually significant [p. 435]."

Rather than relying upon objective clock time when assessing the changes that occur in temporal perception with advancing age, we might well find it more profitable to explore the nature of aging as it relates to the social factors that modify subjective evaluations of temporal experience. Biological rhythms are acted out through a social medium; many who are externally defined as aged create their own time, actively constructing their lives and perspectives in the light of their own awareness of time. In previous research, temporal perceptions that differed greatly from external clock time were considered symptomatic of abnormality, whether it took the form of mental disorder, boredom, mind-altered conceptions of the present, or advanced age. This orientation may in fact prove deleterious to the interdisciplinary focus of social gerontology. Time *per se* is not confined to one aspect of life; no singular definition exists. The fact that individuals agree on an objective, external measure of time does not obviate the differential experiences that arise in the course of individual development. Man can be instructed in the subjective awareness and control of previously defined autonomic responses, and this paves the way for active participation in temporal construction.

A singular illustration of this is provided by the experiments of Zimbardo, Marshall, and Maslach (1971) on hypnosis. They have been able to modify temporal perspective by suggesting to trained hypnotic individuals that they "allow the present to expand and the past and future to become distanced and insignificant [p. 309]." Those whose temporal perspectives were altered differed significantly in their task performances and their perceptions from the members of three other nonhypnotized control groups. Zimbardo et al. hypothesize that older people who live in a past temporal perspective may do so because the present is meaningless or painful, and hence they seek escape. Hypnotic suggestion or other techniques "might induce a sense of expanded present or future in old people [which] would be an antidote to retrograde amnesia phenomena and might even increase longevity [p. 322]."

Objective measures of time are individually appropriated in terms of personal experiences, though the measures themselves provide a consensually validated basis upon which we share interpersonal relationships. Because the mind possesses time and remembers events out of their chronological contexts, temporal experience becomes a personal project (Sartre, 1963). According to Pollock (1971), "the acceptance of time is the acceptance of change and therefore of death, but it is also the acceptance of multiplicity, growth, and further development [p. 445]."

Most gerontological research has emphasized the legitimacy of one temporal orientation. Feifel (1957) averred "a normal sense of time aids in our adjustment and is an important means of establishing contact with and controlling the material universe [p. 71]." We continually seek a model of aging that may in fact be applicable to only one category of elderly individuals. A broader perspective on the issue might allow us to formulate a typology of aging similar to the one Mann, Siegler, and Osmond (1972, p. 145) have developed about personality types and temporal orientations. They have postulated four temporal orientations exist, which arise out of Jung's personality types. The four temporal experiential worlds differ to such a degree that channels of communication and interaction become potentially conflicting. For an individual of the Jungian feeling personality type, perceptions of past time rule, and time is perceived as continuous and circular. One who is predominantly a thinking type will perceive all events as couched within a historical flow; thus the continuity of time becomes crucial. If sensation marks the personality type, temporal experiences are conditioned by and interpreted in the light of the immediate, the present; for the sensation personality type, duration is experienced as an interruption of the flow of time. Finally the intuitive type experiences time as flowing backward; he continually introjects the future into the present.

If the existence of these temporal orientations is supported by further research, questions on what constitutes the "healthy, adjusted" style of aging must expand to incorporate the multidimensional nature of temporal experiences. Some individuals become increasingly preoccupied with past time as they age; this may be a feature of a particular type of personality, rather than a result of the aging process itself. Other individuals may place themselves within the flow of historical time and thus evaluate their relative worth in terms of sociocultural values. Still others may react to the process of aging in immediate terms, relinquishing any emphasis on historical influences. Within certain bounds, each individual has the freedom to construct his own temporal world, if he becomes aware of the potential avenues of temporal expression. This is not to say the road is any easier if consciously selected; indeed Meerloo (1970) saw it as hard and complex:

There is great security in submission to Father Time and in accepting tradition. Tradition regulates man's life. . . . Every man who breaks through the habit bonds of his own time is a rebel, but not necessarily a rebel against group, class, or political authority. He is rebelling also against time and its relentlessness. [pp. 40–41]

The possibility that there are numerous temporal dimensions in the individual's experiential world opens more doors to gerontological research than the dominant conception of a unilinear, physical time. Man is able to transcend his role of a timekeeper who records the passage of physical events, and who has difficulty in separating time from motion, as his very language uses spatial images to convey temporal impressions. The individual is able to distinguish between the world that he observes, to which he applies his sense of time, and the world in which he is a participant (Watanabe, 1972; Meerloo, 1970).

Bergson (1965) maintained that man experiences a continuous flow of time, in which all past impressions accumulate to form the present. This experiential time, *durée*, differs from the physical time, marked by a succession of instants, that man often records. *Durée* may be lived without reflection, yet physical time severs the continuity of temporal flow. Gerontological investigators usually ask the individual to perceive or estimate indicators of physical time, rather than to document his own inner temporal world. Kuhlen and Monge (1968) reported that the direct question, "How rapidly does time seem to pass for you now?" elicited more valid responses than a time metaphor test. Shakespeare appreciated this phenomenon; in *As You Like It*, Rosalind observes "Time travels in divers paces with divers persons [1957, Act III, Sc. 2, 305–6]."

Researchers might reasonably turn to an examination of the individual's own awareness of temporal flow and duration without first determining the physical measures to be used in the investigation. Many individuals will be bound by a physical conception of time, which they see as superior to their own existence. Yet it is possible to highlight alternative avenues of temporal experience, in order to open new models of aging that emphasize the creative role of the individual. The dialectical nature of temporal construction calls for more dynamic conceptions of time than those currently apparent in the literature. Time is currently cast in the role of an object, a concrete phenomenon that is everywhere the same, while only individual perspectives differ in the perception of this object. Time is depicted as a line, on which the present is the dividing point between the past and future. As the individual ages, the amount of future time decreases, and thus past time is increased. The resulting implications rest on the objective nature of the aging processes to which man must adjust. The qualities identified with the experience of time are reduced to mechanical measurement. Quantitative time determines the essence of qualitative temporal experience. This overriding theme tends to deny the possibility of creative action, as time does not truly belong to the individual. Yet how much farther we could explore if we accepted this:

> Man is not a passive piece of world time. He is the participant-creator of his history. Man is neither the biological clock, nor a succession of time spans. He is neither the time-bound words he speaks, nor the history that speaks in him. . . . He endures life and creates and recreates his own time. Man, the hierarchy of structures, lives in many stories and in many time coordinates. He does not live through one evolution, but emerges from many. Man is the father of his own time. [Meerloo, 1970, p. 264]

CONCLUSION

Jean-Paul Sartre (1963) suggests a viable avenue through which we may modify the unilinear, mechanical definition of time that is intrinsic to most gerontological research. Sartre sees man as engaged in projects, acting creatively, and determining temporal flow. The linear model of time denies that alternatives are potentially available to the actor. Sartre recognizes man's projects are defined in terms of past (memory) and future (imagination) times, plus the personal and social spheres. It is only through the construction of projects that man's time becomes his own.

"As time gives us the world so with the same motion it takes it from us [de Beauvoir, 1972, p. 566]." Man does not experience completed periods of time; Husserl maintains that memory allows us continually to re-turn to objects, Augustine that imagination structures the future. Men differ in their experience of temporal speed and duration. This item we admit to commonsense knowledge, that chronological age is not the best indicator of man's feelings of age, now provides the impetus for a consideration of the multiplicity of time.

Linear, clock time is but one of the relevant dimensions of temporal experience. The society's view of time influences the actor's orientation in his life world. The typifications constructed to make sense of the social may in turn assume an objective status in the actor's experience (Schutz, 1967; Berger and Pullberg, 1965). The objective, physical concept of time routinely used in technological societies determines the value of man's experience. Biological rhythms, durations associated with emotions, and social times are all presumed to be inferior to this objective time (de Grazia, 1964; Mumford, 1967; Rioux, 1970). Numerous cross-cultural investigations have revealed that different statuses are accorded to the elderly in different cultures. The value accorded experience, and by extension the depth of temporal experience, are more highly thought of in traditional (often agrarian-based) societies than in industrialized countries (Simmons, 1945; Burgess, 1960). The impact of science in technological societies has apparently fostered the adoption of a restricted definition of time, which tends to denigrate the individual's temporal experience.

Initially, the adoption by social scientists of the concept that arises from physical science time may have reflected the search for neutrality and objective truth. Yet when physical scientists themselves realized the limited nature of their concept, social scientists looked the other way, and continued to base their research on abstract, quantitative time. Gurvitch (1964), noting this paradox, commented, "But if the multiplicity of time forces itself on the natural sciences, how can we take exception to it in the social sciences where the conflicts of time are much sharper and much more striking? [p. 25]"

Since Einstein and Bohr propounded their theories, physical scientists have recognized the plurality of time and the subjective involvement of the scientist in his observations. Total neutrality presupposes a position of omniscient observation, which is rejected as impossible by natural scientists, but seemingly is still assumed by some social scientists. Physicists now concede it likely that other times besides unidirectional time exist, but as yet they lack the tools to identify them (Whitrow, 1961). When the influence of perspective upon knowledge and the multiplicity of time are ignored, man becomes a reactive subject rather than a participating actor. Obviously this focus on monolinear time often leads to conclusions of inevitability in reference to the status of social situations.

The convenience of a mechanical model of time in research is clear; quantitative measures are easy to apply and are highly reliable. However the implications of such models in social research are far-reaching. The mechanical model of time has a normative character, within which human action is explained. The historicity of social objects is discarded in favor of the replicability of human events. Social life in general, and aging in particular, are explained in terms of discrete data that exhibit repetitive patterns, and these are linked with theoretical language that rarely includes references to time. This limited approach to temporal experience in aging strains and reduces the holistic view of man's development.

Due to its interdisciplinary parentage, gerontology is ready to consider new descriptions of time. To do so, we must explore the possibility of returning the control of temporal construction to the actor in our analysis of his experiences. Not all will be able to transcend the limited view of time now prevalent, but some will readily assume a central role in defining different measures of temporality in human experience. Time varies qualitatively, and emotional moments are uneven: some time feels like no time at all (that is, in it we do not experience duration), while other time seems of unending duration. An examination of our implicit assumptions and a restructuring of our research instruments will lead us to new theoretical and practical orientations in the study of aging.

If we posit that man stands in dialectical relation to his social world, and actively constructs temporal experience, many issues in gerontology can be redefined. At present the economic institutions of society convey to the retiring individual that he has outlived his usefulness, and is now embarking on the last phase of his existence, destined to be marked by work-like activities (Anderson, 1959). Time appears to be "running out" for the aged; thus many refuse to actively appropriate time, and focus instead on past experiences. The routines of everyday life are disrupted by retirement; hence individuals feel incapable of creating new schedules.

These problems might be alleviated by new considerations of time and aging. The individual could establish the legitimacy of differential measures of time, emphasizing those that allow him greatest freedom of choice. Since he can never escape the experience of time, he should clearly establish his relation to objective time. Man is able to live in objectified, mechanical time only in a secondary fashion. This form of time is established in the reflective consciousness of man by his life and experience. Merleau-Ponty (1962, p. 240) has clearly specified the relation of the knower to his intentional world: a knower must recognize his ties to the intentional world before he can construct knowledge. The world extends in time and space, which are first experienced by the knower, and then are mathematically formulated. Objective, clock time is known but not lived as an entity present in the world; it is instead a particular order of signification.

The knowledge of objective clock time and its units presupposes that the structures of the social world are grounded in the temporal modes of human existence. Objective time may be based on measures of sequences in nature, but its origins are found in a sociocultural milieu and lived experience (Sorokin, 1964; Merleau-Ponty, 1962). Merleau-Ponty states:

> It is of the essence of time to be in process of self production, and not to be; never, that is, to be completely constituted. Constituted time, the series of possible relations in terms of before and after, is not time itself, but the ultimate recording of time, the result of its passage which objective thinking always presupposes yet never manages to fasten on to. [p. 415]

When time is seen as a process, continually becoming, a man is free to attribute a variety of meanings to his temporal experience. The imposition of quantitative measures on temporal flow exerts a restrictive force on man's experience. Unfortunately the latter approach does not take account of man's active participation in the construction of his temporal world. Students of aging, whatever discipline they represent, would increase the scope of their understanding if they adopted a more flexible conception of the part played by time in aging processes. It does not require an astute observer to realize that the biological, psychological, and social aspects of aging are interactive. Therefore more innovative conceptual frameworks are called for in order that we may appreciate man's holistic nature and the temporally determined dynamics of aging.

Part II

ON THE MEANING OF DISENGAGEMENT

Introduction

In its original formulation (1961), disengagement theory was a functional approach to the place of the aged in social orders. Its basic concept was that it is functional for a social system to disengage its elders, since a system, especially an urban-industrial one, is only as sound as its members' work in a variety of social roles. If we assume that the quality and quantity of a person's work diminishes as he ages, it is "best for all" that he voluntarily withdraw from a number of social roles, so that they can be filled by younger, more efficient occupants.

Immediately after the theory emerged, it received extensive criticism. Some of this came from adherents of what has come to be called activity theory. The central proposition of this is that life satisfaction ("adjustment") results from the maintenance of active involvement in any number of work-like roles in old age. Other criticism came from social environmentalists. They challenged disengagement theory because it ignored the social contexts of growing old. From the environmentalists' viewpoint, growing old has no universal meaning. Rather, its meaning and its subsequent impact on self-conception are tied to the situations in which it occurs.

In this section, disengagement theory holds the center of the stage. First, it is criticized from the point of view of a social phenomenologist. Rather than aging being an "objective" process of functional disengagement, it is suggested that it is an affair the meaning of which is defined and accomplished by all persons involved in it, both young and old. This criticism has the same roots as the subjective, existential idea of time discussed in Part I. Second, a more objective criticism is offered in the presentation of data on the realizations of disengagement theory's withdrawal hypothesis in various cultures. It is suggested that the universal feature of disengagement is not withdrawal from socially recognized roles, but the disengagement of the self from the active mastery of one's activity, and a withdrawal to passive and magical mastery.

chapter 2

Disengagement Theory: A Logical, Empirical, and Phenomenological Critique

ARLIE RUSSELL HOCHSCHILD

The beginning of social theory in a new field is often marked by the publication of some global theory that sets up a central question, makes a good try at answering it, and simplifies reality in some useful way. This is often followed by a period of critical reaction, which is followed in turn by a third stage, an attempt to restructure the general theory. In the field of aging, I suggest, we are in the middle of the second stage. Our global theory was Cumming and Henry's now classic disengagement theory, published in 1961.[1] Throughout the sixties there was a plethora of research reports, which criticized or confirmed this and that part of the theory, disassembled the variables, suggested alternative explanations, and tested the theory on different populations. Now the question is, where do we go from here?[2]

If we are not to start in the wilderness again, with new beginnings detached from past efforts, if we are not to let

I would like to acknowledge the helpful comments of Irving Rosow, John Clausen, and Guy Swanson on an earlier draft of this paper. Footnotes to this chapter appear at end of chapter.

53

the theory fade through lack of interest without learning something from it, we must take a hard look at it, with an eye to the following fundamental questions. Did the theory pose an important question? Was the theory logically constructed in a tight and consistent way? Are the borders of its categories drawn in an analytically useful way? What are the heuristic assumptions which determine the *level* of reality that is to be the domain of social gerontology? I will first try to answer these questions, then in the final section I will suggest that the original question can be posed in the light of new heuristic assumptions about socially situated behavior and meaning in old age.

THE BASIC QUESTION

I take the basic question to which the theory addresses itself to be this: How is age related to the way in which the individual is integrated into society? In the theory, engagement refers to both the "what" and the "how much" of social integration. To be sure, there are problems in the conceptualization of engagement. It refers more to the measurable lengths of behavior, as in the number of visits per month, than it does to the nature or meaning of the visit. It refers more to what people do than what they think about what they do. It refers more to the fulfillment of roles than to the function or power attached to them.[3]

I do not think Cumming and Henry answered the questions well, for logical reasons (the escape clause problem), theoretical reasons (the omnibus variable problem), and heuristic reasons (the assumption of meaning problem). But the fundamental question remains important. It is important if we extend the meaning of the term to include political, social, and experiential integration. It then becomes a social-gerontological approach to the question of social order. This, in turn, can be a point of focus for theories of age stratification, social psychology, and developmental theories of aging.

THE ESCAPE CLAUSE PROBLEM

One problem in the answer of the disengagement theorists to the basic question propounded above lies in the logic of the theory.[4] Let me start with one of the most important and controversial series of propositions in the theory. The first of these is that disengagement is universal, which I take to mean that it happens everywhere and in all historical eras. It is also held to be inevitable, which I take to mean that it must happen at some time in the individual's future if it is not happening now. It is also held to be intrinsic, which I take to mean that social factors alone do not cause it. These claims have throughout the sixties come under the most vigorous attack[5] (for example, see Kutner, 1962; Desroches and Kaiman, 1964; Maddox, 1964; Prasad, 1964; Rose, 1965; Tunstall, 1965; Videbeck and Knox, 1965; Youmans, 1967; Brehm, 1968). The attack, however, has been directed more against the substance of the claim than against its logical connection to other more flexible propositions presented elsewhere in the theory; namely, that there will be variations in the "form" and "timing" of disengagement. When we put these two propositions together, the immediate question becomes: which aspects of disengagement are constant (that is, universal, inevitable, and intrinsic) and which are variable (such as form and timing). Unless this is specified (and it is not specified in the theory), we have an escape clause problem.

The escape clause problem is essentially this: what would constitute counterevidence? Even in the Kansas City sample on which disengagement theory is based, not all very old people were disengaged; 22 per cent of those between the ages of 70 and 74 had "a large number of roles." Over a third (34 per cent) had "high daily interaction with others" and nearly a fifth (18 per cent) had "large lifespace [p. 40]," while 16 per cent did not perceive their lifespace as constricted. (p. 97).[6] Since the data are cross-sectional, we do not know how these particular people would have been gauged on these measures 20 years ago. We do know that it is hard to conceive of them being more active formerly than they are now.

In *Growing Old,* several types of escape-clause explanation are offered that prevent these anomalous older people from being counted as evidence against the theory. First, old engagers are said to be "unsuccessful" disengagers. They have not "achieved" the final psychological stages of "fixed conformity," described as "ego defect" for men and "internalized rigidity" and "externalized ego defect" for women (pp. 120, 125). According to the theorists, these older engaged people are not evidence of the theory's lack of universality; instead they provide evidence that bears on "success" defined, as it is, in this unique way. A person is either a successful disengager or an unsuccessful disengager, but in neither case is he engaged.

Alternatively, the engaged old person can be said to be off in his or her "timing."[7] Again, as their data show, a higher proportion of women in their sixties actually have a larger "lifespace" than do women in their fifties (Cumming and Henry, 1961, p. 40). Here one is either a disengager on time or a disengager off time, but in either case, these women are "on the way" to disengagement.[8] Again, the old engager can be explained away as a member of "a biological and possible psychological elite."[9] In the formal statement of the theory (p. 215), Bertrand Russell is cited as an example of re-engagement, as if his case did not bear on the statement that disengagement is intrinsic, inevitable, and universal. Surely, if we are going to talk about exceptional individuals, we should also entertain the possibility of "exceptional" opportunity structures (Atchley, 1971; Roman and Taietz, 1967).

If counterevidence cannot be dismissed through any of these three back doors, it has yet a fourth opinion: it may be treated as an example of "variation in the form" of disengagement. As the authors put it, "The concept of disengagement is culture-free, but the form it takes will always be culture-bound [p. 218]." The question of form is in turn related to the omnibus variable problem. For example, like most studies that claim to refute disengagement theory, a three-nation study of 2,500 older people in the United States, Great Britain, and Denmark (Shanas, Townsend, Wedderburn, Friis, Milhøj, and Stehouwer, 1968) offered evidence of continual social engagement. On none of their many measures of social contact are more than 40 per cent of those in their eighties isolated, and no more than 25 per cent of those in their sixties are isolated. In fact, the older the person, the less likely that person is (if single or widowed) to be living alone. Older women were found to be more likely than younger women to have seen one of their children on the same or the previous day.[10]

To be active in the sense of "seeing people," however, is not necessarily to be engaged. As Cumming points out in a footnote in her later article on disengagement theory (1963), active people can actually be "relatively disengaged impingers."[11] To say that no more than 40 per cent of the eighty-year-olds in Shanas' sample were isolated is not the same thing as saying that no more than 40 per cent were disengaged. The burden of proof seems to be on those who wish to make a case for continued engagement. If, as Cumming tells us, activity is not the same thing as engagement, then much of the counterevidence offered is invalid (Zborowski, 1962; Havighurst, 1964; Rosow, 1967; Hochschild, 1973). Like Shanas et al., many investigators are essentially concerned with isolation, not with disengagement, and their information, despite what they claim it means, does not measure up to the stringent requirements of counterevidence.

Henry (1964, 1965) likewise discounts counterevidence by stressing some criteria and belittling others. It is interesting to note just how Henry deals with counterevidence proferred in the study by Reichard, Livson, and Peterson (1962). The study cites examples of older people (the "mature," in their typology) who maintain high activity levels in roles indistinguishable from those of middle age, and maintain high morale. Henry (1965) comments on one engaged man in his sixties who is an "enthusiastic breeder of chinchillas."

> I saw one of the most beautiful chinchilla herds; I didn't know they existed. This fellow has been in it eight years. And he has the most beautiful animals. I could just sit there and watch them all day. And I was glad I went down to see him. It gives me something to work for. [p. 25]

Henry comments further:

> The Chinchilla breeder . . . in this quotation, strongly suggests that his ego energy has been displaced from active instrumentality and that the still active work involved in chinchilla raising serves him quite differently. Its meaning is not instrumentality in the usual sense, but rather an occasion for unassertive emotional experience and for sensuous, even voyeuristic, observation. [p. 26]

It remains unclear from this whether a similar slip in focus could be used to discount every other respondent of the same sort, or whether this man is in fact engaged in one way but not in another. If, when we lack one dimension, we can always resort to one of the many other possible dimensions in search of some change since youth, and if such extravagant inferences can be devised about the meaning of chinchilla-raising for such a man, when he was 50 or 60 or 90, then counterevidence will always be hard to come by.

One could argue that a full-scale replication of the theory is the only possible answer, and a few have been made: for example, there is a replication by Chellam (1964), which supports the theory; there is another by Tallmer (1967), and a partial replication by Lipman and Smith (1968), which do not. But since the replications follow the logic as well as the methodology of the original, we find that some interpret counterevidence in one way, and others interpret it in another way. If we were to produce yet another replication on, say, the Mundugumor of New Guinea, and were to find their old people engaged, we might also "find" that they were an example of cultural variation, of "off-timing," or of "unsuccessful engagement," or that the Mundugumor are a tribe of biological specialities." We do not need more replications of an unfalsifiable theory; rather we need a theory that offers clear criteria for counterevidence. This is an important lesson to bear in mind when we go about the construction of a new theory based on different assumptions.

THE OMNIBUS VARIABLE PROBLEM AND ITS CONSEQUENCES

Not only the logic of the connections between one variable and another, but also the size and shape of each, have been exposed as a problem by the research of the sixties. Essentially, the theory posits two independent variables and one dependent variable. The independent variables are the individual's age (with its implied relation to death) and society's stance toward disengagement. The dependent variable is disengagement. Society's stance toward disengagement (the degree of freedom from constraint, and the normative permission to disengage) is ultimately

not a variable, but a constant. One promising type of sociological criticism has converted this constant into a cross-
cultural or historical variable; I will take this point up again
later.

In between the independent and dependent variables,
there are many intervening variables that are said to modify
the relation of age to disengagement. These are said to be
"sources of variation" in the "form" of disengagement,
rather than sources of variation in engagement itself. Such
sources include physiology, personality, type of initial engagement, life situation, and sex role. These modifying
variables seem to be giant, catch-all categories, which encompass most of the classical sociological categories such
as class, race, urbanity, religion, and mobility: consider, for
example, the inclusiveness of the variable, "life situation."
A second type of follow-up research has raised these intervening variables to the status of full, competing, independent variables.

The omnibus variable problem, however, is more pronounced when we come to the dependent variable of disengagement itself. In fact, the characterization of
disengagement as a unitary process has proved to be one
of the weakest parts of the theory, and its exposure is the
most significant result of the follow-up research. Both variables turn out to be "umbrellas," which crowd many discrete phenomena together under single titles. When
researchers begin to unweave the parts from the whole, we
find (a) that different dimensions of disengagement
become dozens of discrete dependent variables, (b) that
when they are broken up by this continual binary fission,
some parts of the former omnibus dependent variable are
transformed into promising new independent variables,
and (c) that different parts of the central independent variable (age and related phenomena) have separate links to
disengagement. I shall now give some examples of these
patterns, from some of the research of the sixties.

First of all, the theory claims that all of the psychological and sociological forms of disengagement go together; but apparently they do not do so empirically. This seems to be more than a variation in "form." Atchley's study (1971) of professors emeritus, for example, shows that social disengagement can occur without its psychological counterpart. Carp (1969) further distinguishes between various kinds of social disengagement. In her study, disengagement from the family was negatively correlated with disengagement from material possessions, mental stimulation, social activities, and relations with other people. She concludes the following: "Some inconsistencies from study to study regarding the nature of disengagement . . . may result from the use of different partial criteria and of compound criteria with different elements [p. 346]."

The same problem exists in relation to the various components of the psychological side of disengagement (See Neugarten, 1964). This raises the following question: Precisely what, from the responses to thematic apperception test (TAT) cards, are we talking about? If we are talking about "adaptive powers and personal adjustment" (Peck and Berowitz, in Neugarten, 1964), we find no age differences. If we are talking about "ego energy available to the ego for maintaining involvements in the outer world" or "affect intensity," we do find age differences. If we are talking about active, passive, or magical mastery, again we find age differences (Gutmann, 1969). If we mean "seclusiveness and repression in the service of the ego," we do not find age differences. Neugarten suggests that whether we find age differences (in four studies in her book) or do not find them (in three), all depends on the overtness of personality expression. But over 100 different variables, types, dimensions, and factors are introduced into the quest for "disengagement," and as Rabin (1965) points out, many of them are often idiosyncratically defined.

I would like to briefly digress to discuss an assumption one often finds here; that social conditioning is associated with consciousness, and innate tendencies with the "unconscious." If there are intrinsic, developmental features in aging, the data based on covert measures suggest that these features are different for men and for women (Neugarten, 1968). The TAT data suggests that men, as they age become increasingly passive and dependent, whereas women become increasingly active and dominant. Neugarten reasoned that with old age, there is a "return of the repressed." If this is so, it may be that what was repressed in youth for women (dominance and mastery) differs from what was repressed in youth for men (passivity and dependence), for social reasons. In these covert measures, that which comes up in old age may be what was earlier "put down." The crossing of paths in old age may be an unconscious expression of equally unconscious social conditioning in youth. Thus, when we examine data that tell us about unconscious social processes in youth, we are not necessarily discovering innate or intrinsic psychological "givens." Rather, we may be finding the unconscious expression of social conditioning.[12] We cannot automatically equate social conditioning with conscious behavior, nor can we equate innate tendencies with unconscious factors.

Despite the problems that arise in the measuring and interpreting of covert processes, we no longer have one polyglot phenomenon called disengagement; and this means that new causal arrangements become apparent. For example, Rose (1965) suggests that economic disengagement can precipitate social and psychological disengagement. As he notes, "Those males who remain at work past age 65 do not disengage socially [p. 363]." Those who continue to work do not retire from the associations linked with work, such as trade unions, businessmen's associations, professional organizations, and service clubs auxiliary to work. Frankel, pursuing this line of argument (1962;

see also Carp, 1966, pp. 5–6), compares the psychological indicators of disengagement in old people with the psychological traits of the unemployed in the village of Marienthal, Austria, during the Depression (Lazarsfeld, 1932). The unemployed, young and old alike, showed, according to Frankel, "a narrowing of the psychological sphere of wants . . . so that the pressure of external conditions is not felt in its full force. We defined this psychic attitude as resignation [p. 149]." In spite of increased leisure time, the unemployed gave up many of their former activities. They did not read newspapers, even though they received them free, and the number of books borrowed from the library decreased by 50 per cent. In a subsequent study of 57 cases of unemployed, Zawadski and Lazarsfeld (1935) found the following reactions: "An especially depressing feeling of humiliation and of being superfluous; an increased sensitivity; aggressiveness, which is nevertheless marked by a peculiar inertia [p. 250]." As the duration of his unemployment increased, the individual progressed from optimism first to pessimism, then to fatalism, while his lifespace gradually narrowed. Lewin (1948) has also noted the effect of unemployment on all parts of a person's life. The unemployed "may cease to leave his immediate neighborhood; even his thinking and his wishes become narrow . . . Only when the person gives up hope does he stop . . . Only then does he shrink to a primitive and passive life [p. 103]." Thus, if we argue by analogy, one part of the dependent variable (economic disengagement) can be carved out and posited as an independent variable, to explain psychological phenomena remarkably close to the tell tale signs of "successful" disengagement, i.e. passive and magical mastery.

There is a similar argument about social isolation, which (though the authors do not use the term) is an essential part of social disengagement. Again, the researchers of the sixties have chipped off part of the dependent variable and set it up as a possible explanation for the remainder of the dependent variable. As Rosow (1967), Messer (1966), Blau (1961), Carp (1966), Lowenthal and Boler (1965), and others have shown, when old people for various reasons are socially isolated, for example by living in old nuclear families that are surrounded by young nuclear families, this has social and psychological manifestations.

Another way of dividing the omnibus dependent variable is to separate the loss of role from what remains of the indicators of disengagement. Tallmer (1967) and Tallmer and Kutner (1969), for example, have cogently argued and empirically shown by using Cumming and Henry's measures on a sample of 181 people aged 50 to 90, that when loss of role (that is, widowhood, poor health, or retirement) remains constant, the relationship between age and disengagement disappears. In their partial correlations between engagement measures, age, and role loss, they found that even when age was partially discounted, the association between disengagement and loss of role remained. In fact, when the association between age and loss of role was statistically partialled out, the link between age and disengagement dropped to zero.

Tallmer (1967) has essentially interposed certain existential imperatives (for example, widowhood and poor health) as independent phenomena that mediate the relationship between age and disengagement. Gutmann (1969) offers a similar argument:

> We do not automatically prove the developmental theory by refuting the socio-cultural alternative. There are existential necessities that impinge on most men, especially in later life —the exigencies of illness, of failing strength, of approaching death, of reduced opportunity and hope—that are independent of specific cultural circumstances just as they may be independent of any prior psychological or developmental events. These *existential* imperatives may be the independent variables, the independent engines of psychological change in later life. [pp. 35–36]

The variable of age and closeness to death has been subjected to the same kind of differentiation and reintegration. In the original statement of the theory, the distinction between being old, being close to death, and being aware that one is close to death was blurred. Furthermore, all these factors were assumed to be crucial for some 25 to 30 years before death. Since they were treated as if they were the "same thing," the theorists could not ask: Is it age *per se,* distance from death, or awareness of death that induces disengagement? Lieberman and Coplan (1970) conducted a series of studies in which they compared people who, as it later turned out, were going to die with a matched group who two years later were still alive.[13] They found that the individual's distance from death is more important than his age *per se,* and that his actual distance from death is only loosely linked to the individual's conscious concern about it. They also found that those who were two years away from death did show signs of disengagement, while those who were not, did not. This suggests that disengagement may be more a 2-year than a 20- or 30-year process, and that age, distance from death, and awareness of it are crucially different.[14]

In sum, there are good reasons to divide up this umbrella variable. In doing so, we see that the aging individual may become, say, more expressive, but no more oriented toward his psychic interior; he may become less oriented to others, but no more passive; he can be more internally oriented, but no less socially involved in the church; he may become more involved with the church, but less with his former work buddies; and so forth. Moreover, intricate new causal webs, yet to be fully explored, come into view where there once stood an apparently solid, seductively simple omnibus variable. This may not simply be the story of why a theory is discarded but of how any theory of aging can grow into something more complex than the simple propositions with which we inevitably begin.

THE ASSUMPTION OF MEANING

Whereas the escape clause problem involves the logic of disengagement theory, and the omnibus variable problem involves the question of how a theory slices reality into variables, the problem of the assumption of meaning deals with the question of what *level* of reality should properly be considered the domain of social gerontology. The disengagement theorists and many of their critics have detached social and psychological behavior from the meanings people ascribe to it. In this study whether a person is deemed disengaged or not depended primarily on two sorts of evidence: what respondents say they do and whom they see for how often (indicators of social disengagement), and what respondents say the TAT cards depict (indicators of psychological disengagement). In addition, to ascertain morale, the authors asked respondents twelve general questions (for example, is there any use in writing to public officials . . .) from the Kutner-Srole scale.

What is missing is evidence about the *meaning* of the daily acts that constitute engagement or disengagement. Lacking this phenomenological level of inquiry, we cannot see how two individuals with identical "role counts" apply different meanings to these roles, or how two people psychologically disengaged see the world and themselves differently as a result. In this study, disengagement is *of* persons but not *by* persons.

The problem of the level of reality is not, as in the logical and theoretical problems examined earlier, a problem of commission, but one of omission, and in my view it is even more serious. Were we to reformulate disengagement theory so as to eliminate the first two problems, there would still remain the more pervasive absence of the actor's own definition and meaning of the experience of aging. We would have, even without the first two problems, only a theory of disengagement *behavior* but not a theory of the personal *meanings* of disengagement.

I would not trouble with such a simple point if I did not sense that it had been forgotten in what has been the major theory of aging over the last ten years. I would not trouble with it were it not also *especially* crucial in the study of aging. The actor's definition of reality is, after all, not equally salient in all subjects of social inquiry, but it is extremely important for the understanding of old age in modern society. To some, death is an ending, to others a mysterious beginning; to some old age is a hanging onto productivity and a sense of efficacy, and to others an induction into a consummatory orientation. In one breath we comment that old age in modern society is a "normless" age, and in the next breath we study it as if norms and meanings were shared and apparent from behavior. The sharedness of meaning is perhaps more legitimately taken for granted in the study of old people in pre-industrial societies. But in my view one of the most basic and profound features of "modern" old age is precisely the diversity of personal meanings imputed to the impersonal facts of disengagement and death. To study behavior and ignore its personal meaning is to miss this most profound dimension of aging.

I shall offer two examples of how the missing "personal meanings" of the actor have led theorists to ignore questions they might have posed concerning the discrepancy and congruity between behavior and meaning. For it is just such discrepancies and congruities we miss when, as in disengagement theory, meaning is *inferred* from behavior.

One major concept in disengagement theory is that of normative control.[15] According to the theory, as old people grow older, they interact with others less. The less they interact, the less they are normatively controlled by others. The less normatively controlled, the more they become desocialized. The more desocialized, the more they exhibit eccentric or egocentric behavior. Desocialization is, in a sense, an "extra" mechanism which assures the inevitable progress of disengagement and prevents any return to previous states of engagement. One might parenthetically argue that, if disengagement is intrinsic and inevitable, this extra social mechanism is unnecessary. It is nonetheless part of the theory.

The hypothetical process would fail to come about if three things were not true: if social interaction did not decrease with age, if social control remained in the absence of social integration, or if normative control was weak despite some type of social integration. I shall focus on the latter two cases.

Cumming and Henry (1961) took the concept of normative control into account when they composed their measure of "social lifespace." In devising this, they asked the respondents questions about their social contact with others. But, as they note in the appendix, "Consideration was given to the relative amount of normative control generally expected in the situation when the weighting was worked out [p. 246]." It was generally expected, of course, by the researchers themselves, not by the respondent. Presumably the researchers reasoned in the composition of the measure, as they reasoned in the theory, that the more friends and relatives one sees a week, the more one is normatively controlled.

This might be a reasonable assumption in a study of mentally healthy children, aged four or five, who have not completely internalized many social norms. However, it is highly questionable whether or not a sixty-year-old adult, even if he is not subject to the sociological policemen of everyday life, an adult who is capable of independently experiencing guilt for violations invisible to others, is normatively controlled in proportion to the number of visitors he receives each week. After all, an insane person may receive many vistors each week, and may even have a very large "lifespace," yet he may not be normatively controlled in the sense in which Cumming and Henry mean the term.

The authors did not ask their subjects whether their behavior when they were alone differed from their behavior when they were not alone, or what meaning this had for them. In my own study (Hochschild, 1973), in which I also did not ask these questions, the residents of a low-income housing project wanted, by and large, to watch others and to be watched. Even the eccentric behavior (for example, the wearing of diamond earrings and tight slacks in the recreation room) was enacted more *in spite of* considerable normative control than because of the lack of it. In fact, one resident in particular took great pride in "getting a rise" out of her more conventional, fundamentalist midwestern neighbors.

We can no more reason backward that eccentric behavior arises from the lack of normative control than we can reason forward that lack of normative control produces the eccentricities of a desocialized old person.[16] Nor can we assume that social interaction and normative control are in direct proportion to one another. Instead, we need to recognize meaning and behavior as two discrete levels of phenomena which are interrelated in a great variety of ways. The combination of behavior and meaning might give rise to a typology of aging styles (Williams and Wirths, 1965). These may, in turn, have different social determinants than do pure, one-dimensional behavioral styles.

Far from recognizing two distinct levels of phenomena, the disengagement theorists infer meaning from behavior. Let me give a second example to illustrate this. The authors describe as disengaged some people in their sample who by all indications were fully engaged in an active social life. They were said to be active in *roles* "appropriate to the disengaged state." This may be a good characterization of their roles—horizontally oriented, somewhat fragile, temporary and lacking in deep commitment. But how do we characterize an engaged *person* in a disengaged *role*? Consider the following case: a person finds that her lifelong friends and her spouse have died. She moves into a public housing project for older people, goes to meetings, finds new friends, and takes up some new hobbies with these new friends, one of whom she is seriously thinking of marrying. Cumming and Henry would point out that her new relationships do not compare in depth with her former ones, and that this stage of re-engagement is to be temporary. But what evidence is there, apart from the fact that her friends are necessarily new, that the woman is not asking of her new relationships what she did of her former ones? In such a case, the crucial test is what she wants from these relationships that she did not want from her earlier ones, and what they mean for her. Without questioning the meaning of her behavior, we can really only comment on the role and not on the person. It is of little help to ask her general questions about life (the morale scale)[17] or to examine her TAT scores. These are no substitutes for data on the personal meanings she attaches to what she does. Without these personal meanings, we can construct a theory of behavior, but not a theory of the interrelation between meaning and behavior in old age.

PHENOMENOLOGICAL REBEGINNINGS

The focus on what people do, rather than on what meanings they attach to what they do, has deep roots in the assumptions about social science with which the theorists began. These assumptions conjure up an implicit image of the actor as an object of meaning, rather than as an assigner of meaning.

In this respect, *Growing Old* is a very strange book to

read, and it was probably a strange book to write. The text, especially after a direct quotation from an older person, often gives one the impression that a phenomenologist is at work, whereas the tables and formal propositions retire into the verbless language of the behaviorist. In one place we read that it is the "recognition" of aging and death that precipitates disengagement, but in another place we read that it is aging or nearness to death "itself." In one place we read "society," and in the next breath "his [the old person's] society." In general, the further away the text is from interview material, the more behaviorist the language and the stronger becomes the implicit image of the actor as an object of meaning. Herbert Blumer (1969) sums up this problem in disengagement theory when he notes of sociology in general: "Meaning is either taken for granted and thus pushed aside as unimportant or it is regarded as a mere neutral link between the factors responsible for human behavior and this behavior as the product of such factors [p. 2]."

It is worthwhile to trace the history of this image of the actor as an object of meaning. Disengagement theory draws heavily from the theoretical framework of Talcott Parsons.[18] Parsons, in turn, assimilated aspects of Max Weber's works into that framework, interpreting Weber in his own particular way. If we return directly to Weber, bypassing Parsons and Cumming and Henry, we discover a different approach to what the subject matter of gerontology as a sociological enterprise might be. To Weber (1966 edition), sociology is

> a science which attempts the interpretive understanding of social action in order thereby to arrive at a causal explanation of its course and effects. . . . [Social action, in turn, is defined as that which includes] all human behavior when and in so far as the acting individual attaches a subjective meaning to it. . . . Action is social in so far as, by virtue of the

subjective meaning attached to it by the acting individual (or
individuals), it takes account of the behavior of others and
is thereby oriented in its course. [p.88]

This simple notion, once filtered through Parsons'
work, is almost entirely lost in disengagement theory, and
in most of the criticisms of it that have dominated the
literature for the last decade. Social phenomenologists
have developed a second understanding of Weber, which
applied here, suggests a more comprehensive conceptualization of engagement, one which brings subjective meaning back in.[19] If we are to reintroduce meaning, there are
two approaches we might take. Following the ethnome-
thodologists,[20] we might examine the social determinants
of various modes of constructing reality, of making accounts of social action. At its extreme this approach leads
us to conceive of engagement as "nothing but" the actor's
account of it, regardless of such things as TAT tests and
morale scores. The story of old age *is* the telling of it. This
seems to me to move as far in the direction of subjective
reductionism as the disengagement theorists moved in the
direction of objective reductionism. (See Dreitzel, 1970).

The second approach[21] is to join the accounts of behavior with the accounts of their meaning for the individual
and to discern patterns woven from the two levels of reality.
(See Crawford, 1971; Birren, Butler, Greenhouse and Yarrow, 1963; and others.) The term "meaning" refers to both
cognitive and emotional dimensions of the actors response
to his social world.[22] Both are elements of the meaning
structures through which the individual perceives, values
and orients himself to his social world.

Moreover, behind the assignment of meaning to an act
is a latent comparison of that perceived act to what is often
a taken-for-granted expectation, one that makes the act
stand out as either extraordinary and important or not.

Here we might focus on expectations concerning relatedness, activity and a sense of efficacy. If, as the disengagement theorists tell us, the disengaged people they studied
were well adjusted to their situation, we might ask what
their background expectations were, and study *them* too as
a sociological phenomenon. The authors mention in passing that "aging people . . . apparently subscribe to the activity value" of aging (1961, p.72). If disengaged people do
not value the disengaged life they seem to live out, there
may be some discrepancy between what they value and
what they expect. This must affect the many private meanings old people attach to their daily acts.

I shall return now to the central question the disengagement theorists posed: how is age related to various
patterns of integration between the individual and his society. To illustrate some of the above, I shall draw on one
particular study by Crawford (1971), a study which examines three meanings or orientations associated with the
same behavior—retirement. These meanings are not
evenly distributed among the working and middle classes
studied. In interpreting why they are not, I would like to
suggest that these meanings are related to different background expectations about old age, which are different in
the two classes. These expectations, in turn, are linked to
a principle I take to be constant: that within the individual's
realm of perceived choices, he will be oriented toward that
sphere in which his sense of efficacy, or power[23] is greatest.
In other words, his sense of efficacy or power is closely
related to what is meaningful for him, however reduced or
redirected that sense of efficacy may be. Expectations concerning power are, in turn, rooted differently in the structure of work and family in the two classes.

In the first part of an exploratory and longitudinal
study of 99 English couples before and after retirement,
Crawford focused on their feelings and attitudes toward

retirement. The first wave of interviews took place before the men had actually retired, and it is to this section of the report that I am referring here.

Crawford elaborated three prototypes (ideal types in Weber's terms) of the meaning of retirement.[24] In the first, the individual feels that he is retiring back to something he already has, for example the family. As Crawford (1971) put it,

> The first group of men are those who identify retirement with disengagement and who are quite content to think of it in this way. They are looking forward to spending most of their time at home, either relaxing, enjoying semi-hobbies such as decorating or gardening, helping their wives with the running of the home or spending time with their families. They are going to concentrate their energies on intra-familial relationships and activities—to re-engage in the family—and to a considerable extent to withdraw from extra-familial networks. [p. 273][25]

In the second type, the individual identifies retirement with a form of disengagement, but in contrast, he dreads retirement because he feels that when the work role is removed, constraints are placed upon him. Retirement to him means a series of losses: "loss of money, loss of things to do, and most importantly loss of a meaningful role, loss of a place in the social structure." Crawford elaborates, "They will from henceforth be almost entirely dependent on their wives for company. They can no longer be part of a group of working men, either in the sense of working alongside them or in the sense of joining them in their leisure hours [pp. 274–5]." These losses all mean constraints on his behavior, because they imply a forced withdrawal from relationships and roles that he has up to now enjoyed. "This withdrawal is not of their own choosing, as they perceive it; it is imposed upon them [p. 275]." These individuals are retiring *from* something.

In the third type, the individual is looking forward to retirement because it releases him from pressures at work, and so frees him for re-engagement in a different set of activities. "Far from seeing it as a time when they will withdraw or disengage, they see it as time for extending their life in different directions, as a time for re-alignment [p. 275]." This type is retiring *for* something.

As Table 2-1 suggests, these three types were not randomly distributed across social classes in the sample population. Nearly half of both the middle and working classes interpret retirement as an externally imposed punishment of some sort. But a higher proportion of the working class see retirement as a return to the home, (type 1) and a higher proportion of the middle class see retirement as a realignment to leisure or another occupation (type 3). Thus, quite apart from the economic or social characteristics of retired life, the meaning of retirement appears to vary sociologically. Not all men who are similarly located in the social structure (for example, the English working class), and are about to do the same thing (that is, to retire), assign the same meaning to this event. If the individual in retirement integrates himself socially where he is least pow-

Table 2-1*

PROPORTIONS OF MANUAL AND NONMANUAL WORKERS WITH
THE THREE RETIRING ATTITUDES

	Manual		Nonmanual	
	percentage	*number*	*percentage*	*number*
Type 1	43	62	27	14
Retiring back to				
Type 2	49	71	48	25
Retiring from				
Type 3	8	11	25	13
Retiring for				
Total	100	144	100	52

*From Crawford (1971, p. 275). The figures are based on my recomputation of her data. Crawford asked what proportion of all "retiring to" types are manual or nonmanual workers. This table tells you what proportion of all manual or non-manual workers fit each type.

erless, how do we account for this difference between classes in their orientation toward retirement?

I suggest that it has to do with class differences in the location of the sphere of power, and the background assumptions concerning this. We should turn to assumptions about the power of men in the world of work and in the home in the two classes. William Goode (1970), when discussing egalitarianism, presents the following analysis of the male role in the family and working life of working- and middle-class men:

> Lower-class men concede fewer rights ideologically than their women in fact obtain, and the more educated men are likely to concede more rights ideologically than they in fact grant. One partial resolution of the latter tension is to be found in the frequent assertion from families of professional men that they should not make demands which would interfere with his *work*. He takes precedence as a *professional*, not as family head or as male; nevertheless, the precedence is his. By contrast, lower-class men demand deference as *men*, as heads of families. [p. 22]

Men in both classes have power in the family, but its location and basis differ. The relevant environment for the middle-class male's sense of power is his profession; that is what makes him the "man" of the family. It may be the background assumptions upon this relevant environment that then lead him as a retiree to avoid the family, and unlike his working-class counterpart, to seek some realignment, an alternative mode of social integration, somewhere else. It may be that both his expectations of reduced power and his ideas on what his immediate social environment (his wife and her expectations) offers are conducive to his resolution. By contrast, the working-class man's power in the home is not so contingent on work; he holds this power by virtue of being male. Thus retirement to the home does not change his sense of efficacy as he has formerly defined it. His expectations and his immediate social environment are different; and so he need not seek realignment. Behind each orientation to retirement there are background assumptions concerning one's sphere of power and efficacy.

There may be other background assumptions and structural features that appear as *givens* and are common to both classes of men, for both classes exist in a modern industrial society, and some of the features of this society may affect them in similar ways. As I have pointed out, the disengagement theorists treated social structure as a constant, not as a variable, and this prevented them from asking what the relationship is between the institutions of work and the family, and how this relationship affects orientations toward retirement.

Family and work are more clearly differentiated in American society than they are in preindustrial societies, and this very differentiation sets up cultural contradictions, a socially situated necessity to unlearn previous modes of orientation to both family and work. It is this schism between family and work that the retiring worker deals with by either returning to the family or seeking realignment outside it. It was this schism that led Eisenstadt (1956), in his discussion of adolescence, to posit that a cultural bridge is needed between the two, in the form of peer groups neither in the family nor in the work place. Perhaps it is just such a cultural bridge that type 3 realigners are seeking (Rosow, 1967). For both classes, the meaning of being oriented back to the family depends on what family there is left to be oriented toward. This varies, too, from society to society, and from class to class. Surely the men of Liebow's *Tally's Corner* and the men of Park Forest in Whyte's book *The Organization Man* have as they grow older different family structures toward which to orient themselves.

The meaning of one's detachment from work is connected with the meaning of one's former attachment to it. Morse and Weiss (1955) asked a sample of men, "If you inherited enough money to live comfortably without working do you think that you would work anyway or not? Eight out of ten said they would, but only nine per cent said this was because they enjoyed their work. The rest mentioned, for example, that they wanted to keep occupied, or to keep from feeling lost. They wanted to do *some* sort of work, even if not because they intrinsically enjoyed it. If more middle-class men in Crawford's study liked their work as young men, this may account for why proportionately more sought re-alignment outside the family, a sort of substitute work, as old men.

If we set out to explain the difference between people in one class and another in their orientation toward retirement, we must examine two things: a) the different structures of work and family in the two classes, structures which set real boundaries around the alternatives available, and assumed or perceived to be available, and b) the constant features, common to both classes, which limit the alternatives they assume or perceive.

Finally, attached to the three general conceptions of retirement for these men are a range of different types of behavior. Perhaps those who conceptualize retirement as disengagement (Types 1 and 2) will actually disengage, but perhaps, by virtue of opportunity or circumstance, not. Perhaps those who conceptualize retirement as engagement (type 3) will actually remain engaged, but perhaps not. But we cannot discern patterns of correspondence between what old people do and what things mean for them, unless we take both fully into account.

CONCLUSION AND IMPLICATIONS

In this essay I have tried to address the question of why the follow-up research of the 1960s has left disengagement theory, taken as a whole, in an indeterminant state. Part of the problem, I suggest, lies in its logical construction (the escape clause problem). We can remedy this problem by assuming that disengagement is a variable and not a constant which varies only in form and timing. Another part of the problem lies in the way in which reality was carved into variables (the omnibus variable problem). We can avoid this by recognizing various distinct and independent levels of disengagement. Finally there remains what I take to be a more serious problem—the level of reality which the theorists took to be the domain of social gerontology.

In addressing again the central question of the social integration of the aged in society, we might start with a more phenomenological image of the actor, as an assigner of meaning rather than an object of meaning. In doing so, I suggest we try two things. First, we try to locate social types of older people, types based not only on what people say they *do*, or on how TAT tests suggest they psychologically *are*, but on what they say is meaningful in the daily acts that constitute their particular form and degree of engagement in social life. Second, we try to explain why these types are distributed as they are in the social structure. In this way we may begin to understand engagement or disengagement not as behavior, but as meaningful experience.

NOTES

1. Disengagement theory first evolved from an article by Cumming, Dean, and Newell (1960), which was later developed in *Growing Old* (1961) by Elaine Cumming and William Henry. Twice revised, once by Cumming (1963) and once by Henry (1964), the theory has attracted several replications and many bodies of data have been linked to various parts of the theory. As various review articles point out (Maddox, 1964; Streib, 1968; Koller, 1969; Youmans, 1969), critics often disagree not only with the theory, but with each other; thus they pose a secondary problem of reconciling different criticisms with each other. For those readers who are not familiar with disengagement theory,

the outline is briefly this: Growing old involves a gradual and "inevitable mutual withdrawal or disengagement, resulting in decreased interaction between an aging person and others in the social systems he belongs to [1961, p. 14]." In every culture and every historical period, the society and individual have prepared in advance for the ultimate disengagement of death by an inevitable, gradual, and mutually satisfying process of social disengagement before death. This is a double withdrawal: of the individual from society, and of the society from the individual. On the one hand the individual "wants" to disengage, and does so by reducing the number of roles he plays, lessening the variety of his roles and relationships, and weakening the intensity of those that remain. The remaining relationships are, in addition, qualitatively different; they become more socioemotional and expressive. On the other hand, society offers the individual freedom from structural constraints and "permission" to withdraw. Once set in motion, the process is irreversible. The individual retreats from the social world, which in turn relieves him of normative control. He becomes desocialized. This ensures the linear progression of disengagement. This process is functional for the individual, in the sense that it can give him a high morale, and it is functional for society in that it retires the aged echelon from roles that young people can then fill. The process is universal and inevitable, although variations in timing and style occur according to the individual's physiology, personality, initial type of engagement, and life situation.

2. To this day the assessors disagree. In the mid-sixties we find Maddox (1964) saying, "In balance, disengagement theory has been found wanting empirically and its original formulation is rarely defended by anyone," while on the other hand, Streib (1968) both defends the claim to universality (the usual target point in the theory) and concludes that it "does have value in understanding aging and the aged in settings very different from that in which the theory was originally developed [p. 76]."

3. Cumming and Henry do not discuss power, and indeed the word "power" does not appear in their index. They focus on the extent to which old people are normatively controlled, but not on whether or how they control others. In their theory the lack of power of old people, especially the retired and widowed,

becomes a parameter, not an independent variable, and the unspoken assumption of their low status underlies the notion that there is a syntonic relation between the old person and society.
4. I will refer to the theory in its latest revised version. This is not the version to which much of the research of the sixties addressed itself. Much of the latter is not really a reaction to disengagement theory; it often takes the form of two or three prefatory paragraphs attached to ongoing research. The operationalization of the concepts, and sometimes the concepts themselves, differ from those of the original theory. Actual replications often apply only to fragments of the theory, and often the results contradict both the theory and other follow-up research.
5. Cumming, in her revision of the theory (1963), ignores the universality claim, while Henry (1964) defends it.
6. On the psychological measures, 5.9 per cent of the men aged 64–70 fell into the "engaged" pattern of "focused active mastery," whereas 17 per cent of the women fell into the "externalized personal mastery" pattern, said to be the corresponding state for women.
7. Although they do not appear in the formal statement of the theory, Cumming and Henry actually describe regularities in time variation:

> Our findings . . . suggest that, following a plateau in the late forties and through the fifties, there is a crisis, marked by anxiety, between sixty and sixty-five. After this, most people become more contented. Again, in the seventies, there is a restlessness and irritability that, if not resolved by death, may lead, for the special few survivors, to a period of tranquility and satisfaction in very old age. [p. 202]

8. In any case, as we shall see, not all of the many dimensions of disengagement need have the same "timing." Ego energy could be hypothesized to obey one schedule, changes of affectivity another, self-absorption yet another, and loss of social role still other schedules. Thus not all the dimensions of the omnibus variable (disengagement) need necessarily occur at the same time.

9. The authors put it thus:

> Many observers have commented on the special qualities of
> the very old. Riesman draws attention to Bertrand Russell
> and Toscanini; others talk of Bernard Baruch and Bernard
> Shaw. There is some evidence that living to be over eighty,
> whether or not you are famous, is associated with being a
> member of a biological, and possibly psychological, elite.
> Furthermore, very old people often have a surprisingly high
> level of social competence and seem able to maintain high
> spirits. [p. 201]

10. "The data . . . do not suggest that, independent of growing
infirmity, social disengagement is a widespread phenomenon [p.
442]." As the authors put it, "The evidence on attitudes is sparse,
but does not in general suggest that as old people get older they
disengage subjectively. . . . There may be a contraction in the
number of 'peripheral' social relationships . . . but there is little
change in the number of central relationships [p. 442]." Only 3
per cent more of the very old (80 and over) than of the moder-
ately old (65–69) had seen no relative in the last week. While
fewer of the older group went out to visit, almost as high a
proportion were visited by others.
11. Cumming (1963) states:

> [This raises a problem of the] difference between the *appear-
> ance* of engagement and the *experience* of it. This problem is
> enhanced by the tendency to contrast disengagement with
> activity. In fact, activity and engagement are not in the same
> dimension. A disengaged person often maintains a high
> level of activity in a small number and narrow variety of
> roles, although it is doubtful if it is possible to be at once
> firmly engaged and inactive. In any event, the opposite of
> disengagement is engagement, a concept different from,
> though related to, the concept of activity. [p. 380]

12. Support for this comes from Mark Zborowski's study (1969)
of the response to pain of old Americans (Jews, Italians, Protestants, and Irishmen) in a Bronx hospital. He found that even
when he controlled for the various types of illness or ailment,

different ethnic groups expressed their pain in different ways (the Jews moaned and groaned, the Protestants stoically and silently withdrew). But it was not only the expression, but also the actual experience of pain (as reflected in physiological tests) that varied with the ethnic group. Some ethnic groups had higher pain thresholds than others. If a sociological category as common as the ethnic group is correlated with a variable as profound as the pain threshold, it is entirely possible that sex and class are correlated with unconscious processes (which are as impossible to control as is the experience of pain) quite as much as they so obviously are with conscious and behavioral characteristics.

13. The 80 subjects, whose average age was 83, came from a variety of socioeconomic backgrounds and social contexts. He did find differences between those who turned out to be close to death and those who did not. These differences showed up in attitudinal scales and TAT tests, and most were compatible with disengagement theory. Those near death were less affectively complex, less assertive and aggressive, and more docile, dependent, and intimacy-oriented than those far from death. They were also, however, less introspective, which disengagement theory would not predict.

14. Distance from death can again be distinguished not only from age, but also from the *awareness* of it. It was this awareness that Challam (1964), in a replication of the theory, found to be related to both social and psychological disengagement. It is always possible, of course, that disengaged people tend to be the sort of people who often think about death.

15. Cumming (1963) elaborates thus:

> "Because interactions create and reaffirm norms, a reduction in the number and variety of interactions leads to an increased freedom from the control of the norms governing every-day behavior. Consequently, once begun, disengagement becomes a circular, or self-perpetuating process [p. 384]."

16. A later test of this portion of the theory (Neugarten, 1964, chapter 7) did not bear it out. Ten variables supposed to indicate disengagement from the social network (some from TAT data

and some from questionnaire data) did not bear out the notion that disengagement from social network leads to eccentric and egocentric behavior.

17. The measure of "morale" poses another problem. We have no way of knowing whether the items on the Kutner-Srole scale ("There is little use writing to public officials because often they aren't interested in the problems of the average man") are in any way connected with experiential morale, or with the life issues to which it is attached. Other problems arise from the morale scale; its questionable link to individual "needs" (on which the argument that disengagement is "functional" rests), and its link to issues other than age, such as poverty. But these have been covered elsewhere.

18. Parsonian categories are generally difficult to operationalize. This problem becomes especially acute in a study such as this, which is otherwise finely tuned to the social psychological level. In the Cumming and Henry study (1961), global distinctions such as that between specificity and diffuseness were operationalized by simple questions such as this: "First tell me the one you think resembles you most, then the one that resembles you second most, a) a person who is esteemed by others and takes a continual interest in human welfare in general" (diffuse) and so on [p. 253].

19. I should mention a third theoretical issue, which applies as much to the behavioral as to the phenomenological approach to old age: atomism. In the Kansas City study, evidence on social structure pretty much boiled down to the number of visits and the labels (such as "role") assigned by the researchers to behavior. There was no feeling for social context or structure, with its own emergent properties. While I think this also poses a problem for phenomenologists, I think they are more likely to handle it subtly through their attention to the meanings people assign to these emergent properties, and through their focus on multiple realities and the different meanings people can assign to such properties.

20. Dreitzel (1970) points to a difference between symbolic interactionism and ethnomethodology:

> The method of "documentary interpretation" should not be misunderstood as a method to reveal patterns that underlie appearances, actions, events and the life, *and* have an existence independent of the interpretation procedures. This is where ethnomethodologists radically depart from the established approaches in sociology, *including* symbolic interactionism which still concentrates on the shared symbols and meanings of everyday activities, even if these symbols are seen as the result of negotiations and interpretations and, therefore, have a precarious, constantly shifting existence. Ethnomethodologists, on the other hand, maintain that the social order, including all its symbols and meanings, exists not only precariously but has no existence at all independent of the member's accounting and describing practices. [p. xv]

21. With this approach, we make our assumptions as clear as possible, and also make the actors' assumptions as clear as possible. We can then go back and forth between the sets of assumptions, taking neither for granted, and negotiating between one construction of reality and another. If this sets us adrift from our positivist moorings, it also gets us closer to a drifty and messy reality, and closer to the unmet challenge of social gerontology.
22. When I use the term "meaning," I refer to three things: (1) a more or less coherent philosophy of aging, proscriptive and explanatory schemas that either legitimize or interpret the events and conditions of old age, (2) an orientation toward the self and the environment in the final stage of the life cycle, roughly commensurate in level of generality with Erikson's notion of integrity, and (3) a multitude of specific attitudes toward a variety of salient events and conditions, which together constitute an orientation, and from which a philosophy is often articulated.
23. The concept of power also has other implications. In their study of TAT cards, Neugarten and Gutmann (1958) found that a trend from active to passive and then to magical mastery was associated with the increasing age of the respondent. Magical mastery may be closely associated with a sense of powerlessness. Malinowski discusses the belief in magic in primitive societies as something related to anxiety, which in turn is related to power-

lessness. One might find this in other cases of powerlessness, regardless of age. In his phenomenological theory of the emotions, Sartre (1948) suggests that emotions involve a departure into "the magical attitude" on just those occasions when one is powerless to resolve some problem.

24. Crawford combines two dimensions in these prototypes, one that involves orientation to and away from something and toward something else, and one that involves the positive or negative value in that orientation. Thus, logically, there are two evaluative possibilities for each of the three orientations, even though Crawford found that there was an empirical clustering of the three types. These three types might be linked to the different meanings associated with an awareness of aging, which Cumming and Henry gratuitously associate with the beginning of disengagement. Only in the second type (retiring from something) do we get a perceptual and affective focus on the significance of "ending." This assignment of meaning might be compared to other cases in the sociology of endings; unemployment (mentioned earlier), divorce, and partings of any kind. It may well share certain structural properties with other types of ending. (I am indebted to Professor Marcia Millman for this idea.) Some of these structural features, in turn, may resemble the telltale signs of disengagement: a withdrawal of interest from objects before the actual end, a dedifferentiation of psychic and social aspects of the individual, in order to reconstitute a more self-sufficient unity, more fully separate from those with whom one is parting. Many divorcees speak of recapturing parts of themselves they had previously relinquished to the other, when they end the relationship. By contrast, in the first and third types, retirement is perceived as a "beginning" of something else. In the first case it is the beginning of a new relation to the family. It is comparable in this sense to other "beginnings," such as marriage or a new job. In the third case, too, retirement means a beginning, a new realignment of involvements. Alternatively, one *could* see retirement, in some areas of life, as a continuation, not remarkably different from what has gone before. In some existential sense, perhaps it is all three (an ending, a beginning, and a continuation), but the question is how the actor himself sees retirement.

25. Crawford also interviewed wives. He found that they assigned very different meanings to retirement than did their husbands. Of the men, 33 per cent fit Type 1, 54 per cent fit Type 2, and 12 per cent fit Type 3. For the women, the corresponding figures were 52, 44, and 3 per cent. In other words, the women were much more likely to see retirement as a return to the family, and much less likely to see it as a realignment to a new activity. Moreover, half of the working-class women, but only a third of the middle-class women, saw retirement as a return to the home, while 11 per cent of the middle-class women and virtually none of the working-class women saw retirement as a realignment. We have no data on men's reactions to women's retirement.

chapter 3

Alternatives to Disengagement: The Old Men of the Highland Druze

DAVID GUTMANN

INTRODUCTION: RESEARCH INTO THE COMPARATIVE PSYCHOLOGY OF LATER LIFE

This paper reports some recent results derived from a study on the middle-aged and older men of the Druze sect, resident in highland villages of the Golan, Galilee, and Carmel regions of Syria and Israel. The overall aim of the research of which this study is a part has been to establish, through application of the comparative method, some basis on which to formulate a developmental psychology of aging. Generally, the research program has involved intensive interviewing and projective testing of the younger men (aged 35–54) and older men (aged 55 and over) of traditional and usually preliterate societies: the Lowland and Highland Maya of Mexico, the traditional or Western Navajo, and the Druze of Israel (including the Golan Heights).[1] These societies differ from each other in lan-

[1]The overall program of cross-cultural research has been supported by Career Development Award 5-K3-Hd-6043 from the National Institutes of Child Health and Human Development. Field expenses for Indian studies in Mexico and America were covered by Faculty Research grants 1344 and 1412 from the Rackham School of Graduate Studies, the University of Michigan, and by grant MH 13031-01 from the National Institutes of Mental Health. Fieldwork expenses among the Druze were covered by grant M66-345 from the Foundation's Fund for Research in Psychiatry.

guage, ethnic composition, cultural contents, and physical environment. They are alike in that they are composed of marginal agriculturalists who dwell in relatively remote communities and hold to their traditional life ways. Given their traditional orientations, these societies tend to be culturally homogeneous across the generations, and the pace of social change is fairly slow. Accordingly, if the analysis shows that there are standard cross-cultural differences between the psychological functioning of the younger and older men of such societies, the variation can be attributed to intrinsic developmental factors, rather than to extrinsic social influences. The guiding hypothesis of this research program was originally developed from findings in an urban study made in the United States; briefly stated, it holds that important psychological orientations, based on the parameters of passivity and aggressiveness, dependence and autonomy, would discriminate age groups within culturally different societies—in effect, that these orientations would be governed more reliably by age than by culture. Accordingly, a hypothesis was set up that younger men across cultures would reveal motives, attitudes, and images characteristic of an active, production-centered, and competitive stance, while other men would show the converse pattern. They would give priority to community rather than agency, to receptivity rather than productivity, and to mildness and humility rather than competition. The predicted age shift, then, is from the mode of *active mastery* in younger men, to the mode of *passive mastery* in older men. It was further expected that the oldest men of the various samples (those aged 65 and over), would protect their retreat from action and maintain their tenuous sense of security in the face of oncoming death through a reliance on *magical mastery,* a conformation based on the primitive, reality-distorting defense mechanisms of denial and projection. Thus far the hypothesis has been borne out, by both cross-sectional and longitudinal data derived from study sites in the United

States, Mexico, and the Middle East (Gutmann, 1964, 1966, 1967, 1969; Krohn and Gutmann, 1971; Goldstine and Gutmann 1972). Though the societies surveyed vary in the degree to which they emphasize or sponsor active, passive, or magical mastery and toward the passive and/or magical orientations with increasing age. Thus, despite the profound cultural differences in our samples, age accounts for a greater part of the variation in the personality measures than cultural differences; and this independent effect of age would seem to indicate that intrinsic, or "developmental," factors contribute to the psychology of aging men.

Nature and Nurture: Their Impact in Later Life

The finding that there are intrinsic age-related influences does not rule out the influence of sociocultural factors over the psychic life. Men who are partly shaped by intrinsic processes must still find the setting for their development in socially organized worlds; and they are continually influenced by the age norms set by their society over their behaviors and attitudes. Covert, universal influences do not make men less sensitive to overt social influences; they only direct that sensitivity to particular subsets of the available social norms, usages, and understandings. Thus younger men might recognize the existence of a religious tradition in their society, and be knowledgeable about its precepts, but their *subjective* relation to this tradition would differ from that of their fathers. The younger men could report (as anthropological informants, for example) on the rules of the religious tradition, but they would not always turn to those rules for regulation of their behavior. By the same token, the aging fathers of these young men would know a good deal about the social usages that govern the productive life in their society, but would find these less personally relevant than the rules that govern the religious life, and the relationship to God. Thus, owing to the influence of emerging developmental dispositions, older men would give personal reality to social norms and conventions that had far less impact upon them when they were younger.

The nature versus nurture issue is perhaps the central question in the behavioral sciences, and cannot be put to rest by a single study; nevertheless, the case of the Highland Druze of the Middle East perhaps offers an integrating model: it suggests the ways in which age-graded role requirements and developmental potentials and co-exist, as reciprocals and metaphors of each other, in the traditional community. This discussion begins with a description (necessarily brief) of the Druze history, culture, and modal personality.[2]

THE HIGHLAND DRUZE

The villages of the Druze, which are sited for defense, are scattered through the highland regions of Lebanon, Syria, and Galilean Israel. The Druze people are mainly agriculturalists, involved in the cultivation of fruits, olives, wheat, and tobacco. Throughout their history, however, individual Druze have been prominent in the political and particularly in the military affairs of the Middle East. The Druze are a people who chose a minority status, on religious grounds, within the larger Arab world. They speak Arabic, and their life-style is in most respects similar to that of the patriarchal Muslim villagers of the Levant. The Druze broke with the Muslim religion on doctrinal points,

[2]The Druze study reported here would have been impossible had it not been for the friendship and dedicated help of Mr. Kassem Y. Kassem, a Druze social worker and resident of the Galilean village of Rami, who worked closely with me during three field trips among his people. The entire Kassem family gave me their help and hospitality on these occasions, and this too is most gratefully acknowledged.

however, and thereby exposed themselves to the difficulties that go with self-elected minority status. Over the past 800 years the Druze have suffered many episodes of religious persecution at the hands of the Muslim majority; and they have managed to develop the personal and cultural traits that generally characterize a minority that survives in the face of odds. Since they could not take the goodwill of the majority for granted, they learned as a group to trust mainly themselves: the courage, strength, and wit of the Druze people. Each individual Druze tends to reproduce in his personality the general stance of the culture. Individual Druze are fiercely self-reliant, and will allow themselves to depend only on their own strengths, or on resources that they themselves have cultivated: the produce of their fields, or the strength of their sons. They trust very little that comes from outside of themselves as gift or gratuity, and this mistrust of whatever is not under their own control extends even to their mental life. Thus the Druze are extremely stubborn and refractory as individuals, not only against coercion from the will of others; but even against coercion from their own willfulness, their own spontaneous emotions. They do not allow themselves to become excited, and even illiterate Druze peasants set rationality above emotionality. In effect, they value the mental resource that they have created for themselves over the emotions that have been "foisted" on them. As part of their self-reliance, they must deny any needfulness within themselves, and must hold themselves in the position of the giver rather than the receiver. Hence they are unfailingly and sometimes even aggressively hospitable.

A major political problem for the Druze is the coordination of their own community life, which is centered around their religion, with the requirements and demands of the non-Druze majority, which has frequently been hostile to their faith. Over the centuries they have learned to blend flexibility and accommodation with firmness and traditional rigidity. So they change and compromise in minor ways that do not touch on the core of their religious tradition, in order to maintain that same core inviolate and unchanged. Thus, they typically raise their sons to be career soldiers and policemen for the majority government—in effect, they trade their sons for political security—and they are usually meticulously loyal to the letter of the secular law. But they will not tolerate any violation, by the majority, of the core of their religion or their tradition. For example, they will not tolerate any attack on the honor of their women or of their priests. If their minor compliances do not succeed in staving off dishonor and sacrilege, then the Druze will, almost to the last man, go to war. Though their villages have always been scattered over different countries, the Druze say of themselves that they are like a large brass plate: "Strike one corner, then the whole will vibrate." True to this motto, the Druze led the revolution against the French after World War I that gave rise to the establishment of modern Syria; and they are famous throughout the Middle East for their ardor in battle.

Druze Age Roles

Since the Druze people form a religious sect, their religion is central to the workings of their society, and to the sense of Druze identity. Yet it is kept a secret, not only from the outside world, but also from Druze women and from the younger men of the community. Thus the schedules that govern admission to the inner circles of the Druze religion also determine the age-grade systems, the social norms and shared understandings that partially order the latter half of the life-cycle for the typical Druze male. The Druze have learned to treat their heretical religion as a kind of conspiracy within the body of Islam; traditionally, therefore, the younger Druze (who might rashly reveal their identity to non-Druze neighbors) were not instructed in the religion or even told that they were Druze until they reached the age of discretion. This tradition of keeping the religion secret from the younger members of the community has survived even into these more liberal times. Younger Druze men, those not yet initiated to the secret books, are known as *Jahil*, the "unknowing" ones. The older men, those who have been accepted into the religious society, and who have received their copy of the secret text, are known as *Aqil*: literally, those who know. In the more traditional villages some men may become *Aqil* in early middle age, after they have established their family of procreation, and there are even a few *Aqil* youths, seminary-trained sons of famous religious leaders. But for the most part, men are not invited to become *Aqil* until late middle age, after they have led an exemplary life. As was noted earlier, Druze men of any age are generally formal and punctilious, but this is intensified after a man becomes *Aqil*: he shaves his head, he adopts special garb, and there is a notable shift towards even greater propriety in his behavior. Furthermore, he gives up alcohol and tobacco, he devotes much time to prayer, and he is expected to appear at all important social functions. Even the inner life of the *Aqil* is regulated: he is expected to devote himself to good and pious thoughts and to forget the errors and stupidities of his past life, committed before he was introduced to true knowledge. Hence it is very difficult to interview an old *Aqil* on his childhood experiences. He becomes remote or evasive, and at times even angry: "Why do you ask me about the time when I was ignorant, before I became close to God? I was like an animal then, I did not think of God, and it is a shame to remember such things!"

In sum, the old *Aqil* purge themselves, consciously at least, of the appetites (and even the memories of the appetites) that do not fit the prescriptions of the religious life. As the typical Druze man passes into late middle life and old age, he appears to shunt into the behavioral and attitudinal tracks that have been prepared for him by the age-grade system of Druze society. His life appears to be almost completely governed by parochial requirements of a kind that have meaning only to the religious Druze.

Universal Trends in Druze Aging

The projective data on these same Druze men suggest, however, that in later years their inner, subjective lives change in accordance with universal developments as well as with extrinsic, parochial constraints. These data indicate a pattern of psychological changes that conforms with the patterns observed in their age peers from radically different cultures, in which older men do *not* necessarily enter a rigorous religious subculture. The comparative analysis of the Druze projective materials, between age cohorts and across cultures, supports the hypothesis that there are universal psychological patterns in aging, developments that are mandatory regardless of the requirements set by particular cultures.

Thus, if we inspect Table 3-I, and compare the age/ theme distribution of Druze responses to the "rope climber" card of the thematic apperception test (TAT),[3] a card used in its original form at all sites, we find that this distribution replicates that developed toward the same card by the younger and older men of the Mayan (both Highland and Lowland), Navajo, and United States cultures. The younger men, whether urban American, Navajo, Mayan, or Druze, tend to interpret this stimulus in the ways listed in categories 1 and 2, which reflect the various components (competitive, rebellious, and productive) of the active mastery orientation. For them, the rope climber competes

[3]The rope-climber card, card 17BM of the standard Murray TAT shows a muscular man, possibly clad in tight-fitting gymnast's clothing, in the position of one who either climbs or descends a rope; the card is ambiguous as to the direction of movement.

Table 3-I

DISTRIBUTION OF RESPONSES TO THE ROPE-CLIMBER CARD, BY AGE, CULTURE, AND THEME

Theme	Culture	Age Group Distribution		
		35-49	50-59	60+
1. The climber demonstrates his strength, often in the face of competition. However, triumph has its price: the rope may break at the moment of victory.	Kansas City	21	35	10
	Navajo	5	1	6
	Lowland Maya	3	2	2
	Highland Maya	2	0	1
	Druze	11	5	6
	Totals	42*	43	25
2. The climber acts in the service of relatively limited but productive goals: he searches for a shortcut, for food, or for herds. He trains for future competition. If he is thwarted, it is by the physical environment, not by other men or by his own weakness.	Kansas City	4	13	7
	Navajo	6	7	10
	Lowland Maya	9	2	2
	Highland Maya	3	1	1
	Druze	21	19	23
	Totals	43	42	43
3. The climber indulges his physical weakness, or his wish for pleasure: he rests, he enjoys the view, he dives into water, he plays on the rope.	Kansas City	2	3	7
	Navajo	3	4	12
	Lowland Maya	3	5	14
	Highland Maya	4	7	7
	Druze	1	1	1
	Totals	13	20	41
4. The climber is menaced by external forces, or by his own weakness: he flees from enemy, beast, or fire; he is too tired to climb, and clings to the rope; he is on a rope, but not in motion.	Kansas City	4	18	17
	Navajo	4	5	16
	Lowland Maya	3	6	8
	Highland Maya	5	2	6
	Druze	8	4	12
	Totals	24	35	59
5. Either the rope or the climber is grossly misperceived: the climber is lying down, or dead; the rope is a snake, etc.	Kansas City	—	—	2
	Navajo	—	—	3
	Lowland Maya	—	1	2
	Highland Maya	1	1	1
	Druze	2	—	14
	Totals	3	2	22
	Age group totals	125	142	190
	Kansas City	N=143		
	Navajo	N= 82		
	Lowland Maya	N= 62		
	Highland Maya	N= 42		
	Druze	N=128		
	Overall total	N=457		

* Chi square (of cell totals) = 48.712. Degree of freedom (DF) = 8; $P < 0.001$.

† The Druze group includes Golan, (Syrian) Galilean and Carmel (Israeli) subjects.

against other climbers, trains for future contests, or escapes from prison (category 1); if the hero is seen to be in danger, it is a risk that he has incurred for himself, by virtue of his own initiative or boldness. While substantial numbers of older men continue to see the climber as active, they no longer see him as an aggressive figure. The age totals in category 2 indicate that for them, the hero may struggle against physical nature, or against his own weakness; but he does not struggle against society, or against other men. Among older men, the shift away from aggressive interpretations of the rope-climber card is matched by their notably greater tendency to see in him the expressions of passive mastery: he is relaxed and pleasure-seeking (category 3); or he is menaced either by his own fatigue and weakness or by the superior strength of some external agent—human enemy, beast, or fire (category 4). In addition, older men, including the older Druze, far outweigh younger men in their use of the magical mastery interpretation, represented by images of the rope climber as dead, asleep, or penetrated by a spear (category 5).

Equivalent age differences in the distribution of active, passive, and magical perceptions are developed by the "heterosexual-conflict" card of the standard TAT. The card depicts a young woman reaching toward a young man, who is turned away from her. Again, as is shown in Table 3–II, the younger Druze, like the younger men of other societies, see the male figure as representing active mastery: for them, he is impelled out of the picture by his own intrinsic energy, on some *Macho* mission: he is fighting a man who has insulted his woman, he is going to work, or he has a more desirable woman (category 1). For the younger men, the sex roles are sharply distinguished: any concern about the possibly dangerous consequences of the young man's assertive behavior is lodged in the timorous woman; the young man is all restlessness and fire. But the older Druze, like other older men, shape their perceptions

Table 3-II

THE HETEROSEXUAL CONFLICT CARD: DISTRIBUTION
OF RESPONSES BY AGE, CULTURE, AND THEME

Theme	Culture	Age Group Distribution		
		35-49	50-59	60+
1. *Male initiative and dominance.* Young man's intrinsic sex, aggression and autonomy must constitute a problem for a gentle, nurturant young woman, and potential danger for himself.	Kansas City	21	12	10
	Navajo	9	7	9
	Lowland Maya	4	1	2
	Highland Maya	2	—	—
	Druze	20	13	7
	Totals	56*	33	28
2. *Domestic problems.* Problem is centered around young man's aggression; but direction, scope, nature of cause, or outcome of this aggression is unclear	Kansas City	1	3	—
	Navajo	4	4	4
	Lowland Maya	7	5	7
	Highland Maya	—	2	1
	Druze	8	8	8
	Totals	20	22	20
3. *Female initiatives and dominance.* Young man's anger is reactive to young woman's rejection of him, or her dominance over him.	Kansas City	6	5	6
	Navajo	—	3	9
	Lowland Maya	—	—	2
	Highland Maya	3	1	2
	Druze	5	4	8
	Totals	14	13	27
4. *Rationalized male succorance.* Menaced by external forces, or defeated in his strivings for outer-world achievement, the young man looks for or accepts female nurturance and control.	Kansas City	—	1	4
	Navajo	—	1	12
	Lowland Maya	—	1	2
	Highland Maya	1	—	2
	Druze	18	5	22
	Totals	19	8	42
5. *Untroubled affiliation (or syntonic dependency).* Mild, untroubled affiliation between the relatively undifferentiated young man and woman.	Kansas City	—	—	—
	Navajo	1	6	6
	Lowland Maya	3	7	12
	Highland Maya	8	3	3
	Druze	11	9	32
	Totals	23	25	53
	Age group totals	132	101	170

Kansas City	N=69
Navajo	N=75
Lowland Maya	N=53
Highland Maya	N=28
Druze	N=178
Overall total	N=403

* Chi square (of cell totals) = 42.165, DF = 8; $P < 0.001$.
† The Druze group includes Golan, (Syrian) Galilean, and Carmel (Israeli) Druze.

of these figures according to the passive mastery principles: for them, the younger woman becomes the dominant, initiating figure (category 3); or the young man, impelled by sickness or fear, moves back "into" the picture, to find comfort in the young woman's arms; or else the man and woman are looking out, with equal apprehension, toward some menacing agent that is not visible in the picture (category 4). Finally, the oldest men tend to deny the presence of conflict, either between the man and woman or between the couple and the world, and perceive instead a mildly affectionate unisex couple, alike in their qualities and feelings for each other (category 5). As with the rope-climber card, young men locate energy and assertion within the male figure, older men locate them in the environment, and the oldest men overlook or deny their presence altogether.

The transcultural age trends elicited by the rope-climber and heterosexual-conflict cards reflect the response to the majority of TAT cards used at all sites. Despite the relative unanimity on the card themes among age peers of different societies, however, the criticism has been raised that such divergences in card interpretations at different ages reflect cohort differences between generations, rather than intraindividual developmental shifts. Longitudinal studies undertaken with both Navajo and Druze subjects indicate, however, that variations in card perceptions of the *same* individuals over a five-year interval replicate those already found between age cohorts in both these societies. Thus, when we contrast the responses of the same individuals to the same cards at times 1 and 2 (see Tables 3-III and 3-IV), we find the predicted appearance of more passive or magical interpretations at time 2 in a significant percentage of the subjects. Navajo or Druze men who saw the rope climber as moving vigorously for some productive purpose at time 1 may see him as clinging anxiously to that same rope, or as fleeing from some wild beast, at time 2. By the same token, subjects who saw the young man of the heterosexual card as taking some active role at time 1 have in many cases come to see him as more subdued, as dominated by his wife, or as gravely ill, by time 2. Clearly, the statistically significant age differences that we have been picking up across cultures appear to be the artifacts of developmental changes in later life, rather than of socially induced differences between generations.

The Social and the Personal in Druze Religious Life

If the passive leanings that emerge openly in the TAT interpretations of elderly Druze are universal in scope, we could argue that they should also be powerful: they should have a peremptory effect on behavior. Yet, as was noted earlier, behavior of the older *Aqil,* or at least his public behavior, seems to be completely ordered by his local culture, not by some species-wide undertow toward passivity. When we look at the conventional behavior of the religious man, we find him going busily from place to place and from one ceremonial visit to another, praying, or receiving guests with elaborate hospitality. In his social relations he is not submissive; on the contrary, he is even dogmatic and dictatorial, laying down the law to his younger relations. Within the framework of the religious life, the older *Aqil* seems to behave in an active rather than a passive fashion.

When we ask the *Aqil* what he does as a religious man, he describes an energetic life; but, when we ask him about the meaning that the religious life holds for him, about his subjective relation to the religious life, and to God, we get a different picture. It is at this level that the passive yearnings shown in the TAT seem to make their appearance, and it is here that the *Aqil* resembles his overtly passive age peers in other societies, not only his Druze co-religionists. When they talk about their relationship to Allah, fierce, patriarchal old Druze, who dominate their grown sons, will

Table 3-III

LONGITUDINAL CHANGES IN TAT IMAGERY OF NAVAJO AND DRUZE
SUBJECTS, ELICITED BY THE ROPE-CLIMBER CARD

	Number of passive images discarded in favor of more active images after Time 1*			Number of passive images that appear only at Time 2		
	Navajo	Druze	Total	Navajo	Druze	Total
Climber's activity is discredited; he does some evil or crazy thing.	2	2	4	6	3	9
Climber descends on the rope.	8	1	9	13	3	16
Climber flees from beast, fire, flood or enemy.	1	1	2	9	4	13
Tired climber, unable to ascend, clutches the rope.	2	1	3	3	4	7
Menaced by external threats, or by his own weariness, the climber looks for help.	3	2	5	6	4	10
The climber is dead, sick, or crippled.	—	1	1	4	—	4
The climber seeks pleasure; he looks at pleasant scenes, or plays on the rope.	4	1	5	7	4	11

Total number of passive images discarded by Time 2: 29

Total number of new passive images adopted by Time 2: 70 †

* The time 1-time 2 interval is four years in the Navajo case, and five years in the Druze case. The Galilean and Carmel Druze, but not the Golan Druze, were reinterviewed in the time 2 study.
† Note: these are not independent entries. A single story may be entered under more than one heading.

completely adopt the posture and tone of the passive, self-effacing supplicant: "Allah is all and I am nothing; I live only in his will, and by his will. . . . I do not question his will. . . . I do not complain about my illness, because this is from God; and to complain about my illness is to question God." These older men are not merely playing back the prescription for conventional religious behavior: when we ask young *Aqil* about the meaning of the religious life, they tell us that their task is to seek out sinners, to correct their ways,

Table 3-IV

LONGITUDINAL CHANGES IN TAT IMAGERY OF NAVAJO AND DRUZE
SUBJECTS ELICITED BY THE HETEROSEXUAL CONFLICT CARD

	Number of passive images discarded in favor of more active images after Time 1*			Number of passive images that appear only at Time 2		
	Navajo	Druze	Total	Navajo	Druze	Total
Male aggression is in reaction to female dominance.	3	1	4	8	3	11
Man is inactive; woman is active and/or dominant.	2	2	4	4	7	11
Man and woman both look at troubling or pleasant scene.	3	2	5	5	7	12
Man is sick; woman is his nurse, or is concerned about him.	1	3	4	6	4	10
Man is tired, or old (the woman may be his daughter).	1	2	3	2	5	7
Man and woman like or love each other. There is no conflict or role distinction.	1	9†	10	8	4	12

Total number of passive images discarded by Time 2: 30

Total number of new passive images adopted by Time 2: 63**

* The time 1- time 2 interval is four years in the Navajo case, and five years in the Druze case. The Galilean and Carmel Druze, but not the Golan Druze, were reinterviewed in the time 2 study.
† Two-thirds of the Druze reversals in this category toward more "active" imagery occur among men below the age of 65; three-quarters of the new perceptions of an affiliative and undifferentiated couple occur in men aged 65 and over.
** Note: these are not independent entries. A single story may be entered under more than one heading.

and through this action to make the village acceptable in the eyes of God. In effect, the younger *Aqil* are social workers for God; and their relationship to Allah is mediated by their action in his service. It is only among the old *Aqil* that we get the sense of a direct and personal relation to Allah, mediated not by work, but by supplication and prayer. Allah is for them an intensely felt and loving presence: as they talk of God their eyes shine, and the voices of these old patriarchs tremble with emotion. They become not unlike the stereotype of a submissive woman who speaks fearfully and yearningly of her master. There are no rules in Druze society that tell young *Aqil* to center their relationship to Allah in their own action, or that tell older men to center their relationship to Allah in the power and actions of that same Allah. Clearly, a range of permissible postures toward Allah is available to the Druze, regardless of age, but each age cohort finds certain stances within this range more congenial than others. The relationship of the younger *Aqil* to Allah conforms with the principles of active mastery, while older *Aqil* enact the themes of passive mastery; and these age preferences reflect intrinsic rather than social coercion. Evidently, then, the religious role allows the passive strivings noted in the older men's TAT to find their dramatic expression and their outlet.

This example illustrates the relatively seamless fit that often exists in the traditional community between particular social roles and psychic potentials that are developmental in nature. As we have seen, the older Druze shares with his age peers in other societies the tendency toward what might be called the normal bisexuality of later life. He does not need, however, to make some final and conflict-ridden choice between active and passive, "masculine" and "feminine" relational styles. The traditional religious structure of the society provides him with a particular psychosocial niche in which he can live out passive and even "feminine" strivings, while he continues to domineer his sons. The religious role requires and gives definition to the psychic potentials that are released by the older man's withdrawal from the active tasks of parenthood and production. The yearnings that men in secular societies might manifest in the form of neurotic symptoms, the old traditional Druze expresses in his worshipful link to God.

THE SOCIAL UTILITY OF PASSIVE MASTERY

The religious role fits the special needs of older men; their tendencies toward mildness and accommodation are particularly fitted to the requirements of the religious role. For the preliterate mind, life-sustaining vitality or power does not originate in the mundane, everyday world. It has its ultimate origin in supernatural sources outside and beyond the community: in the spirits of ancestral dead, in totemic animals, in the enemy, and particularly in the gods. The particular source of power varies by cultural prescription, but the idea that the prosaic world is kept "real" and vital by power imported from supernatural sources is general across the preliterate world. Wherever this world view is institutionalized, specially anointed figures are required to live on the interface between the mundane and supernatural worlds, in order to "attract" the benevolent aspect of supernatural power, to contain it, and to make it available to the life forms of the community and its ecosystem. Roheim (1930) has cited a large body of data on preliterate societies to document the point that this role of the "transformer" or "power-bringer" is enacted through submissive and even masochistic behavior: in many cultures, the gods give power mainly to those who approach them humbly, sometimes even in the guise of women. Thus, in the religious community it is not the competitive, Promethean young men, but the older men, the potential reservoirs of humility and receptivity, who can draw good influences from the gods for the benefit of the community, without offending the divinity. In this case, the office does not create the worshipful old man; in common with the old men of less traditional, less prayerful societies, he has ego potentials that are reciprocal to the prayerful role, and so the office seeks him.

In sum, in the traditional society, as exemplified by the Druze, the potentially destructive passivity of the older man is reformed, through the religious role, into a vehicle of social power: the old man's emerging humility and submissiveness fit him to live on the dangerous interface between the gods and the mundane community, and, through his prayers, to bring life-sustaining forces into the community, in order to maintain and increase children, flocks, and crops. The passivity that in other settings could lead to vulnerability, depression, and psychosomatic illness becomes in the traditional society the very core and pivot of the older man's social prestige and personal identity.[4]

DISENGAGEMENT OR ROLE TRANSITION?

The theory of disengagement in later life put forward by Cumming and Henry (1961) is perhaps the most important current concept in the social psychology of aging. In essence, it pictures a mutual disengagement whereby the agencies of society withdraw their attention from the aged, and the aged likewise withdraw from society's normative restraints, to become more idiosyncratic, but also more "liberated." Though the theory was developed exclusively on the basis of urban studies made in the United States, and

[4]We should not be surprised by this finding in the Druze community, namely, that in the traditional society, the emergent propensities of later life mortise into those age-specific roles that both require them and sponsor their further development, as identity resources. By far the longest period of human history was passed in isolated, preliterate, traditionally oriented communities. These were the species-specific settings in which human characteristics, and particularly those ego-executive capacities that organize personal-communal relationships, evolved. The personal-social integrations that we find among older traditions are not accidental, and in human prehistory they were the rule rather than the exception. They may register a process of interlocking evolution that over the millennia selected viable human traits and viable institutions, roles and conventions that lifted crude human potentials to the level of communication and social utility. Thus the study of the old traditional societies may constitute a kind of social archaeology: they may reveal to us the close, almost umbilical articulation between man and the folk community that was once the general human condition.

was not tested cross-culturally, the authors claim that disengagement is both mandatory and universal.[5] As such, disengagement is a developmental event; the older person who sets himself up in opposition to this dictate of nature is fighting a losing battle, and may even do so at his peril.

Cumming and Henry partly justify their argument that disengagement is a developmental (and hence universal) process by relating it to another presumably developmental event: the emergence of passive ego states in later life. Various associates of Cumming and Henry (the present author among them) examined the TAT protocols of their United States subjects for various indicators of the passive state, and found that older subjects scored consistently higher on these: they were more likely than younger subjects to introduce themes of passive mastery into their stories, they were less likely to infuse stimulus figures with assertive energy or emotional intensity, or to introduce outside figures or possibilities of conflict (Ch. VI). Since the age trend toward TAT metaphors of passivity matched the age trend toward disengagement on other "social" barometers in the population studied, Cumming and Henry concluded that the two trends were combined into one developmental event, so that the increased passivity of later life represented the inner, subjective correlate of the total disengagement process.

The case of the Druze *Aqil* indicates, however, that disengagement need not be compulsory; and in particular it demonstrates that passivity is not inextricably tied to disengagement. Quite the contrary; in the Druze case (and

[5]The authors state it thus: "This theory is intended to apply to the aging process in all societies, although the initiation of the process may vary from culture to culture, as may the pattern of the process itself. For example, in those traditional cultures in which the old are valued for their wisdom, it may well be that the aging person openly initiates the process; in primitive, and especially in impoverished cultures, he may resist the process until it is forced upon him." [p. 17]

probably in other traditional folk societies that have a strong religious orientation), the so-called passivity of the older man can be the central, necessary component of his engagement in age-appropriate social roles, traditions, and associated normative controls. Clearly the older Druze *Aqil* switches his allegiance from the norms that govern the productive and secular life to those that govern the traditional and moral life but in this transition he does not stray from the influence of normative controls as such. If anything, they gain increased influence over him. The older Druze may detach his interest and allegiance from those social codes that are no longer congenial to his passive needs, but he certainly does not detach himself from society *per se*. Rather, he links himself subjectively to the religious dimension of his society, and in so doing he plays out the theme of passive mastery, the need to be in personal touch with a powerful, benevolent, and productive agent. He relinquishes his own productivity, but does not detach himself from productivity *per se*. Instead of being the center of enterprise, he is now the bridge between the community and the productive, life-sustaining potencies of Allah. The old *Aqil* now carries forward the moral rather than the material work of the community. Thus, guided by needs and sensibilities that reflect his emerging passivity, the older Druze transfers himself from one normative order to another *within* society; and in that transition he becomes, quite completely, the instrument and the representative of the traditional moral order that he has adopted, and that has adopted him.

Incidentally, what is true of the Druze is also in general true of the men of other tradition-oriented societies. As Simmons (1945) reports, the traditional elders of preliterate groups do not usually disengage from the social order and its normative prescriptions; on the contrary, they often become the interpreters and administrators of the moral sector of society. They become the bearers of the norms.

Hence the disengagement that Cumming and Henry found in our society is not found in all versions of the human condition; it is the exception rather than the rule. The disengagement that Cumming and Henry found is only the first step in a total process of transition: a process that can reach its natural terminus in a traditional society, but is interrupted or aborted in a secular society. It may well be that disengagement is only an artifact of secular society, which does not offer the old man a moral order based on tradition; hence he has nothing to relate to once he has decoupled from those social norms that regulate the parental and productive life periods.

In sum, it is the movement toward passive and magical mastery that appears to be universal, not the movement toward disengagement. It now appears that the inner, subjective shift is general and transcultural, but it does not necessarily lead to disengagement. The case of the Druze shows that the inexorable psychic developments of later life are not necessarily a prelude to social withdrawal and physical death; given a society that recognizes the emerging dispositions, values them, and gives them articulation in a valid role, the so-called passivity of later life can provide the ground for a revival in later life, a kind of social rebirth.

Part III

ROLE CONSISTENCY

Introduction

In the actual playing of their own roles and in symbolically taking the roles of others, individuals come to know themselves. For most people, most of the time, it is probably safe to say that the roles they play and those they take are fairly consistent with each other. If they are not consistent, contradictory roles are often insulated from each other by situational boundaries.

An important link between the self and roles is expectation. Roles are social entities that define a certain range of behaviors for their occupants. To people both in and out of roles, these definitions are expectations that publicly locate their selves. Self-expectation, at least as regards one's public self, is bound to the playing and taking of roles.

The individual's performances are facilitated by consistency between the expectations set up by his various roles. A person who occupies a set of roles that impose inconsistent expectations on his performances is more likely to be, or to become aware of, "social strain" than one whose social life is relatively consistent. A great many of what are sometimes considered personal problems are located in the stress imposed by the patterning of social life.

Roles in old age may be inconsistent in a variety of ways. Age-appropriate sets of roles may be out of line for some people, so that they may occupy one major role typical of early adulthood, and another typical of later life. Or a person may become the occupant of a role that is not a "just reward" for good work in another role. Or some people may continuously occupy a single role over an entire lifetime, while others do not. Each of these forms of role inconsistency poses a problem for the self. The papers in this section deal with these issues.

chapter 4

Suggestions for the Examination of Time-Disordered Relationships

MILDRED M. SELTZER

The interest in time as a variable in the analysis of social and psychological phenomena has been shown in gerontological literature, as well as in the literature written for other disciplines (Cain, 1967, 1968; Cottrell, 1940, 1961; Gioscia, 1972; Hendricks and Hendricks, 1972; Neugarten, 1965, 1968; Reichenbach and Mather, 1959; Riegel, 1961, 1973; Roth, 1963). In fact, Gioscia (1972) proposes that a new cross-disciplinary science called "chronetics" should be developed, and sees the founding of this field as his task. It is the purpose of this paper to discuss, in a speculative fashion, an aspect of the effects of time on social and psychological matters, that of time-disordered relationships. Our interest is in the sources and consequences of such relationships, particularly as these occur in middle and old age. Time-disordered relationships are those relationships that arise when an individual's various

Dr. Robert Sherwin, of the Department of Sociology and Anthropology, Miami University, suggested the phrase "time-disordered relationships," and also coined the term "position-set congruence."

social spheres and role sets are not temporally synchronized.

Most people are integrated into society through at
least three ties: family, work, and age-grade categories.
Each of these three provides us with generalized sets of
expectations for ourselves and for others. Essentially these
are socially rather than individually defined activities. If
Roth (1963) is correct in his suggestion that "It may well
be possible, and for some purposes useful, to conceive of
the life cycle as an interacting bundle of career timetables,"
then people expect and need position-set congruence in
the career patterning of their various social spheres of family, work, and age-grade categories. (This "fitting together" of our various positions in the primary and highly
valued spheres of life is position-set congruence.) The lack
of fit is what Cain (1964) refers to as asynchronization.
Most people expect that their family, career, and age-
related positions should be conterminous with one another
in their social clocks (Neugarten, 1965). We expect to
achieve success in our careers at about the time that our
children are in college (if we are middle-class), and this
should be when we are in our late forties or early fifties. We
assume that there is a sequence of positions in each sphere,
and we expect the ordering of these positions to be relatively similar in our various spheres of social interaction.
Position-set congruence does not exist when our roles are
not synchronized in terms of career phases. In cases of
asynchronization, the social timing of events is irregular,
and the interacting bundle of career timetables do not fit
together temporally. This lack of fit is a source of potential
role conflict. An example of an individual whose social
timing is relatively atypical is one who "marries late," returns to school in his mid-forties, starts a family in his late
forties, and retires early or dies young. These are numeri-
cally and normatively atypical patterns of behavior, which

may be a source of conflict or discomfort for individuals. The offbeat timing that appears in the life of an individual who reaches a career peak in his forties, when he has just been divorced, can produce even more conflict, or at least is more significant as a source of potential conflict. Remarried, he may become a father at the same time that a child by his first wife makes him a grandfather. (Grandparenthood is a position that one is given by the actions of others, actions over which one usually has no control.) In this kind of situation, timing is out of phase both within and between the family cycle and the career cycle.

For the most part, an individual in our society marries in his early twenties, completes the childbearing period in his late twenties, reaches a career and income peak in his late forties or early fifties, retires by his mid-sixties, is widowed sometime thereafter, and begins to consider himself old in his mid-seventies. Glick and Parke (1965) describe the twentieth-century trends in the stages of the family life cycle. They note that:

> As the family moves through its life cycle, marked changes generally occur in the family's place of residence, its composition, and its economic well-being. These changes tend to take place in a systematic pattern which is essentially the same when portrayed by various methods. In the modern day, the wife may work for a while after marriage, the couple establishes a separate home, children enter and eventually leave the family, and in the meantime the level of family income usually rises with the increasing skill and experience of the family breadwinner(s) but eventually falls as gainful employment of the earner(s) becomes intermittent or discontinues. [p. 196]

This is the normative pattern, but sociologists increasingly note that the range of variation about the norms is growing. Nonetheless, it is implicitly assumed that there are observable and predictable patterns in which the various positions an individual occupies and the roles he plays "fit together" for him, and are socially sanctioned by others. He and his age cohorts tend to follow essentially the same pattern. As a consequence, he undergoes the same experiences, trials, and tribulations as his peers, and gains support and insight from them. One need only go to a party, a meeting, or a family get-together to hear age-mates sharing problems. Wives share wifely problems, young mothers share information and problem-solving activities, and occupational cohorts share work-oriented discussions. This, in a broad sense, is a kind of concurrent adult socialization. The social bonding is of an "all in the same boat at the same time" nature. Such sharing and bonding is based on experience, rather than on skills and knowledge. The stage of life and the shared timing of events are more important than the chronological ages of the participants. Generally, however, those involved are expected to be both at the same ages and at the same stages of life. As a result of these double similarities, the nature of the sharing tends to be egalitarian and relatively tension-free. What happens, then, when the individual is thrown off the predictable sociotemporal schedule, either by choice or as a result of externally imposed factors? What happens, for example, when the middle-aged man or woman goes to graduate school relatively late in life, and is faced with the problems usually experienced by graduate students in their twenties? Some research has been undertaken in this area, specifically on the woman who returns to college. Zatlin, Storandt, and Botwinick (1973), expecting that women who returned to college relatively late in life (35–50) would have some unique characteristics, compared these women with others of the same age who had never gone to college, with women who had gone earlier, and with young women (18–25) currently in college. This, however, was what they found:

The hypothesis that women returning to college in their mid-years are a unique group in terms of personality characteristics, job values, and interest and agreement with the feminist movement was not supported. They were, instead, quite similar to their age peers who received their college education at the normal time, prior to the age of 25. They were also similar to women of like age who had never been exposed to the college experience, when the confounding effect of socioeconomic status was statistically eliminated. [p. 221]

On the other hand, some people do find that those who return to school are in some ways unique. One of the women interviewed by Likert (1967) said, "So, at early middle age, I think I've finally found my niche. This discovery really reflects, of course, a kind of self-knowledge that I never had before [p. 9]." Another commented:

In the first place, I want to suggest that the returning woman really has some advantages as a student, for the following reasons. First of all, many of the problems that relate to the multi-university campus really apply to all students today; they are not exclusively the problems of the returning woman. Secondly, in terms of older women who go back, I don't think for the most part they have as many problems as the undergraduate or as other graduate students do. I am a sample of one woman, to be sure, and you can't generalize from a sample of one woman. But many problems such as selection of a career, finding a man, holding down a responsible job, the draft, that confront the undergraduate and graduate students, the older woman doesn't have. These younger students have much more anxiety than I have. If I had failed, it would have been my ego which would have suffered, that's all. The graduate student or undergraduate who has an over-ambitious parent or who has a real problem of earning money on the side in order to progress in school, has a much tougher problem than I do. Furthermore, the average woman returning to school doesn't take as many hours; that is, you can't! If you're in the fortunate situation that I was, you can take fewer hours so you have more time on some of these problems.

My personal experiences and conversations with others involved in such situations have shown, however, that they do face some unique problems. For example, many individuals in their late thirties and forties have achieved a modicum of success in their lives: in business, with families, in community activities. In the positions they have occupied and the roles they have played, they have achieved competence and been given recognition. Now the individual is faced with occupying the relatively powerless position of graduate student, and with playing a role similar in many respects to the role that his or her children may be playing. I recall one middle-aged woman telling me that her children found her crying when she received her first set of grades, because she didn't get A's. The children reminded her of what she had always told them: "It's not the grades you get, but what you've learned." She found this a less reassuring statement than her children had done, because to be evaluated for academic work in one's thirties or forties is a qualitatively different experience from being scholastically evaluated in one's teens or twenties. The returning student sometimes points out that he has already been evaluated and found adequate in other areas of life; so why is this process necessary in this particular fashion at this stage of his life? The examination processes and the studying mystique are an old experience, with new overtones. One is not only faced with one's own feelings and attitudes about this experience; also, today's definition of the situation is somewhat different from the views that were held by one's age cohorts.

Another area in which people make changes in their middle years is the occupational sphere. Haug and Sussman (1970) observe that:

> Career switches are not a rare phenomenon in contemporary society and are likely to become more common in the future. . . . There has been no systematic examination of the

factors associated with the choice and entrance into a second career and no attempt to test tentative explanations empirically. [p. 124]

In their discussion of factors that may create a "push" into a second career, they point out the following as important: the individual may feel unable to continue in a field, or may recognize that the original career has reached a dead end; rapid social change may have eliminated his initial career, he may feel a quest for change from a rutted career (particularly if there are no economic risks involved), or he may be dissatisfied with the prestige, pay, or security of the original career. As factors that produce a "pull" into a second career, they comment upon the importance of prestige, pay, mobility, and security. There is another factor that affects the choice of the second career: "[Because] persons entering a second career will generally be older than those embarking on their first, the issue of entrance requirements is salient. Careers demanding long courses of training are usually ruled out [p. 125]."

They were able to test some of their hypotheses about the characteristics of those involved in second careers by using data available in the Professions Project. The data were collected in 1965. Their conclusions are based upon a remarkable response rate—out of 326 students who were graduating from 38 training programs in rehabilitation counseling, 324 responded. Haug and Sussman found that those who were entering a second career differed from those who were entering a career for the first time not only with respect to age, but also with respect to sex. A disproportionate number of those who were entering a second career were women. When they entered their second careers they were economically better off than those in the first-career group, although the social class origins of those aged 35 and over were lower than those of the first-career group. They concluded that:

In general, these findings suggest that the second career phenomenon is most common among married women, among those who have already achieved middle class occupational status, and among younger persons seeking upward mobility. Two of these groups may be presumed to have a minimum of risk in entering a second career. The married women are not likely to be the sole earners in their families and are probably not endangering their livelihoods by a job change. Younger persons are apt to have a relatively low investment in a prior career and thus are risking less in tenure and status by seeking advancement in a different line of work. It is apparent that the element of risk is one variable to be considered in studying the second career phenomenon. [pp. 130–131]

The problems faced by middle-aged federal employees are amply documented in a report to a special United States Senate subcommittee, entitled *Cancelled Careers* (1972). Other literature, both technical and slick, describes the problems faced by successful businessmen who lose jobs because of mergers, shutdowns of programs, or cutbacks in funds. We also anticipate a new problem area among academic people who are working for private colleges that are cutting back or closing down.

There is nothing sociologically startling in the statement that often the individual's social spheres are not temporally congruent, and as a consequence he experiences strain. What is important is to isolate the significant variables and develop a paradigm that will make the sources of strain more predictable and hence more amenable to reduction. It is also important to examine this lack of temporal synchronization as a potential source of social change.

One of the things we should look at first, perhaps, is how society defines the cause of the time-disordered relationships, and how the involved individual defines his situation. If an individual regards his lack of temporal congruence as the result of his own decisions, rather than as being externally imposed, we would expect him to be less threatened and less anxious about the lack of fit. On the other hand, the situation could still give rise to problems. For example, a man who is successful in one career decides to enter a new one, and so returns to school. Unlike many other students, he is less likely to have an academic "patron," more impatient with immediate lack of success and recognition, and less satisfied with small achievements. Such individuals are caught between the Scylla of age and the Charybdis of youth. They are competing at a disadvantage with the powerful middle-aged who are their age peers, and identify with the career problems of their powerless younger colleagues, whose career stage they share. They are out of phase with their age-grade.

If we examine more specifically other variables that could be involved in a paradigm for the study of time-disordered relationships, we might want to include the following as major independent variables:

1. the time in life when a lack of congruence is experienced
2. the specific situation in which it is experienced
3. the sex of the subject
4. the chronological age of the subject
5. the social class of the subject
6. the particular dimension that is out of sequence
7. the degree of asynchronization.

Sources of time-disordered relationships are:

1. inconsistencies within social spheres (for example, a career that is not normatively patterned)
2. inconsistencies between social spheres (for example, late parenthood, at the time of one's career peak and financial success)
3. both (for example, late parenthood, a late career peak, and early retirement).

It seems highly probable that the more career milestones an individual has successfully achieved in specific spheres, the more difficult it will be to give up these

Table 4-I

RESPONSES TO TIME-DISORDERED RELATIONSHIPS
(based on Merton, 1938)

	Career Goals	Goal Timing
1. Conformity	+	+
2. Innovation	+	−
3. Ritualism	−	+
4. Retreatism	−	−
5. Rebellion	±	±

(+) signifies "acceptance," (−) signifies "rejected," and (±) signifies "rejection and substitution of something else."

achievements and begin anew in another sphere. Difficulties will arise from two sources: the individual is removed from a position in which rewards have been assured, and he is placed in a time-disordered relationship. There may be an inverse relationship between the degree of success achieved in a particular sphere and one's feelings about "starting again" in another sphere. In other words, the more an individual has accomplished in a career schedule, the further back he will feel he is placed if he begins another career. If such time-disordered relationships occur during middle or old age, they may produce particularly severe stress. These are the times in an individual's life cycle when it is most important for his self-esteem that his spheres should be congruent. If offbeat timing occurs then, noncongruence replaces congruence, and this results in lower self-esteem.

When we begin to examine the causes of and the responses to time-disordered relationships, one possible approach is a modification of Merton's (1938) paradigm, as shown in Table 4-I.

Conformity.—This is found among those who follow the normative, "built-in" social calendar. On the whole, these people will not experience time-disordered relationships by choice. If external circumstances result in a temporally inappropriate change of position (early widowhood or forced early retirement), the impact of such an event may be devastating. In part, the difficulty experienced by such individuals results from their acceptance of the culturally defined temporal patterning and temporally bound definitions of what constitutes an acceptable situation. Because we learn our definitions of acceptable situations at a given time in our lives, and carry these definitions relatively unchanged with us throughout the rest of our lives, our behavior remains stable and our patterns of accommodation relatively unchanged. We may modify our definitions to some extent, but we tend to keep the essence of these definitions relatively unchanged. This is one of the factors that account for stability in social systems. Thus, if an individual learns a worker's role in the 1940s, but is forced to find a new kind of job that has a lower status and a different work ethic in the 1970s, he may find that his new situation not only involves role reversals, but also clashes with his outdated role definitions and expectations. Because his definitions of the situation are relatively unchanged, he perceives and defines the current situation in terms of the past definitions. He is, therefore, shaken by what he views as the inappropriateness of his situation. The events he is experiencing are "too early," "too late," or "off schedule." He is "out of phase with the times." His situation is the result of external forces, not of internal choice.

Some social mechanisms are provided to help individuals to cope with their time-disordered relationships: preretirement programs, centers for continuing education, widows-to-widows groups, and other such organizations.

Innovation. As a mechanism of adaptation, innovation is characteristic of those who accept the normative goals, but do not follow or are prevented from following the culturally prescribed timing for the achievement of these goals. Some are individuals who create their own timetables, and one would speculate that these people tend to perceive their own ages as younger than do their conforming age mates. To a certain extent these are the people whom Cain (1968) describes when he writes the following:

> Implicit in much of the discussion of achievement in old age has been the assertion that the aged are quite capable of providing for their own socialization into old age roles. In a vital sense, as mentioned above, the aged in America today are called upon to be the most inventive and adaptive group in the society. The ability to redesign their own status and to socialize themselves to fit it is surely a major achievement. [p. 253]

Others are prevented from meeting cultural timetables by wars, depressions, or other social events. It should be noted that there is institutional support and sanction for some rescheduling of goals; this is evidenced, for example, in the expression "He's (she's) a late bloomer."

Ritualism.—Merton (1938) describes ritualism as the result of "an extreme assimilation of institutional demands." However, "The goal is dropped as beyond one's reach while conformity to the mores persists." This is essentially a situation in which form without content prevails; one goes through the motions, or more specifically, one concentrates on the motions without expecting to achieve the goals. Among such individuals are the middle-aged or older people who no longer expect to achieve age-appropriate work goals, but continue to go through the motions of working as if they were related to achievement, and engage in family activities as though they will achieve familial goals.

Retreatism.—This reaction is found in individuals who accept neither the culturally prescribed goals nor their timing. Their behavior is non-normative. They are life-long isolates, isolates at every age. They do not want to marry at any age, they may work out of necessity but have no other motivation to do so, and their behavior is rarely age-grade-oriented. In fact, age is an irrelevant and insignificant factor in their lives, except insofar as it may affect how others behave toward them. The number of people who react in this way is relatively small.

Rebellion.—On this last mechanism of adaptation to time-disordered relationships described in Merton's mode, he writes thus:

> This fifth alternative is on a plane clearly different from that of the others. It represents a *transitional* response which seeks to *institutionalize* new procedures oriented toward re vamped cultural goals shared by the members of the society. It thus involves efforts to *change* the existing structure rather than to perform accommodative action *within* this structure, and introduces additional problems with which we are not at the moment concerned. [p. 775]

Here we find people who, we suspect, experience stress because they have both accepted and rejected the cultural goals and their timing. They march to the beat of a different time, as well as a different tune. These individuals are usually given little social support and sanction for those aspects of their behavior that deviate from the established and expected. One is tempted to describe such people as temporal immigrants, an analogy which offers a somewhat different image from the picture of old people as a minority category. Temporal immigrants may also be temporal marginal men, who both accept and reject the goals and timing of the world in which they live, and of the world they are creating. These are people who "start all over again." Such individuals may have a high potential for engagement or re-engagement, but not for disengagement. Among these people we find our most active agents of change: the Gray Panthers, the senior power advocates.

Obviously, the ideas suggested above are based primarily upon a linear model of time. Other models would provide different ideas about time-disordered relationships. In this discussion our focus has been primarily upon the sources of the stress that people experience when they do not follow culturally defined timetables and/or when there is a discrepancy in their "interacting bundle of career timetables." In addition to the discussion of some of the sources of stress and possible modes of accommodation to temporal asynchronization, some suggestions have been made on the extent of stress experienced. Significant variables have been noted which should be considered in an examination of time-disordered relationships. The variables that are perhaps particularly important in this area are the social definitions of the factors that are believed to cause a particular time-disordered phenomenon. Another variable that critically affects how an individual feels about his particular time-disordered situation is whether or not he sees it as being under his own control. If he sees his situation as externally imposed, he will experience greater stress than if he views it as resulting from internally motivated causes.

Although we are still at the exploratory stage in the study of asynchronization and time-disordered relationships, we are beginning to amass data that will enable us to define more precisely some of the most significant variables.

As a preliminary step in evaluating the usefulness of some of the ideas expressed in this paper, the following hypotheses are suggested:

1. The greater the degree of temporal asynchronization among his various social spheres, the greater the number of time-disordered relationships an individual will have, and the greater will be his sense of stress.

2. Temporal asynchronization within a single social sphere produces less stress for an individual than does temporal asynchronization between spheres. The latter, in turn, is less stress-producing than the two in combination: asynchronization both within and between spheres.

3. The more an individual values a social sphere, the more stress will be produced by events that are temporally off schedule.

4. The more an individual views events that are temporally off schedule as being under his control, rather than as being externally imposed, the less stress will be produced by these events.

5. The greater the success experienced in a given social sphere, the more are activities that are off schedule in that sphere a source of stress.

6. Middle-aged and older people who view the scheduling of events as under their control perceive themselves as younger than do those who view the scheduling as externally imposed.

chapter 5

Status Inconsistency and Political Action in Old Age

JAMES E. TRELA

Comparatively little sociological knowledge has been brought to bear on the phenomenon of aging in general, or on old age in particular. Due to the increasing visibility of the aged, and to the "social problem" label that has been applied to their position, however, this condition is in the early stages of being remedied. In this paper an attempt is made to develop a framework that will enable us to view the process of aging in terms of status consistency theory. This framework is used first to conceptualize the transition from middle to old age, and to explore the effects of the aging experience on the political beliefs and attitudes of several different categories of older people, and second, to examine how much potential the aged possess for concerted political action in contemporary American life.

The concept of status consistency is essentially theoretical; it was developed to supplement the unidimensional, vertical view of stratification as a composite hierarchy in which a person occupies a single position. Although the recognition of multiple hierarchies of stratification can be traced to Max Weber (1946), the basis of status consistency theory was the work of Benoit-Smullyan (1944) who speculated on the processes involved in the equilibration of ranks held by a single person or by a group over several status hierarchies. Lenski (1954, 1956) further developed this line of thinking with his concept of "status crystallization," which calls attention to the "nonvertical" dimension of stratification by focusing on inconsistencies in the several rank positions that individuals hold either simultaneously or sequentially over a period of time. It is assumed that behavior and attitudes are influenced not only by the separate effects of each status (occupation or ethnicity, for example), but that particular combinations of ranks on these status hierarchies may produce conditions that independently affect behavior and attitudes.[1] Regard less of their overall status rank *per se,* individuals whose discrete ranks on various status hierarchies are inconsistent will exhibit different attitudes and behavior than will those whose ranks are consistent. Here are the (summarized) propositions that sketch the theoretical outlines of this framework:

1. The status or rank structure of a group is not a unidi-mensional phenomenon; it has both vertical and horizontal dimensions.

2. The status of any individual (or group) normally in-volves the coexistence of a number of imperfectly corre-lated ranks, on parallel vertical hierarchies.

3. The possession of discrepant ranks in various status hierarchies creates social and psychological strain or stress.

4. The stress generated by the holding of discrepant ranks causes an individual or group to adopt a course of action designed to bring their ranks in line with one another.

---

[1]This phenomenon has also been called status congruence, status equili bration, status contradiction, and status consistency. The term status consistency is used throughout this paper, except when we are referring to authors who prefer another term.

These propositions focus on a causal sequence that begins with the condition of status inconsistency, and proceeds through some stressful social and psychological state to responses of attitude and behavior that are intended to reduce stress by equilibrating ranks. The intervening stressful state has been variously thought to arise from unstable self-images (Fenchel, 1951; Goffman, 1957), rewards that are out of line with aspirations (Zaleznik, 1958), unsatisfactory social relationships (Hughes, 1944–45), social ambiguity (Lenski, 1956; Hughes, 1944–45; Goffman, 1957), or conflicting expectations and demands (Jackson, 1962). Among the political responses thought to result from the stressful state that accompanies status inconsistency are a preference for change in the social order, political liberalism, and extremism (Benoit-Smullyan, 1944; Lenski, 1954; Goffman, 1957; Jackson, 1962; Olsen and Tully, 1972).

Recent research indicates that inconsistency on the parameters of socioeconomic achievement and ascribed status are most likely to elicit political responses. Inconsistency within a given nexus, achieved or ascribed, appears to be less important (Lenski, 1956; Jackson, 1962). For example, a combination of low racial or ethnic status (ascribed) and high occupational and educational status (achieved) appears to be an especially significant profile (Hughes, 1944–45); those who possess it seem exceptionally prone to liberal political responses (Jackson, 1962). To capitalize on the unique characteristics of the aged in terms of status inconsistency theory, age may be treated as an ascribed status and then related to various ranks on the achieved status hierarchies.[2] If we accept this, the rank of

[2]The task of specifying the components of status that are relevant in old age (that is, the hierarchies along which the independent variables will be measured) may be approached in one of two ways. Either general societal status hierarchies (those that are known to be important, for example income and education) may be selected, or the most appropriate statuses may be selected on

the aged in Western urban cultures is unequivocally low. This lowered status is a result of the emphasis placed on youth and employment in contemporary American culture. As Linden (1954) states, "Our values have been values of youth—vigor, physical beauty, motion, quantitative productivity, and, to some degree, arrogance." Advanced age really means retirement, with the loss of social contacts, of opportunities to express creative impulses, and of social prestige (Roucek, 1957). Since our values are those of youthfulness, to be too old is to have a lessened status.[3]

The consequences of a sharp reduction in rank on the ascribed status hierarchy of age are not, however, the same for all individuals. As middle-aged persons come to be defined as old, they present diverse status profiles to this abrupt devaluation, and these condition their perception and definition of aging. The problem, then, is to determine the different reactions of middle-aged individuals of the various status types to the severe status dislocations on the ascribed age hierarchy that come with what is conventionally thought to be old age. Figure 5-I shows this loss of status in terms of a status consistency model. This figure

---

an *ad hoc* basis, depending on what the salient status variables are thought to be. Lenski (1954), for example, included standard socioeconomic achievement variables as well as race. His argument was that these are of critical importance to all social groups. Adams (1953), on the other hand, employed status variables peculiarly relevant to the group he studied (bomber crews). Interviews with group members showed the major status hierarchies along which individuals could be evaluated. Almost any variable may thus prove to be important in some specific group or situational context. Although the latter course could easily have been followed, our interest in political participation dictated that important common societal status variables be emphasized.

[3]The low status of the contemporary American aged is especially notable when contrasted with the aged of other generations and cultures (Roucek, 1957; Simmons, 1945). We are, of course, speaking of the aged as a group, and are ignoring those few persons who remain the custodians of great wealth and power. Because our cultural ethos dictates that obsolescence rather than wisdom comes with age, most older people do not occupy important positions in the social structure.

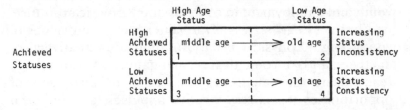

Fig. 5–I. Status consistency in old age.

describes what happens to people in two group categories, those of high and low socioeconomic status (SES), as they pass from middle to old age. Assuming, for the present, that achieved statuses remain relatively constant after middle life, individual aging may be conceived as a passage through either the upper or lower cells of the figure. The status profile of a person of high SES (who moves from cell 1 to cell 2) changes from consistent to inconsistent, while that of a person of lower SES (who moves from cell 3 to cell 4) changes from inconsistent to consistent. Although there are many variations of profile between the completely consistent and the completely inconsistent types, it will be useful to focus only on the political consequences that result when an individual belongs to one or the other of these polar types. This will allow us to avoid becoming involved, at present, with the large number of profiles that emerge when differential ranks within the achieved nexus are considered.

The first profile type is epitomized by the person who has consistently achieved high statuses before he comes to be defined as old. He is ranked high on the occupation, education, and income hierarchies (this would be true of a business executive, for example), but after a long period of stable or rising achievement he is suddenly ranked low on the age hierarchy. This may be symbolized by forced retirement at the age of 65. His former highly consistent status now becomes increasingly inconsistent; high achieved status is combined with low ascribed status. The second profile type (for example, the unskilled laborer who perhaps has worked sporadically during his middle years) has consistently been ranked low on the achievement hierarchies, and low status on the age hierarchy serves to crystallize his status profile further. During middle life his profile was inconsistent; he was ranked low on the achievement hierarchies, but high on the ascribed age status hierarchy. But the expectations generally associated with middle age were not matched by success on the achievement criteria. He has not met the cultural expectation that middle-aged men should be "successful," and has felt insecure, unfulfilled, and insufficiently rewarded in his job. Old age removes this disparity between his expectations and achievement.

In general, then, for those who are ranked high on the various achievement hierarchies, the loss of age status results in status inconsistency, while for those who have low ranks on the achievement hierarchies it results in increased consistency. If this is true, it can be shown that (1) a political response to the stress of status inconsistency is highly probable, while other responses are largely precluded; (2) past political movements of the aged can be partially explained by the status inconsistency framework; and (3) the conversion of stress into collective political action by the aged who are suffering from status inconsistency is largely contingent upon the prevailing political conditions and other factors.

ALTERNATIVE RESPONSES

If it is true that old age is a stressful time in the life cycle for those who are achievement-oriented and have been successful during middle life, we should ask why the effects of status inconsistency will be manifested in political action rather than in some alternative form of behavior. Although it is not possible to anticipate all the possible responses to status inconsistency, the literature indicates that striving for upward mobility, psychosomatic symptoms of stress, social withdrawal, and preference for change in the social order are among those that deserve consideration.

Benoit-Smullyan (1944) posited the existence of a tendency toward the equilibration of ranks; we would therefore anticipate that individuals who have discrepant statuses will strive to equilibrate them by seeking upward mobility on those statuses that are ranked low. It is immediately apparent however, that the rank of older persons is low on the ascribed age status hierarchy, and their ranks on most other status hierarchies are either fixed or are tending downward. The loss of employment, for example, threatens socioeconomic rank in that income almost universally declines in old age. Although their ranks on the educational, racial-ethnic, and religious hierarchies are not subject to decline, they have no significant prospects of upward mobility.

If upward mobility is not possible, several kinds of adaptive or compensatory behavior might be anticipated. Stress caused by status inconsistency may manifest itself physically in psychosomatic symptoms. With advancing age, mobility is perceived as less likely; thus Jackson (1962) found that younger individuals with inconsistent profiles, whose status profiles could however become equilibrated through mobility, had lower symptom rates than did older persons with similar profiles. When the possibility of mobility is lessened, the response to inconsistency may be turned inward, although this depends largely upon whether people regard themselves or the social order as the source of their social deprivation and ambiguous standing.

If individuals see themselves as the source of their problems, their responses to status inconsistency may be manifested in high symptom rates. Jackson (1962) found high rates of psychosomatic symptoms in individuals with high racial-ethnic ranks and low occupational ranks. Under such circumstances, it would be difficult for the individual to blame the social order. This suggests that those who have high ascribed and low achieved statuses may perceive themselves as failures, and hence will respond inwardly, and will subsequently manifest high symptom rates. Support for this thesis is indirectly supplied by Lenski (1954), who noted that persons with low ascribed and high achieved statuses may see themselves as successful, yet victimized by the system. He found that such individuals gave liberal political responses, which suggests that they feel a desire for change in the social order.

The sense of personal failure may also strain social interaction and lead to social isolation. It may be assumed that interaction which is negatively sanctioned or unrewarded will decline in frequency. To the degree that individuals whose status is poorly crystallized are vulnerable to disturbing experiences in interaction with others ("rebuffs," "embarrassments," and "disappointments") they will find it difficult to establish and maintain rewarding patterns of social interaction. To compensate, they may attempt to support their social interaction by presenting that status on which they are ranked highest as their "master status," the one most representative of their total makeup. The retired executive, for example, may continually remind his aged associates of his former rank, and seek the deference that he was accorded during his occupational career. If this is not successful, some degree of social withdrawal may result. When examining the relationship between status inconsistency and tendencies toward social isolation, Lenski (1954) found that individuals of inconsistent status were less likely than those of consistent status to interact with their neighbors and fellow-workers after business hours, and were less likely to be members of voluntary associations, or to be regular participants in the activities of those voluntary associations of which they were members. It should be emphasized, however, that withdrawal may be selective. The individual of inconsistent status may withdraw only from groups in which his patterns of interaction have become strained, and may seek other groups in which he can reintegrate himself. We would think that the aged of inconsistent status would withdraw from those organizations that provide unrewarding social relations, but would be inclined to join those that promise either social change or a redefinition of status. The latter would presumably compensate for inconsistencies by redefining age and initiating an alternative value system. Age-graded voluntary associations, for example, provide an atmosphere which does not set up the conflicting expectations that may cause interaction to become unpleasant, and to be broken off.

If the stress that accompanies status inconsistency is not manifested in psychosomatic symptoms or in social withdrawal, it may generate resentment toward the social order, and manifest itself in liberal political attitudes and a high desire for social and political change. Benoit-Smullyan (1944) suggested that as a result of the status coversion processes that are normally at work in any society, the different types of status tend to reach a common level; he states that "there are historical grounds for supposing that when legal, customary, or other barriers seriously hamper the equilibrating tendency, social tensions of revolutionary magnitude may be generated." Similarly, Lenski (1954) predicted that the more frequently acute status inconsistencies occur within a population, the more people within that population will be willing to support programs of social change. Thus, persons of inconsistent status may respond to institutional barriers that block status equilibration by generating pressures for change within the social structure. This pressure may assume a political form. Goffman (1957), for example, related status inconsistency to a desire for change in the distribution of power in society. He reasoned that one way in which the individual can reduce the stress caused by status inconsistency is by attempting to change his environment. Gross status inconsistency was measured on the educational, occupational, and income hierarchies. In order to assess their attitudes to change, subjects were asked to identify the agencies that now exercise power, and to indicate what distribution of power they would choose. It was found that status consistency was inversely related to the desire for change in the distribution of power in society. Further, it has been shown that political liberalism may be an expression of status inconsistency. The persons of least consistent status are more liberal than those of most consistent status in their attitudes toward government health insurance and price controls and their choice of political party (Lenski, 1954).[4]

We might also predict that groups of inconsistent status would be an important source of leadership for social and political movements, in that they often combine personal motivation (stress from status inconsistency) with necessary leadership skills. This is most notably true when low ascribed rank is combined with high achieved rank. Leadership in the civil rights movement, for example, is supplied not by those of consistently low status, but by

[4]Lenski (1954) suggests that the political liberalism of diverse historical groups in American society can be interpreted within the context of status inconsistency theory. In recent years, political observers have reported that relatively strong support for liberal political programs is provided by such diverse groups as college professors, Jewish businessmen, actors, and Protestant clergy. Each of these groups is characterized by a lack of status consistency. Professors and clergy enjoy high occupational and educational ranks, yet their income is often lower than that of skilled manual laborers. Actors frequently combine high income with low educational and ethnic ranks. Jewish businessmen combine high economic, occupational, and educational ranks with low ethnic rank.

those who have a high rank on some achievement hierarchy, such as education or occupation. Support for organizations such as the Urban League and the NAACP tends to come from the middle-class Negroes rather than from the most disadvantaged Negro groups (Frazier, 1959). This thesis is also supported by Michels (1959), who noted that middle-class Jews were prominent in European Socialist parties. It may be noted that in the cases of both the European Jew and the American Negro, individuals are seen in the framework of the subgroups of their respective religious and racial groups. In each case, the most salient status was ascribed. Similarly, we may anticipate that support and leadership for political movements of the aged will come from the middle-class aged, who possess high achieved statuses.[5]

If a political response to status inconsistency is likely, political satisfaction or apathy is a probable response to consistency. This results both from the correlates of low socioeconomic status and from the effects of status consistency. Characteristics such as "psychological underprivilege," habits of submission, lack of information, and verbal facility are linked with low status and economic underprivilege. Such persons, furthermore, are least likely to vote, and those who do not vote are less willing to criticize the *status quo,* or even to believe that newspapers should be allowed to criticize governmental decisions (Knupfer, 1953). Bell (1962), who regards political action by the poor as improbable, has written, "It is not poverty *per se* that leads people to revolt; poverty most often induces fatalism and despair. . . . Social tensions are an expression of unfulfilled expectations." This thesis is supported by evi-

[5]The relationship between status inconsistency and liberal attitudes and behavior is by no means thoroughly established. Several studies have found that status inconsistency explains only a small part of the variation in several dependent variables, including political liberalism (Jackson and Curtis, 1972; Olsen and Tully, 1972).

dence that political movements of both the left and right sometimes fail because they are initially unable to enlist the support of people of low status—the group that presumably would benefit most from implementation of the programs of at least some of these movements (Pinard, 1967). To the degree that the expectations of individuals of consistent status are in line with their objective circumstances, increasing status consistency in old age will probably accentuate the tendencies toward indifference and nonparticipation that characterize low-status groups during middle life. Presumably, also, aged and poor people of low status will not play a significant part in the initial stages of any political movements of the aged. Since they have not achieved tangible social or economic status, these are the people least threatened by the loss of status due to old age; and because they have continuity of status from middle to old age, they find the deprivations and uncertainties of aging comparatively mild and unstressful.

PENSION MOVEMENTS

Crane Brinton (1960) has described the groups that typically seek radical political change as those whose rank in one status hierarchy is rising, while their upward mobility in other hierarchies is frustrated. While this description is not applicable in every detail to the aged, it does emphasize that status inconsistency and frustrated expectations are important causes of collective disenchantment and political mobilization. The status of older persons in the age hierarchy is declining, and this threatens their other statuses, while their expectations generally remain at previous levels. This loss of status produces an increasing sense of relative deprivation in the individuals we have labeled as having inconsistent status—those who have achieved measurable social and economic status during their middle years. In that the well-being of such persons is largely dependent upon their position in the occupational hierarchy, retirement (and thus removal from the means of maintaining their advantages) constitutes a severe status dislocation. The stress produced by this threat to status may manifest itself in patterns of political participation.

The viability of these assertions, and of the status inconsistency model, may be partially and indirectly tested by analysis of the Townsend and McLain movements. The case of the Townsend Movement shows that an aloof posture on the part of the political and governmental structures, coupled with the inconsistent status characteristics of a disenchanted subgroup of the aged, can lead to independent old-age politics. During the five most critical years of the depression the condition of the aged population deteriorated, and the federal government failed to respond. This lack of sensitivity was a major cause of the rise of the Townsend Movement. More important than this, however, were the status characteristics of those who entered the ranks of the dependent. As jobs disappeared, and as businesses were ruined and savings were wiped out, those who had formerly been professional men, independent businessmen, or skilled workers were increasingly driven into the ranks of the dependent aged. These were people who had achieved a high degree of success in various achievement hierarchies, and had experienced economic security and social independence during their middle years. Holtzman (1954) puts it thus: "These new accretions to the ranks of dependent aged represented a sensitive force receptive to protest thinking." This sensitivity, however, was not wholly economically inspired; it was also the result of severe status loss (and thus of status inconsistency) and the concomitant frustration of cherished expectations.

The importance of social status in old age may be further illustrated by the McLain Movement in California. Pinner, Jacobs, and Selznick (1959) studied the California

Institute of Social Welfare (CISW), a political pressure group composed chiefly of recipients of old-age assistance, and sought to discover whether the aged develop their own values, attitudes, and forms of political expression—all dominated by the experience of old age. The authors report that the recipients of old-age assistance whom they studied showed evidence of status anxiety, and were more concerned to remedy this felt loss than to improve their personal relations with others. The most notable proof of the status inconsistency model, however, is that members of the McLain Movement closely fit the status-inconsistent type described earlier, and showed more status anxiety than did nonmembers. The California old-age security laws permit some pensioners to enjoy a "slightly privileged" status, and this group supplied a disproportionately high proportion of the CISW members. This slightly privileged group includes people whose spouses are still living, and who are therefore benefiting from combined grants; it also includes owners of modest homes and those who have an allowable additional income. The members of the McLain Movement tended to come from the privileged group; indeed, the more deeply involved a member was, the more likely he was to possess some such advantage. The fact that members were not the most disadvantaged aged indicates again that a consistently low status is associated with apathetic withdrawal rather than political activism. Those who joined this political pressure group tended to have some status or material advantage that was threatened by aging. As Pinner (1959) suggests, "Those who have some hold upon the material foundations of respectability are more likely to sustain the aspiration and resent the loss." Strong feelings about loss of status stir resentments and motivate people to engage in political activity. Furthermore, membership in such organizations has the reciprocal effect of strengthening an individual's political and social views, and causing an increased concern for his social status.

The McLain study illustrates that social status is a potent motivating force in old age, that loss of status produces stress or anxiety, and that concern about status may manifest itself in political behavior. Although it was found that members of the McLain Movement did not display a high level of age-group consciousness, they were prone to regard other groups as the enemies of older people. Thus political action was rationalized in that other elements of the social structure were identified as the source of stress. In spite of a lack of group cohesiveness, there was a high demand for the development of special groups or organizations that would seek to ameliorate the problems of older people. Only 7 per cent of the members of the McLain Movement, as opposed to 16 per cent of the nonmembers, explicitly rejected the idea of special groups. Pinner noted that it was not identification with older people or a general desire for political action that impelled participation in these organizations. Rather, such organizations appeared to appeal to those threatened by status loss, whom they serve as instruments of political expression.

COLLECTIVE POLITICAL ACTION

It has been submitted that the stress produced by low status on the age hierarchy and concomitant devaluation on other status hierarchies, particularly if this follows a generally high achieved status prior to old age, will manifest itself in political activities and attitudes. The Townsend and McLain movements illustrate the importance of status inconsistency. It appears to be the aged of inconsistent status who are most discontented and politically active. We may ask what the existence of an increasingly large bloc of older people of inconsistent status portends for political life in America. Havighurst (1949) held that if the aged were to form a voting bloc, they could secure anything they might demand of governments, and Clague (1940) contended that the old-age movements of the depression were pastoral in comparison with the pension movements of the future. The existence of old-age political movements, however, is clearly not dependent upon the stress of status inconsistency alone. A sufficient examination of old-age politics must also consider levels of political interest and activity among older people, the degree to which they support common political interests based upon age status, the actual and perceived responsiveness of political institutions, and the availability of suitable political organizations.

Political interest may be expressed in many ways: by voting, lobbying, and providing financial support for candidates, and also by influencing the opinion of others. The aged do not lobby (a mechanism that implies collective pressure), but otherwise they exhibit strong political orientations. For example, they vote more or at least as often as other age groups in contemporary American society. Insofar as voting involves a conscious, positive commitment and expenditure of time and energy (Lane, 1959), older people, contrary to the disengagement thesis, display high political involvement and relatedness to society. Whereas only 50 per cent of those in their early twenties vote in presidential elections, fully 80 per cent of those over the age of 60 vote, and in the 1956 presidential election, the aged had the lowest percentage of nonvoters. Furthermore, Hoar (1961) reports that 83 per cent said they had voted in a recent national election; nearly 93 per cent of men in their sixties and 90 per cent of women in their seventies reported that they had voted.

But voting is only one form of political participation. Working in elections, making financial contributions, and membership in political organizations are all measures of participation in American political life. The percentage of the general population that engages in these activities is small. The American Institute of Public Opinion, for exam-

ple, estimated (after the 1956 election) that 5 million people worked as volunteers; this was a little less than 5 per
cent of the electorate (Lane, 1959). Although the literature
on the aged is barren in this area, there is evidence that
political involvement generally increases with age: older
people are more interested in politics, they follow political
activity in the media more closely, and they participate
more actively than younger people (Campbell, 1962). With
age come increased political exposure and intense interest;
there are significant declines in the reading of sports and
comics, and noteworthy increases in the reading of news
and editorials on public affairs (Schramm and White,
1954). Also, older people are well represented among
opinion leaders, those who feel that others come to them
for information. In cases of intergenerational discussion,
younger people are more likely to seek political orientation
from older people. Whereas opinion leaders comprise
about 22 per cent of the general adult population, 35 per
cent of the retired were so rated. Opinion leaders are more
interested in elections, have more relevant information, are
more exposed to the media, know more about candidates'
positions, and feel that they have more influence on elections (Lane, 1959). Thus, there are real reasons for others
to seek their advice and guidance, and for the older person
to offer it and engage in persuasive discussion.

The high voting levels of the aged population, their
tendency to give rather than to receive political orientation,
and their high levels of interest in political activity on the
media suggest that the aged are intensely interested in and
committed to political processes. That their age compels
older individuals to act alike politically is less certain, however. Two conditions appear to militate against the recognition of common interests and the emergence of unified
political activity among older people. First, the low cultural
value that is associated with old age leads to self-rejection
and a refusal to identify with those of the same age status.

Second, the political system is not seen as indifferent, unresponsive, or illegitimate. The confluence of these two factors robs the aged both of a sense of common identity, and of the recognition of a common enemy against whom action can be directed.

Instead of identifying themselves with their contemporaries, older people consider advanced age a negative reference category. To be old in our society brings low prestige; hence the aged tend to dissociate themselves from the concept of old age and identify themselves with other groups.[6] Blau (1956) found that 60 per cent of those between 65 and 70 years of age labeled themselves as middle-aged rather than as old. The result of this failure to identify with their age peers is that the saliency of other status hierarchies is reflected in political behavior. Socioeconomic status, for example, is a more important factor than age in determining party affiliation (Loether, 1967). The wealthy older person votes as other wealthy individuals do, rather than as an elderly person. The aged with lower incomes, who in the past were blue-collar workers, align themselves with the Democratic Party, while the more affluent are usually Republicans. The degree to which political activity is grounded in status hierarchies other than age indicates the extent to which the aged may be working at political cross-purposes. This is especially notable in rural areas, where the aged are over-represented and their potential political power is most apparent; yet as a rule they are divided, and belong to many (and often opposed) interest groups, most of which do not make the welfare of the aged their primary goal (Cottrell, 1960). Hence, their political potential has never been realized. Even the aged in the

[6]Evidence indicates that the low social evaluations of old age are internalized by older persons, and are reflected in negative self-conceptions. In general, the aged tend to have less favorable self-images than do younger people, and, these unfavorable evaluations lead them to dissociate themselves from their peers (Kogan, 1961; Kogan and Wallach, 1961).

McLain Movement did not display a high level of group identity or consciousness. Pinner, Jacobs, and Selznick (1959) found the following:

> Anxiety concerning their status both as aged and as pensioners manifests itself in several ways: the pensioners hesitate to identify themselves with other aged persons; they are reluctant to identify themselves as aged; they prefer to be called "citizens" rather than "old" and "pensioners." The interviews with the forty-two signature collectors were rated for manifestations of identification with the aged. Criteria for this rating were the use of the pronoun "we" as well as other expressions of we-feeling. In only seven cases could such manifestations be detected, and even in these they occur only occasionally.

In addition, important issues that might cause older people to develop a common political consciousness and guiding ideology are absorbed into the platforms of both political parties. Special-interest groups have historically been unsuccessful, especially in the development of third-party movements, because they are denied the cohesive effects that would be provided if major issues were obviously ignored by the major parties. Although it was partly the concerted political pressure that the aged were able to bring to bear on officials during the early thirties that originally forced politicians to view their political future as affected by the aged, the momentum of the Townsend Movement as an independent political force was neutralized when the Democratic Party developed a social security platform in 1935. The acceptance by governments of a positive role in the protection of the aged resulted in a gradual recession of independent old-age politics.

More recently, Campbell (1962) has noted that national surveys provide evidence that differences of attitude between age groups are far less impressive than those within age groups. Smith (1966), in an examination of the

group status of the aged, found that older people themselves are far from achieving any consensus about common
needs or goals. When they were asked whether they would
approve of efforts by the aged to act as a bloc, only 40 per
cent answered affirmatively. The rejection of this kind of
political participation usually reflects a relative satisfaction
with political affairs, the belief that the needs of the aged
are being adequately met, a reluctance to "burden the
other generations," and the self-reliant attitudes that are
typical of the present generation of older people (Trela,
1971). Older people may at present be politically acqui-
escent for generational reasons, and subsequent aged cohorts may be more activist, but also the present
ambivalence of the aged toward their own status, and the
perceived legitimacy of present political arrangements,
cause the considerable political energies of the aged to be
spent in other ways rather than in pursuit of their age-
related self-interests. Their age is not a salient point of
political reference for most older people; there is no system
of beliefs and values that shapes the political life of the
aged, and except in rudimentary form, the aged have no
effective political organizations.

Although the aged exhibit a low sense of common
identity and perceive the present political processes as le-
gitimate and responsive, one factor that may interact with
the stress of status inconsistency and facilitate the development of a collective political response is the age-grading of
social relations, especially at the level of social interaction.
While some voluntary association activities are reduced in
the latter part of life, the proliferation of associations designed exclusively for the aged, at the national, state, and
especially the local level, suggests that some older people
reorient their associational activities in response to their
changing age status. Such associations are playing an
increasingly important role in the corporate life of older
people. It has been observed that the reduction of inter-

generational relations is being accompanied by increasing interaction and solidarity among age peers (Cumming and Schneider, 1961; Rosow, 1967; Bultena, 1968); this is consistent with both the disengagement (Cumming and Henry, 1961) and the quasi-minority (Barron, 1953) theories of aging, and it is a seminal element in Rose's (1962) tenet that the aged are an emergent subculture. Inasmuch as political attitudes and behaviors are learned through, and legitimized by, friends and fellow-members of organizations (Campbell, Curin, and Miller, 1954), increased interaction and communication with age peers in voluntary organizations may forward the development of a viable political movement based upon age status.

For several reasons, age-graded organizations may heighten political consciousness and activity somewhat more than groups whose members are of mixed age. This is probably true in that a homogeneous social environment reduces exposure to the cross-pressures generated by status inconsistency, which cause people to withdraw from social and political involvement (Lipset, 1963). Because contact with others who share similar life-circumstances lowers the individual's tendency to set up competing requests for political support and competing interpretations of social and political reality, and heightens the ability to act as a group, we may expect those aged who choose to associate with their age peers to be highly involved in political affairs. This thesis is partially supported by the existing evidence, which shows that participants in senior centers are somewhat more likely than those who participate exclusively in groups of mixed ages to profess high political interest, discuss politics, argue with others over political issues, and engage in other forms of political activity both at and outside the center (Trela, 1971).

Furthermore, membership in age-graded groups may be expected to provide sets of reference points from which individuals can define the political problems that confront them, and can identify their interests more clearly. Such settings provide a context (often as a by-product of other activities) in which news stories and the speeches of politicians are interpreted, and a perspective from which various social and political processes can be viewed. Members engage in small, intimate group discussions, which serve to create a climate of opinion, homogenize and crystallize group attitudes, and anchor each person's perceptions and political expectations in his group life. The political implications of this seem clear. Age status is given political meaning, and becomes an important reference point in the development of attitudes and behavior. There is a subsequent recognition of mutual interests and needs that may be satisfied through collective social action. It is not surprising, then, that members of age-graded organizations show a relatively high degree of political self-interest and predisposition toward activism (Trela, 1972). In comparison with aged individuals who participate exclusively in mixed generational groups, members of age-graded organizations record a higher desire for political change that will benefit the aged, greater receptivity to appeals for organized social action, and a greater willingness actually to engage in activity designed to secure change. When asked whether they would join an organization designed to gain benefits for the aged, members of senior centers are more likely than nonmembers to say that they would join. While this may reflect a general preference for affiliation with older people, it may also be that political feelings grounded in age status are activated in age-graded associations. If the stress of status inconsistency renders the individual receptive to appeals for political action, groups of age peers, by separating older people from the diffuse orientations of the larger community and promoting a common orientation toward political life, may provide the organizational basis for political expression.

chapter 6

Role Set Orientations and Life Satisfaction: A New Look at an Old Theory

BILL D. BELL

THE PROBLEM IN PERSPECTIVE

A great deal of the literature in social gerontology focuses on the increasing numbers of elderly people in the population, and also on the decreasing proportion of these individuals in the active labor force (Sheldon, 1958; Donahue, Orbach, and Pollak, 1960; Gordon, 1960; Brotman, 1968a, 1968b). In accordance with this developing pattern, the phenomena associated with occupational retirement have received considerable attention in research. The writings of Friedmann and Havighurst (1954), Lipman (1961), Thompson and Streib (1957), Goodstein (1962), Rosow (1967), Busse and Kreps (1963), Streib and Schneider (1971), and Carp (1972), among others, reflect a growing concern for the effects of retirement on the social adjustment and morale of older persons.

The study from which this analysis is drawn was supported in part by research funds provided by the Midwest Council for Social Research in Aging, a Division of the Institute for Community Studies in Kansas City, Missouri 64111.

While much of the correlational research of an earlier era has been displaced through Merton's (1957) stress on data-based theoretical procedures, many of the traditional orientations in gerontology are observed to overlap one another (Bell, 1973). In addition, contradictory predictions on the same independent variables frequently follow from the simultaneous use of more than one perspective (for example, possession of social status supposedly produces a positive sense of life satisfaction in the case of continuity theory, but reduces it in the case of the crisis perspective). As a consequence, it is difficult to discern in the literature a comprehensive test of the validity of any given theory as applied to the present question. For this reason, the following research selects a single orientation (continuity theory) and examines *only* the assumptions and predictions of this theory with regard to retirement and life satisfaction. The first point of interest is what relationship a continuous or discontinuous pattern of behavior bears to one's phenomenological expression of subjective satisfaction.

CONTINUITY THEORY IN REVIEW

The continuity tradition emphasizes the importance of a relatively stable pattern of previously established role behavior. It is clear from the discussion by Zborowski and Eyde (1962) of differential "living patterns," for example, that one's role set orientation has a significant influence on one's life satisfaction. In this regard, Back and McKinney (1966) have demonstrated that such orientations remain more or less consistent over time. Cavan (1947), Busse, Barnes, Silverman, Thaler, and Frost (1955), and Peck (1956) report that people tend to make preretirement investments of time, energy, and so on, in order to carry over the retirement experience. In similar fashion, the studies of Maddox (1970) and Bultena (1969) have reinforced the thesis that orientational consistency is related to life satisfaction.

While they stress the importance of role set behavior, continuity theorists generally de-emphasize the negative character of retirement. Back and Guptill (1966), for instance, argue that "[while] much of the literature of gerontology speaks of the shock of retirement, especially among those retirees who were very much involved with the work role . . . a closer look shows that the evidence is mainly impressionistic and clinical and does not come from a consideration of objective circumstances [p. 120]." Recent studies by Thompson (1958), Preston (1967), Streib and Schneider (1971), and Carp (1972) have made similar observations, for Streib and Schneider (1971) in particular,

> Retirement does not have the broad negative consequences for the older person that we had expected. The cessation of the work role results in a sharp reduction in income, but there is no significant increase in "worry" about money in the impact year of retirement. There is no sharp decline in health, feelings of usefulness, or *satisfaction in life* after retirement. Neither do respondents suddenly think of themselves as old. [p. 163]

The de-emphasis on the negative aspects of retirement suggested above arises primarily from the belief of continuity theorists that this experience is of an anticipatory character. They view the worker as being continually bombarded with the knowledge that retirement is inevitable. These reminders come through such avenues as the payment of retirement insurance (Orbach, 1963), attendance at company-sponsored "seminars" (Streib and Schneider, 1971), and contacts with retired friends and associates. Under these circumstances, the individual is in a position to become familiar with the role of the retiree well in advance of his own retirement. As a consequence, it is postulated, the behavioral changes that arise from retirement are usually made before employment is relinquished.

A second factor that facilitates the retirement transition is the makeup of the retirement role. Unlike those theorists who see the retired as having an ambiguously defined position in the social structure, the theorists of the continuity tradition not only emphasize the institutionalized nature of retirement (Baker, 1953; Donahue, Orbach, and Pollak, 1960; Orbach, 1963), but also stress that general and also specific expectations exist regarding the behavior of this age group (Anderson, 1967; Breen, 1963; Neugarten, 1968). As a result of both factors, these theorists tend to appraise occupational retirement as a nondisruptive experience.

In summary, then, continuity theory acknowledges that the individual is involved in a variety of roles in his role set (Biddle and Thomas, 1966). Not only are these roles held to vary in importance and significance, but behavior related to any given role is seen as limited by such factors as time, energy, and space. Given these contingencies, the individual purportedly develops a definite temporal orientation with respect to his role set. Role transitions, on the other hand, signal potential changes in these orientations. In relation to these potential changes, continuity theorists posit that orientational stability arises from the anticipatory nature of such transitions. Hence, to the extent that role changes can be anticipated in advance, any "adjustments" or reallocations of resources (personal or otherwise) may be made before the individual is faced with the "loss" or "gain" involved in specific transitions.

THE RESPONDENT SELECTION PROCESS

The data presented here come from interviews with 165 male respondents in an urban area of central Missouri, in the spring of 1973. Respondents were selected from lists submitted by (1) local labor organizations, (2) area churches (including the Salvation Army), (3) the local office of aging, (4) a transportation service for older Americans, (5) the Social Security Administration, (6) a recreational agency for older Americans, and (7) numerous interested individuals in the study community. Information was obtained on the employment status, residence, health, and marital status of each individual. The final sample was composed of white, retired males who lived within the city limits of the study community. Each individual's spouse was alive and lived with the respondent. In addition, each subject was in relatively good health from the standpoint of physical mobility, and owned or had access to appropriate means of transportation. All the interviews were conducted in the subjects' homes.

The individuals in question ranged in age from 53 to 99 years (the mean age was 72.4 years). Some 72.5 per cent of the respondents were between 65 and 79 years of age. Another 13.3 per cent were between 80 and 84 years old. Occupationally, the sample was composed of farmers, service workers, and laborers (29.7 per cent); clerical workers, salesmen, operatives, and craftsmen (31.5 per cent); and professional, technical, and managerial workers (38.8 per cent). The mean educational level of the sample was 12.5 years, a figure slightly above the national average (McKee, 1969). In addition, 55.6 per cent of all the persons interviewed had lived in the study community for 25 years or longer. Finally, the median monthly income was slightly less than $450 ($449.50).

MAJOR VARIABLES AND RESEARCH FOCUS

Role Set.—The role set has been defined as the total collection or set of "public" behaviors that characterize an individual as he goes from context to context (Biddle and Thomas, 1966). This definition implies that he will show an everbroadening complex of behaviors as more settings are added to his experience. Although the role sets of certain persons may differ from those of others, in the present analysis attention was limited to those areas of behavior that are generally common to everyone. In this regard, the four "interactional complexes" of Orbach and Shaw (1957) were pursued. For these writers the areas of occupation, family and kinship, voluntary associations, and community encompass the behavior of all. As the present respondents were retired, however, attention was focused upon the other three areas of interaction. The roles (behaviors) characteristic of these areas were taken to comprise the role sets of the people under study.

From an operational standpoint, family and kinship behavior involved all interaction between the respondent and those persons (with the exception of his spouse) related to him through blood or marital ties. This included visits, telephone calls, letters, or any other means of communication between the respondent and his kin. Voluntary association behavior, on the other hand, encompassed the individual's involvement in such formal organizational structures as civic clubs, professional societies, fraternal organizations, and the church. Included here were activities both directly and indirectly related to organizational goals. Finally, community behavior consisted of interaction with close friends and neighbors (defined as such by the respondent) and involvement in informal civic and political activities (canvassing for civic causes, political campaigning and voting, participation in community events, and so on).

Role Set Orientation.—A role set orientation was defined as the way in which an individual relates himself to the components of his role set. Such orientations involve expenditures of energy, and are limited by contingencies of time and space. In the present research, these orientations were measured by a temporal dimension. That is, the amount of time an individual spent in the component areas of his role set was taken to indicate his behavioral involvement in these settings. To this extent, it was possible to speak of a characteristic attitude or "orientation" toward each of the areas in question.

For operational purposes, respondents were asked to estimate the amount of time spent in each of the three role set areas. In the case of family and kin, the respondents were asked to estimate the amount of time spent visiting, telephoning, or otherwise communicating with their relatives before and after retirement. The unit of time selected was the number of hours per month spent in these activities. (Individuals were instructed to consider only those kin with whom they would have contact every month.) In the area of voluntary associations, they were asked to state the number of hours spent each month in such groupings as civic clubs, professional societies, fraternal organizations, and the church. Finally, in the community area, the number of hours spent each month in interaction with friends and neighbors and in informal civic and political activities were assessed. By comparing the estimates of time spent in each of the component areas before and after retirement, changes in role set orientations were computed. Changes were expressed by the formula $T_2 - T_1 = -, 0,$ or $+$. T_1 and T_2 were the estimates of time spent in specific areas before and after retirement respectively. A minus sign indicated a decrease in temporal involvement after retirement; a zero denoted no change in involvement; and a plus value represented an increase in temporal involvement.

Life Satisfaction.—Life satisfaction was regarded as the subjective experience of pleasure, with self and others, in relation to past or present social circumstances. In essence, satisfaction represented a statement of personal morale with respect to time and place. Because of the need for a comparable measure of degrees of satisfaction before and after retirement, however, the traditional satisfaction scales (for example, those of Neugarten, Havighurst, and Tobin, 1961) were not employed. Instead, life satisfaction was assessed by means of a single item.

In the present research, postretirement satisfaction was measured by means of the following question: "On the whole, how satisfied would you say you are with your way of life today?" In responding, the subject ranked himself along a 5-point scale, which ranged from 1 (not satisfied at all) to 5 (very satisfied). Many of the items suggested by Neugarten et al. were positively correlated with this measure. Specifically, ratings of present happiness, absence of concern over health, and feelings of usefulness, correlated significantly (at the .001 level) with ratings of satisfaction (Tau = + .3533; + .6787; and + .3283 respectively).

Preretirement satisfaction was assessed by the individual's retrospective response to the question: "On the whole, how satisfied would you say you were with your way of life before you stopped working?" Once again, the subject responded by ranking himself along the above-mentioned 5-point scale. In the analysis that follows, scale rankings were used as "measures" of the pre- and postretirement satisfaction of each respondent.

THE RESEARCH HYPOTHESIS

Two aspects of the continuity framework are related to the issue of life satisfaction. The first is the relationship of an anticipated role change to one's role set orientation. For the continuity theorist, an individual shows whether his patterns of behavior are specific and meaningful (that is, satisfying) through the components of his role set. The consistency of these orientations is in turn related to the nature of subsequent role changes, and also to the person's ability to anticipate in advance the behavioral implications of these transitions. Secondly, to the extent that a role change is both significant and clearly defined, theorists of the continuity tradition posit that behavioral reorientation precedes the event itself. As a consequence, pre- and post-transitional orientations and degrees of life satisfaction are expected to be generally consistent.

For the continuity theorist, however, not everyone is equally successful in anticipating or "adjusting to" the implications of an impending role change. Consequently, to the extent that the individual has little success in this regard, observable changes are expected to appear in his role set behaviors after the transition. As one's psychological well-being is thought to be closely related to one's orientational stability, significant disruptions at this point should be accompanied by changes in the level of life satisfaction. In the present instance, the transition from work-related to non-work-related roles should influence life satisfaction to the extent that previous role set orientations have been appreciably altered. In other words, stable (that is, consistent) orientations will be characterized by significantly less change in life satisfaction than will be observed if orientational disruption occurs.

THE RESULTS OF ANALYSIS

The relationship of changed levels of life satisfaction to changes in family orientations is shown in Table 6–I. In this instance, the difference between the proportion of those who experienced a change in family orientation (of either a positive or negative nature) and a subsequent change in life satisfaction did not differ significantly from the proportion of those who had stable, consistent orientations but experienced satisfaction changes ($z = -.7793$;

Table 6-I

RELATION OF CHANGES IN LIFE SATISFACTION
TO CHANGES IN FAMILY ORIENTATIONS

Change in Satisfaction	Change in Family Orientation						Difference between Proportions	Value of Z	Level of Significance
	Decrease		No Change		Increase				
	N	%	N	%	N	%			
Decrease	5	13.9	19	22.4	17	38.6			
No change	25	69.4	55	64.7	22	50.0	6.3	-0.7793	0.2177
Increase	6	16.7	11	12.9	5	11.4			
	36		85		44				

Chi Square = 7.090   .20
Kendall's Tau = – .1645   .001

probability $P < .2177$). From an associational standpoint, however, the correlation of these variables is both significant and negative in direction (Tau = – .1645; $P < .001$). Of those respondents who experienced an increase in family contact, 38.6 per cent evidenced a *decline* in life satisfaction. On the other hand, of those who underwent a decline in family interaction, 16.7 per cent indicated an *increase* in satisfaction. While 55 respondents reported no change in either variable, the present correlation suggests that the more time is invested in the family subsequent to retirement, the more decline occurs in life satisfaction. This finding remained consistent for the various categories of age, retirement duration, health, income, status, and community residence. These observations, then, fail to confirm the continuity hypothesis in the area of family behavior.

Somewhat similar results were obtained in the case of associational orientations. It is clear from Table 6–II that the difference between the proportion of those who experienced a change in voluntary association orientations and a subsequent change in life satisfaction did not differ significantly from the proportion of those who had stable, consistent orientations but experienced satisfaction changes (z = – .0270; $P < .3936$). In this instance, however, the correlation of these variables is significant and positive in direction

Table 6-II

RELATION OF CHANGES IN LIFE SATISFACTION
TO CHANGES IN VOLUNTARY ASSOCIATIONAL ORIENTATIONS

Change in Satisfaction	Change in Associational Orientation						Difference between Proportions	Value of Z	Level of Significance
	Decrease		No Change		Increase				
	N	%	N	%	N	%			
Decrease	16	32.0	20	23.8	5	16.1			
No change	29	58.0	52	61.9	21	67.7	0.2	−0.027	0.3936
Increase	5	10.0	12	14.3	5	16.1			
	50		84		31				

Chi Square = 2.832   .70
Kendall's Tau = + .1184   .012

(Tau $= + .1184$; $P < .012$). Thus, while the association is weak, it does suggest that greater investments of time in this area after retirement are associated with positive changes in life satisfaction. In this regard, 32.0 per cent of those respondents who underwent a decline in associational interaction experienced a *decrease* in life satisfaction. On the other hand, 16.1 per cent of those who reported an increase in associational interaction demonstrated an *increase* in satisfaction. Controls for age, health, status, and duration of retirement revealed that slightly younger respondents, with fair health (Tau $= + .3647$; $P < .009$) and low status (Tau $= + .2622$; $P < .004$) reflected the observed relationship more significantly. Once again, however, one-third of the sample reported no change in either variable. These findings also fail to support the continuity hypothesis.

In the final relationship examined (Table 6–III), the difference between the proportion of those who experienced a change in community orientation and a subsequent change in life satisfaction did not differ significantly from the proportion who had consistent orientations but experienced satisfaction changes ($z = + .1358$; $P < .4443$). While the correlation of these variables was not significant, it did extend in a positive direction (Tau $= + .0781$; $P < .068$):

Table 6-III

RELATION OF CHANGES IN LIFE SATISFACTION
CHANGE TO CHANGES IN COMMUNITY ORIENTATIONS

Change in Satisfaction	Change in Community Orientation						Difference between Proportions	Value of Z	Level of Significance
	Decrease		No Change		Increase				
	N	%	N	%	N	%			
Decrease	19	31.1	9	16.7	13	26.0			
No change	38	62.3	33	61.1	31	62.0	0.9	+ 0.1358	0.4443
Increase	4	6.6	12	22.2	6	12.0			
	61		54		50				

Chi Square = 7.773   .20
Kendall's Tau = + .0781   .068

31.1 per cent of those who underwent a decline in community orientation also indicated a decline in life satisfaction.
On the other hand, 12 per cent of those who increased their
community contact after retirement experienced an increase in satisfaction. Once again, although the correlation
was weak, it does suggest that the more time an individual
invests in community contact after retirement, the more
positive his change in life satisfaction will be. This was
particularly true for the younger, healthier respondents
(Tau = + .5418; $P < .002$). Nevertheless, 54 of the people
in the sample reported no change in either community
orientation or life satisfaction. The continuity explanation,
therefore, would appear inappropriate to the present
findings.

DISCUSSION OF FINDINGS

From the perspective of these data, the more time that
is invested in the family after retirement, the more negative
the life satisfaction will be. Several factors might account
for this finding. In the first place, family interaction is qualitatively different from interaction in the work setting (Lipman, 1961). To this extent, the individual's behavior

toward his co-workers probably involves "rewards" that are unobtainable within the family context. Then, too, increased interaction in the family setting may serve only to magnify hostilities that were previously latent, due to the infrequency of preretirement contacts. In addition, the diminished personal status that accompanies occupational retirement (Reiss, 1961) places the person in a dependent relationship with his family members. "Forced" interaction in this setting, coupled with the prospect of declining interactional opportunities outside the family (Srole, 1956), might be expected to result in lowered satisfaction. In the present instance, this was especially true of persons in poor health (Tau = $-.4170$; $P < .001$), with low incomes (Tau = $-.1620$; $P < .035$), or whose retirement was relatively recent (Tau = $-.2937$; $P < .001$).

In the case of voluntary associations, however, a positive relationship was observed between involvement and satisfaction. The relationship was most pronounced among younger persons of lower status, in fair to good health. These findings also suggest that there is a context-specific reason for satisfaction. It can be argued, for example, that interaction in associational settings is in many respects similar to interaction in an employment situation (Carp, 1967). To the extent that this is true, retirement has not totally removed the individual from a context similar to that of work. Interaction in such settings, then, would result in little or no loss of status for the older person. As a consequence, intensified involvement in this area should be accompanied by increased satisfaction. This was the finding of the present study.

In a similar fashion, interaction in the community area was positively associated with satisfaction. Nevertheless, the association was decidedly weak. In addition, "community interaction" was primarily with friends and neighbors: 61.2 per cent of the respondents, for example, had interacted only with friends and neighbors before retirement. Following retirement, 66.1 per cent of all subjects confined their community behavior to these persons. Given these circumstances, it is possible to see the community setting as a "hybrid" of the previous two. The person's position in relation to his friends and neighbors, for instance, is akin to his position in relation to his family members. On the other hand, many informal facets of community interaction parallel those of associational settings. Hence, to the extent that one's status with friends and neighbors reflects the loss of occupational roles, a negative correlation similar to that evidenced in the family setting would be expected. On the other hand, informal community activities are often associated with formal organizational settings (Carp, 1967), which would give a positive satisfaction change. Consequently, this dual community focus might account for the rather weak correlation observed in this area.

These findings, then, do not substantiate the continuity hypothesis. On the contrary, an activity orientation is seen as a more appropriate explanation. In addition, life satisfaction is observed to be context-related. That is, satisfaction is primarily maintained, increased, or decreased according to the character of specific behavioral settings. In this regard, the contextual milieu helps to insulate the individual from the loss of status that accompanies retirement. In the case of the family, the segment of the role set least like the work setting, status loss effects a decline in satisfaction. In the two remaining areas, however, the character of social interaction does not represent a radical departure from work relations. Consequently, associational and community interaction "insure" the person against status loss. Increased involvement in these areas, therefore, results in relatively stable or increased levels of satisfaction.

LIMITATIONS AND RESEARCH SUGGESTIONS

The present research is not without its limitations. The definition of life satisfaction is a case in point. Neugarten et al. (1961), for example, have incorporated five factors in the satisfaction variable. These include: (1) whether the individual takes pleasure from the round of activities that constitute his everyday life; (2) whether he regards his life as meaningful and accepts resolutely what his life has been; (3) whether he feels he has successfully achieved his major goals; (4) whether he holds a positive image of himself; and (5) whether he is able to maintain happy and optimistic attitudes and moods. In this study, however, life satisfaction was taken to be simply the phenomenological experience of pleasure, with self and others, in past or present social circumstances. Obviously, this definition omitted several of the areas cited by Neugarten et al. To this extent, only a very general picture of satisfaction was obtained from the present data. A more comprehensive examination would include several of the areas cited above. In addition, from a methodological standpoint, an objective rating procedure coupled with these subjective responses would lend more credence to the validity of the reports.

The definition of life satisfaction was modified by problems in the definition of the role set and role set orientations. Initially, the role set was seen as the total collection, or set, of "public" behaviors that characterize an individual as he goes from one context to another. This implied, of course, that he would show an ever-broadening complex of behaviors as he experienced an increasing number of settings. Nevertheless, for present convenience, only three areas of behavior were investigated: the family, voluntary associations, and the community. Clearly, in taking these areas as comprising the "total" role set of all respondents, the researcher was sampling selectively from many possible forms of interaction, and was subsequently constructing artificial boundaries within what is in reality a much broader perspective. Accordingly, the findings of the present research may be altered somewhat by a more extensive investigation of role set components—both components found in all role sets and more personal, idiosyncratic components.

The role set orientation, on the other hand, was viewed as the manner in which an individual interacted with the components of his role set. These orientations supposedly involve expenditures of energy, and are assumed to be limited by contingencies of time and space. Such a concept, again, implies a much broader dimension than was actually studied. For example, one's mode of interaction usually involves a certain "style" or approach. Closely related here are aspects such as dress, demeanor, and so on, which go well beyond the simple assessment of the time spent in specific areas. Also, we cannot assume that retrospective reconstructions of temporal involvement are consistent with actual past behavior. Then, too, "behavior" was never fully defined in relation to the contexts investigated. These points, then, lead to the following suggestions for research: (1) use of a broader concept of "orientation," one that incorporates many of the extra-interactional factors normally associated with the concept of life-style; (2) a more specific enumeration of the behaviors to be considered, with corresponding changes in the research procedure; (3) provision for objective, factual corroboration of the behavior in question; and ideally, (4) use of a longitudinal research design in order to eliminate generational differences.

Finally, a number of methodological problems must be addressed. The first is the choice of research design. Interviews with a purposively selected, cross-sectional sample of retired males may be subject to a series of confounding influences. It was not possible, for example, to examine the influence of generational differences. Even though the respondents were of the same race, sex, marital status, and so on, they nevertheless received their major socialization experiences at different times. Hence there is no simple way to determine whether the results truly represented the

variables examined, or were merely artifacts of generational experience. Subsequent research, therefore, should
perhaps include longitudinal design. For this purpose,
also, thought should be given to the randomness of subject
assignment. It is clear that the present study fails in this
respect. In addition, the researcher would do well to refine
his instruments in a way that would make it possible to use
parametric statistical techniques. The present data did not
justify such procedures.

chapter 7

Effects of Age-Grade Comparisons on Adjustment in Later Life

GORDON BULTENA
EDWARD POWERS

THEORETICAL PERSPECTIVE

Aging is a social as well as a biological process, and entry into old age commonly brings major changes in role and status. In American society, these changes, viewed from the perspective of the dominant cultural values, are largely detrimental. Specifically, when individuals reach old age, they are caught up in a series of life changes (more often involuntary than voluntary) that attenuate their ability to retain, or to attain, important cultural goals. The goals that generally attract Americans (acceptable social status, economic success, good health, youthful appearance, energetic living, and personal independence) continue to be important goals in old age.[1]

The changes in status involved in the passage from

This study was carried out under a grant from the Iowa Commission on the Aging and with funds provided by the Iowa Agriculture and Home Economics Experiment Station, Ames, Iowa (Project No. 1871). A version of this paper was prepared for the Ninth International Congress of Gerontology, Kiev, Russia.

Footnotes to this chapter are at the end of the chapter.

middle to old age is problematic, not only because the life changes are predominantly detrimental, but also because they tend to be compressed into a relatively short period of time. Older individuals not uncommonly find that occupational retirement is followed by a diminished income, lessened physical mobility, a decline in health and vitality, and a constriction of the social world through the death of a spouse, siblings, and close friends.[2] Each of these changes has a distressing impact upon the individual's psychological adaptation; their occurrence in rapid succession makes them an even greater threat to the retention of good morale and mental stability in old age.

This view of aging as a detrimental process suggests that older persons should show considerable demoralization as life changes progressively attenuate their standing in relation to the dominant cultural values.[3] Previous research has often demonstrated that morale diminishes with losses in health, reduced income, constricted social relationships, widowhood, and occupational retirement (for a review of this literature see Adams, 1971). It has also been found, however, that aged persons with deprived statuses often report surprisingly high levels of life satisfaction. Riley and Foner (1968), after making an inventory of the literature on life satisfaction of the aged, conclude that older persons appear to "come to terms" with their deprived statuses, and may even find contentment in their new life situations.

Several alternative explanations have been offered for the retention of relatively high morale in later life. Cumming and Henry (1961), in their disengagement theory, have posited that there is a mutual withdrawal between older persons and society, and that individuals replace many established values with a desire for an isolated, static, self-centered existence. This reorientation results in new contentments, despite the onset of objectively deprived life situations. Another explanation is that American values foster a stoic acceptance of adversity, and encourage individuals to maintain positive outlooks despite their deteriorating life conditions. The explanation considered in this study is that new reference groups emerge for the aged, which serve to buoy morale in the face of what would seem to be demoralizing losses of role and status.

Reference-group theory appears particularly fruitful as a means of explaining the seeming disparity between the deprived life conditions of older persons and their retention of good morale. Kelley (1968) has suggested that reference groups can perform two functions: they can provide the actor with a set of values and norms (the normative function), or provide a point of reference with which he can compare his life situations (the comparative function). As yet there appear to be no reference groups that offer the aged a distinct set of age-appropriate norms (Rose, 1965; Wood, 1971). It would seem, however, that the "aged," as a social category, constitute an important comparative reference group against which older individuals can gauge the desirability of their evolving life situations.

An important aspect of this comparative function is that many negative stereotypes are applied to the "aged" as a social category in American society. Old age is seen by young and old as a time of diminished physical activity, absentmindedness, social isolation, poor health, increased dependency, sexual abstinence, and the like (McTavish, 1971).[4] Comparisons by older persons of their personal situations with those of other "aged" are likely to be cast against these negative stereotypes, rather than against the more positive life patterns that may be normative for their age group. In one sense the stereotypes have a positive function; they reassure persons who are undergoing age-related losses that these experiences are neither uncommon nor, according to the stereotypes, as severe as those experienced by most aged persons. The individual's comparison of his own situation with that of the stereotyped "aged" reference group may thus serve as a buffer against the demoralization that would otherwise be expected to accompany the losses of role and status incurred with aging.

While reference group theory has previously been offered as a fruitful approach to the study of adjustment in later life (Romeis, Albert, and Acuff, 1971), the ability of the theory to explain these adjustments has not been established in empirical literature. Past research on adjustment to age (also referred to as morale and life satisfaction) has concentrated on the "objective" roles and statuses of older persons, that is, their relative positions on such scales as chronological age, income, health, organizational participation, and interaction with relatives and friends. More recently research has focused on the "subjective" assessments older persons make of their "objective" conditions, as reflected in variables of age-identity, health, adequacy of income, and perceived life-space. These subjective assessments undoubtedly reflect reference-group comparisons, but the specific nature of these comparisons has been neglected.

The relevance of reference-group comparisons to the adjustment of the aged was tested in this study. First, it was hypothesized (consistently with previous research) that a favorable position on "objective" statuses would be associated with a high level of life satisfaction in old age. Second, it was hypothesized that older persons, although they occupied relatively deprived objective statuses, would view their various life situations as comparable to, or better than, those of other aged persons. Finally, it was hypothesized that favorable comparisons of their own life situations with those of other older people would be associated with relatively high levels of life satisfaction.

SAMPLE AND PROCEDURES

The data are derived from a ten-year longitudinal study of older persons in Iowa. When first studied in 1960, the respondents were at least 60 years of age. In the 1970 restudy, they ranged in age from 70 to 97; the median age was 76.

The 1960 study was of noninstitutionalized older persons in counties selected to provide a representative cross-section of rural and urban populations. All of the persons interviewed in five of these counties (a total of 611) in 1960 were considered eligible respondents in 1970. Fieldwork revealed, however, that 56 per cent of the original respondents could not be reinterviewed, largely because of death. Of the remaining 269 potential respondents, 235 were reinterviewed. The 34 persons who were not reinterviewed were unavailable because of health and senility problems (16 respondents), absence on vacations (12), or refusals (6).

The following measures were used in 1970 to test the hypotheses posed in this paper.

Health.—Respondents were asked to list their major health problems, if any. The number of different problems listed (which ranged in number from zero to five) was used in this analysis as an overall indicator of general health status.

Income.—The annual family income derived from wages, pensions, insurance, stock, social security, and other sources was found to range from less than $1,000 to over $8,000. The median family income of the respondents was $2,900.

Physical Mobility.—Respondents were asked how often they got out of the house to make visits, do shopping, attend clubs, and the like. The response categories and frequencies were: once a day or more (42 per cent), several times a week (29 per cent), about once a week (13 per cent), and less than once a week (16 per cent).

Social Interaction.—The frequency of face-to-face contact with siblings, other relatives (not a spouse or children), neighbors, and friends was determined. A score was assigned to each respondent that reflected the frequency of interaction (daily = 365, weekly = 52, monthly = 12, less often = 6). The interaction scores of respondents in 1970 varied from 0 to 3,285; the median score was 260.

Organizational Participation.—Information was obtained on the number of clubs and organizations regularly attended. The number of groups that individuals attended ranged from 0 to 7.

Comparative Life Situations.—In addition to the information that was obtained on the respondents' "objective" standing in health, income, physical mobility, social interaction, and organizational participation, they were asked in 1970 how they felt their situations compared with that of other people of their age on each of these variables. For example, the question on health was: "Would you say that you're in better health, in about the same shape, or in poorer health than others your age?"

Life Satisfaction.—The dependent variable in this study, life satisfaction, was measured by a scale of thirteen items; a three-point response format was employed (agree, undecided, disagree). The life satisfaction scale was developed and validated in the Kansas City study of adult life by Neugarten, Havighurst, and Tobin (1961). A shortened version of the original scale (Wood, Wylie, and Sheafor, 1969) was used in this study. Responses to each item were scored, and cumulative scores were derived. These ranged from 13 (which reflected favorable life satisfaction) to 38 (which indicated little satisfaction); the median score was 21.

FINDINGS

Analysis of the life changes of respondents during the 1960–1970 decade revealed considerable deterioration in their collective situations. In 1970 an increased number were found to be living alone or with children, many had lost a spouse, there was a sharp increase in health problems, more help was being received from friends and relatives for personal and nonpersonal tasks, many more were confined to the house, and fewer were gainfully employed (Table 7-I). The actual income levels of the respondents had remained stable over the decade, but inflation meant that many now had diminished purchasing power.[5]

Table 7-I

SELECTED LIFE SITUATIONS OF THE AGED RESPONDENTS
IN 1960 AND 1970

Situation	Percentage	
	1960	1970
Living arrangement:		
Respondent alone	28	36
Respondent with spouse (children)	54	36
Respondent with children	8	14
Other	10	14
Spouse is deceased	43	63
Number of major health problems:		
None	71	36
One	22	31
Two or more	6	32
Assistance required to meet daily needs	8	33
Confined to house	3	13
Gainfully employed	41	14

Despite these adverse changes in situation, the respondents retained a surprisingly high level of general satisfaction with their lives. In response to the question: "How satisfied are you with your way of life today?" 88 per cent in 1960 said they were "very satisfied" or "fairly satisfied" (as compared to "not very satisfied" or "not satisfied at all"). In 1970, 91 per cent reported a similar level of satisfaction. Further, while there was evidence of a slight decline in satisfaction in responses to a set of morale items gauged in both 1960 and 1970, the number of respondents who evaluated their situations favorably in 1970 is striking (Table 7-II).[6]

That high levels of morale were retained by the respondents despite their deteriorating life situations suggests that factors other than their "objective" statuses may be important to their outlooks in later life. These objective statuses, however, were the initial point of attention in this study, due to the prominence they are given in the litera-

Table 7-II

RESPONSES TO QUESTIONS ON ATTITUDE TOWARD
LIFE SITUATIONS IN 1960 AND 1970

Expressions of Attitude		Responses (Percentage)†		
		Agree	Unsure	Disagree
These are the best years	1960:	31*	21	48
of my life	1970:	23	15	62
I just feel miserable	1960:	3	3	94*
most of the time	1970:	7	3	90
I have more free time	1960:	13	3	84*
than I know how to use	1970:	29	3	68
My life is full of	1960:	4	3	93*
worry	1970:	9	5	86
Sometimes I feel there	1960:	1	2	97*
is no point in living	1970:	10	4	86
I have very few friends	1960:	6	2	92*
	1970:	13	1	86
My life is still busy	1960:	89*	3	8
and useful	1970:	79	5	16

* Asterisks indicate responses that represent high life satisfaction.
† These percentages are derived only from persons who responded to these items.

Table 7-III

CORRELATION OF OBJECTIVE STATUSES AND COMPARATIVE
ASSESSMENTS WITH LIFE SATISFACTION

Variable	Correlation with Life Satisfaction		
	Objective Status	Comparative Assessment	Comparative Assessment Governing Objective Status
Health	.39*	.36*	.23*
Income	.29*	.28*	.26*
Physical mobility	.35*	.28*	.10
Social interaction	.02	.34*	.31*
Organizational participation	-.14†	.22*	.26*

* Significant at .001 level.
† Significant at .05 level.

ture on adjustment in later life. The first hypothesis was that a favorable position on the objective status scales of health, income, physical mobility, social interaction, and organizational participation would be associated with high life satisfaction. The data only partly supported his hypothesis. Health status (r = .39), income (r = .29), and physical mobility (r = .35) were found to have a positive relationship to life satisfaction. Contrary to expectations, participation in organizations was inversely associated with life satisfaction (r = − .14) and no significant relationship was found for social interaction (r = .02; Table 7-III, column 1).[7]

The second hypothesis was that respondents would rate their several life situations as comparable to, or better than, that of their age peers. Only in comparing their levels of organizational participation did a majority (60 per cent) perceive themselves as "worse off" or as having a lower level of activity than most older persons (Table 7-IV). This response might be anticipated, since social participation, unlike the other characteristics considered, tends to be expected behavior for older persons; in the stereotypes, many aged are seen as playing fairly active roles in church groups. Only a minority of the respondents perceived their

Table 7-IV

COMPARISONS OF PERSONAL STATUS TO PERCEIVED
LIFE SITUATIONS OF AGE PEERS

Variable	Personal Status (Percentage)*			
	Better Off	Same as Others	Worse Off	Don't Know
Health	48	37	12	3
Income	21	51	18	10
Physical mobility	37	39	20	4
Social interaction	15	52	30	3
Organizational participation	9	25	60	6

* The number of respondents was 235.

situations on health (12 per cent), income (18 per cent), physical mobility (20 per cent), and social interaction (30 per cent) as poorer than that of their age peers (Table 7-IV).

The third hypothesis, which is central to our theoretical argument, is that favorable comparative assessments of status are important to the maintenance of good morale in old age. A test was made of the relationship of assessments on each of these five variables to life satisfaction. As expected, significant relationships were found for health ($r = .36$), income ($r = .28$), physical mobility ($r = .28$), social interaction ($r = .34$), and organizational participation ($r = .22$; Table 7-III, column 2). The correlation between comparative assessments and life satisfaction could be spurious, however, if the comparative variables are merely a function of the respondents' objective positions on status hierarchies. This is suggested by the fact that significant correlations were obtained between the objective and comparative measures of health ($r = .41$), income ($r = .21$), physical mobility ($r = .55$), social interaction ($r = .24$), and organizational participation ($r = .19$).

To determine the independent effects of comparative assessments on life satisfaction, first-order partial correla-

Table 7-V

STEPWISE REGRESSION ANALYSIS OF RELATIONSHIP OF OBJECTIVE
AND COMPARATIVE MEASURES TO LIFE SATISFACTION

Measure	Multiple R	R Square
Objective health	0.36296	0.13174
Comparative income	0.44732	0.20009
Comparative participation	0.49903	0.24903
Comparative interaction	0.52362	0.27418
Objective income	0.54018	0.29179
Comparative health	0.55715	0.31041
Comparative mobility	0.56081	0.31451
Objective participation	0.56136	0.31512
Objective interaction	0.56147	0.31525
Objective mobility	0.56147	0.31525

tions were run between individual comparative items and life satisfaction, and controls were run on the corresponding objective statuses. It was found that, with the exception of physical mobility, the relationship between the comparative items and life satisfaction remained statistically significant (Table 7-III, column 3). This analysis suggests that the relationship of comparative assessments of status to life satisfaction is direct, and is not merely an artifact of objective situations.

A final question to be answered by these data is whether comparative assessments or objective statuses are more important to life satisfaction. Stepwise regression was employed to test the relative contribution of each of the comparative and objective variables to life satisfaction. Objective health was found to be the most important variable, followed by comparative income, comparative participation, and comparative interaction assessments. The three comparative items increased the amount of variance explained beyond that attributable to objective health from 13 to 27 per cent. Overall, the five comparative items ranked in the top seven variables when ordered by the amount of variance they explained in life satisfaction (Table 7-V).

Discussion

Role and status changes incurred in the aging process have been a major concern in previous examinations of psychological adjustment in later life. In particular, the relatively deprived health, income, interaction, participation, and mobility situations of older people have been singled out as possible sources of demoralization. Yet research literature indicates that many older people, while they show some loss of morale, nevertheless tend to retain a surprisingly high level of general satisfaction with their lives.

The psychological adjustment of older persons to deprived statuses is examined in this study from the perspective of reference group theory. The "aged" as a social category are seen as comprising a salient comparative (but not normative) reference group for older individuals. It was posited that they define their life situations in the areas of health, income, interaction, participation, and physical mobility statuses as comparable to, or better than, the patterns perceived as normative for their age group. It was further hypothesized that such favorable comparisons are associated with the maintenance of good morale in old age. The data supported these hypotheses in indicating: (1) that a large majority of the respondents perceived themselves as enjoying a comparable or advantageous position relative to their age peers on four of the five statuses studied, and (2) that favorable comparative evaluations were associated with high levels of life satisfaction. It was also found that comparative evaluations tended to be as important to the life satisfaction of respondents as were their actual objective positions on various status scales.

This finding, that comparative assessments of life conditions are highly important to the maintenance of good morale in old age, is consistent with a basic premise of interactionist theory, which Blumer (1969) stated thus:

"Human beings act toward things on the basis of meanings that the things have for them [2]." The meanings that older persons attribute to role losses in later life, for example, may not coincide with the meanings assigned to these losses by others. Whereas younger persons, operating in terms of the dominant cultural values, perceive many of the changed situations of older persons as critically important, these same situations may be defined as normative by the aged, and hence may not precipitate the demoralization that is otherwise anticipated.[8]

There is a need for social research to determine more definitively the different views that older and younger persons bring to an assessment of the role changes encountered in aging. Reference group theory appears to offer a particularly fruitful perspective for such investigation. Our findings revealed that reference groups may emerge late in the life cycle that serve to cushion the psychological shock of adverse role changes. The types of reference groups that are used in later life, and their differential importance for the aged, however, remain to be explored.[9]

NOTES

1. Several writers (Rose, 1965; Wood, 1971) argue that a set of values are developing among the aged that are more congruent with the structural and personal realities of old age, and are distinct from the values that prevail in society at large. These values, however, are not sufficiently crystallized to provide meaningful alternatives to the current normative patterns for most older persons.

2. In addition to the frequent deterioration in the life situations of aged individuals, the gap between the younger and aged populations is growing in many ways; for example, income differentials have been increasing (Palmore and Whittington, 1071).

3. Merton (1957) and Meier and Bell (1959) argue, for example, that personal pathologies tend to be precipitated by structural

situations in which the individual experiences a disjunction between cultural goals and the institutionalized means for their attainment.

4. The existence of negative stereotypes of the aged is reflected in the resistance of older persons to the concept that they are old (Peters, 1971).

5. Inflation as reflected in the consumer price index was about 30 per cent over the 1960–1970 decade. Thus, merely to "stay even," income had to increase about one-third; yet less than two-fifths of the respondents had received an income gain of this magnitude.

6. Comparison of scores on the life satisfaction scale between the two periods was impossible, since this instrument was not used in the 1960 survey.

7. Further analysis showed that the lack of a relationship between the quantity of social interaction and life satisfaction was a function of the fact that high levels of late life interaction were often made necessary by serious health problems and by the physical dependency of the respondents.

8. In this regard, Neugarten (1970) found that women in menopause or in the empty-nest stage of family life define their experiences as less stressful than cultural definitions of these roles would imply.

9. Townsend (1968) has suggested that several references may be important in the different orientations of older persons toward physical isolation: (1) comparison with contemporaries, (2) comparison with preceding generations of aged, (3) comparison with earlier life statuses, and (4) comparison with the statuses occupied by younger persons.

chapter 8

Being Single in Old Age

JABER F. GUBRIUM

The study of lives has been approached from a variety of perspectives, ranging from the highly personal viewpoint of some psychoanalytic traditions to the situational perspective of the sociological study of social structures. In this paper, the social personality of single elders will be considered. This particular perspective on the study of lives conceives of the person as a rational social being, who has a past and anticipates a future, and who faces a variety of different contingencies in everyday living that constrain him to act in one way or another (Thomas, 1966). Analytically, the social being has two major problems in everyday life: the evaluation and validation of the self, and the consideration of situational contingencies as they affect action, both toward others and the self.

How is social personality located? At least two answers have been offered to this question. Some researchers hunt out a number of people who have particular social characteristics in common, assume that they have experienced

This article also appears in the *International Journal of Aging and Human Development*, 1975.

similar everyday circumstances, and talk to them about themselves as social types. Other researchers choose a situation that affects a number of people in common, assume that they all consider its contingencies, and watch and listen to how they act within it. Both methods have certain procedural problems that raise questions about their validity. Researchers using either technique attempt to resolve these problems within the confines of their own technique. In the research on which this paper reports, single elders were located and interviewed both about themselves and about some aspects of the quality of their everyday lives.

SINGLE ELDERS AS SPECIAL CASES

As an individual grows old, one of the situational contingencies of everyday life is the increasing probability of losing a spouse through death. This, as well as the chances of becoming ill and insolvent, makes it likely that persons will become socially isolated with age. This has led to the hypothesis that social isolation, which is partly an outcome of the death of the spouse, leads to such personal acts as suicide (Berardo, 1968, 1970; Bock and Webber, 1972) and to low morale (Berardo, 1967).

The argument that underlies this hypothesis is that the self is a highly social thing. Throughout the life cycle, a person comes to know who he is, and what he can expect of himself, through contact with others in the various situations in which he participates. The trust he has in himself hinges significantly on these conditions. When their viability is shaken, self-validation loses its routine proving-ground.

It might be argued further that as one grows older, social investment becomes an increasingly important dimension of self-validation. Over the life cycle, a person learns to trust other specific individuals to support and lend credibility to his actions. With age, these others are likely to become relatively stable. Likewise, a person's routine expectations of himself become increasingly stable. The extensive social investments accumulated in others over time provide the ground for personal confidence when they remain secure, and can cause disintegration when they become shaken.

Having a spouse is a major ground of self-validation. It affects a wide range of interpersonal expectations and routines. In old age, a married individual's interpersonal relationships are likely to have developed out of the long-term investments he has made in conjunction with his spouse. For example, his friendships (Blau, 1956, 1961) and his relationships with his kin often hinge on the fact that his spouse participates in them.

If he becomes widowed in old age, the everyday routines previously supported by the spouse's actions are disrupted. The widowed person loses a certain source of validation for these routines. His sudden isolation transforms his trust in others' expectations of him, hitherto taken for granted, into something questionable, and this in turn leads to problems of self-validation.

How general is this process likely to be in old age? Moreover, to what extent does isolation *per se* affect it?

Most older people (65 and over) are married and reside with a spouse (United States Bureau of the Census, 1960). This, of course, changes with age, and it does so sooner for women than for men. By the age of 80, over one-third of the males and about two-thirds of the females in the United States are widowed. On the basis of the foregoing argument on the effects of social isolation, most persons should experience some problems of self-validation as they grow old. The exceptions to this are the single, as a category. They are relatively rare among those over 65 years of age; they represent a proportion of about 8%.

Being single in old age is a kind of premium. Since

such persons have no spouses, they do not experience the social disruptions that come with the death of the spouse. Their everyday routines are more likely than the married to have been generated out of lifelong relative isolation. As Clark and Anderson (1967) state:

> Many old bachelors like Mr. Ebenhauser, who have maintained a social distance from others throughout their lives, often appear to function well, as though they have had a lifetime of practice in the self-reliance and autonomy required of many old people. Since they have never been close to others, they are spared the grief and loneliness of those who, having invested in and been intimate with others, must suffer the loss of a cherished relative, spouse, or friend. [p. 257]

The "crisis" of the decision of whether to marry, if it occurs for the single, is likely to have taken place in early adulthood, when most persons marry, rather than in late life.

The case of the single means we must make the preceding statement on isolation more specific. Rather than claiming that a certain level of isolation *per se* affects the personal and everyday lives of the aged, the argument is really about the effects of changes in the level of isolation, that is, the impact of becoming desolate in old age. The distinction between isolation and desolation has been noted to be important, since without it, important differences between the lives of elderly persons are overlooked (Townsend, 1957, 1968; Tunstall, 1966; Gubrium, 1974).

The single are not only special cases demographically and sociologically, they are also peculiar in the sense that the quality of their lives has seldom been examined. They face everyday circumstances that differ markedly from those of married, widowed, or divorced persons. In old age, their lifelong experiences provide them with rather unusual grounds for self-validation and action, so unusual that they have remained "hidden" exceptions to much discussion about the social psychology of aging and isolation.

PREVIOUS RESEARCH ON SINGLE ELDERS

Research on single elders is sparse. Two kinds of studies have focused on them, at least to some extent. One devotes attention to the relative isolation of the lives of single elders as it affects loneliness. The second considers the impact of marital desolation in old age on the evaluation of everyday life; obviously single elders serve as a control group.

Research on single elders that focuses primarily on their degree of loneliness, as compared to that of elders with other marital statuses, is based on British data. Townsend (1957) developed a social contact index as a measure of social isolation in old age. The index is a weighted sum of weekly contacts with a variety of persons. Of the 203 persons he interviewed, the 10 most isolated were all unmarried or childless. Those living in relative isolation did not always report the greatest loneliness, however. Rather, those who had recently become isolates (desolates) tended to be the loneliest. Half of those persons who said that they were very lonely or sometimes lonely had been recently bereaved. Willmott and Young (1960), using data collected in a London suburb, also found that desolation rather than isolation was related to loneliness in old age. Single and married persons reported similar degrees of loneliness. More than twice as many of the widowed, on the other hand, said that they were lonely. Tunstall (1966), likewise, found that single elders tended to be lifelong isolates. Furthermore, single elders were aware of the advantages of their marital status in old age.

Gubrium (1974) has made a second kind of study of single elders. The hypothesis tested was that the relative isolation (desolation) involved in becoming widowed or divorced, rather than absolute isolation (which includes the widowed, the divorced, and the single) is related to negative evaluations of everyday life in old age. Results showed that the desolate did indeed have a more negative view than

184 JABER F. GUBRIUM

the nondesolate. In the evaluation of everyday life, then, being single resembles being married in its effect. This finding corroborates the preceding British data.

The available data on single elders indicate the following:

1. They tend to be lifelong isolates.
2. They are not especially lonely in old age.
3. Their evaluation of everyday life is similar to that of married elders, in the sense that both have a more positive view than divorced or widowed aged persons.
4. Compared to other marital statuses, being single is a premium in old age in that it avoids the desolating effects of bereavement following the death of the spouse.

The Quality of Single Life in Old Age

In considering the social personality of single elders, we must focus both on the social selves of this type of person and the contingencies of their social situation as they affect their actions. The following descriptions of the quality of single life in old age address two questions: How do single elders define and evaluate themselves at present and over time? And how do they feel their social situation affects their actions? Answers to these questions provide a qualitative portrait of their social personalities.

As part of a larger study of the social behavior of the aged, 22 single elderly persons were intensively interviewed in Detroit. The total sample (210 people), of which the 22 single individuals were a part, was systematically selected and stratified by type of housing. This resulted in a sample of elders whose demographic characteristics were representative of the older American population. The respondents ranged in age from 60 to 94 years.

Self-Definitions

In exploring the ways in which single elders define and evaluate themselves at present and over time, four dimensions of self-definition are probed: the self-conception with respect to age, feelings of loneliness, perception of the life cycle, and conception of one's future. Here is how single elders describe themselves.

Each person was asked how he thinks of himself so far as age goes. It is evident from their responses that the singles, in contrast to persons with other marital statuses, tend to avoid labeling themselves as being at any one period of life. Some imply that their lives are not structured into "ages," but rather that life seems to be as it always has been. Here are some of their responses:

"About the same as always."

"I don't think of it at all. I'm pretty good. I've never compared it. In our Scottish way [from a respondent of Scottish descent], we don't like to analyze ourselves. I don't give it much thought."

"If you've been blessed as I have, you don't think of it."

"I don't think of it at all. I don't know. I don't bother with that."

"I feel pretty good for 73. I feel equal to most others."

"I don't feel old. I don't feel young and I don't feel old either. I'm in between. I get along with 'em. They don't tell me I'm an old man. They never did anyway."

When asked about loneliness, several persons became exasperated with the question. Some of the singles couldn't imagine why such a question was being asked; they reacted as if, somehow, their lives were being stereotyped with a characteristic that to them was quite inappropriate. Here are some of their responses:

"I prefer being alone!"

"I never was lonely."

"I need eight days in the week. I'm so busy now. I'm not unhappy. They're stupid questions, aren't they?"

"Never lonely! You can put that down twice! I've been the *same,* right through! At 45, I was still the same. I'm satisfied. I was all satisfied and I'm still satisfied! I didn't change at all."

"Never, never bored! I've never been lonely."

"I'm never lonely now. I wasn't lonely when I was 45. I think it's rather foolish to answer that—even for the heck of it."

"I'm from a big family. I've always been among people. I don't give loneliness a thought."

"I'm not a lonely person. I like to live alone."

"Never! I have my own TV and do a great deal of religious reading. That makes me satisfied. I never was lonely. I never have that feeling. I have been very contented."

It was analytically significant that single elders tended to be exasperated by the question about loneliness, while others were not. It was not the substance of the question that they disliked, but rather the question *per se.* Such non-substantive replies suggest that the perspectives of those who make them may differ qualitatively from others; this in turn suggests that a particular type of person may have been located.

If they mentioned anyone at all when they were asked whether there was some particular person for whom they felt lonely, it was usually a sibling, parent, or friend. Moreover, their answers showed that their feeling was one of "missing someone," rather than of "feeling lonely for him." "Missing someone" is a less agonizing and desolate recognition of someone's absence than the latter. Single elders were rarely as sorrowful as the widows in the larger sample when they talked of "missing someone," nor, of course, did they gloomily express anticipations of the possible death of the spouse, which several married persons did. Here again are some of the single persons' responses:

> "I miss my brother and sister. Just because you're alone and your own family ain't around. And, I don't brood over it. I make the best of it."

> "All my life, I never felt lonely. Oh, once in a while when it's kind of quiet. I don't feel lonely most of the time. It just comes once in a while. You feel you want to talk to your own relatives. I put the radio on. I never feel very lonely at any time."

> "Not very often. I miss my friend, Lois. We lived together. Well, with Lois, we used to do everything together. We had nice trips together. We lived together for over 30 years."

> "I was just home in Scotland and they wanted me to stay, but I'm too long here. No one getting in touch with you—naturally you get lonesome. I get out and browse around. I call somebody on the phone."

> "Always one thing—financial. I'm lonely because my financial ability doesn't let me do what I want to do. I'm not lonely for people. I'm lonely for a better life. You get what are called 'let-downs.' "

How do single elders perceive their present lives as a whole? Respondents were asked this, and specifically were asked whether or not they saw life as a series of stages with gradual decline in old age ("going downhill"), or as a process of continued personal growth. Here are some of the answers:

> "It's not downhill. It seems to me it stays about average. It's just about the same."

> "From my point of view, I just continue on. My life wasn't that exciting before. So, it's just about the same now. I don't go in for that self-analyzing."

> "I don't think it's downhill. You're not making uphill, but I don't think you're down. As long as you're able to get up and around a little bit. It's a struggle, but I get by."

"I think it's a period of continued personal growth. I can't tell you why. I just do think that way."

"I'd say it's another experience. So, it's continued personal growth. It's not necessarily decline."

"Oh no! I don't agree with you dwelling on this old age business. But, what you people have to worry about old people for, I don't know. If you're prepared to die, you die!"

"I just feel that it's something you got to put up with. It's one thing that you can't miss. So, you got to put up with it. I don't think it's downhill. Oh yeah, it's growth. I figure everybody's got to get old, so I take my share of it too."

"The older you get, naturally you go down. But, on the other hand, you're a more experienced man. You grow as a counselor."

Typically, these single elders did not consider the later years of life as something new or notably different. Again, it became apparent that some of them were puzzled at the age distinctions that were presumed to be salient in questions put to them.

Respondents were asked, further, to consider their future in the coming years. Although their conceptions were probed for both positive and negative aspects, on the whole, most single elders felt that their future would probably be "just an extension" of their past. Some stated simply that they did not worry about it, which implied that they had no reason to believe that "things would change that much":

"Just what I'm doing now. I don't worry about the future."

"I'm not fearin' about the future. I got to take it as comes. Oh, I ain't wishin' for anything."

"I don't wish for anything. There's no use wishing for things you can't get. [laughs] I hope to live as long as I can, I guess."

"I wish to be quiet and by ourselves."

"I don't want nothing. I'm perfectly satisfied. I don't wish
for the better because I know I won't get it. I live from day
to day. It'll be the same."

In thinking about their future, several single elders
even considered impending death as just one more event
in a chain of ordinary, ongoing experiences. Here are some
of their answers to the question of whether they fear death:

"No, I don't. I don't know what it will be. Nobody knows.
I don't think there's any use worrying. I have no fears. I
know where I'm to be buried—near my parents. We all have
tombstones that match each other. My cousin has put up my
tombstone. It has by birth on it and all it needs now is the
date of my death. So, there's a place for me."

"I don't know as I'd want any change. Well, I think the way
I've been thinking these last few years—that's the trouble
with this age—fear. If I don't say another word to you before
you leave, you've got to have a strong faith in yourself. And
I'm not worrying about death. I told people in the hospital
that they were fine even though near death. Fear is a state
of mind."

"I just go on from day to day. I don't know that I've got any
particular fears and worries. People go off so quickly and
suddenly, so why worry about what you don't know."

"I don't care when I'm going. No worries. When your time
comes, there's nothing you can do about it.

Situational Considerations

Persons who represent a specific social type are likely
to have experienced circumstances in common, circumstances that differ from those experienced by other groups.
At the very least, to the extent that the persons studied here
are all single and aged, they represent a particular type of
elder. Moreover, because marital status extensively influences a wide range of social relationships, the single indi-

vidual may be further delineated as a special type of social personality.

Three situational aspects of the lives of single elders were explored: their feelings about nonmarriage, social contacts, and leisure time. Respondents were asked questions about the quality of these.

How do single elders evaluate their circumstances as unmarried persons? What do they say about the routine situations of being single, as compared to those of married life? Typically, in their descriptions of single life they rarely referred to their circumstances as "abnormal" in any way. In their eyes, to be single is not a social stigma. Rather, it is defined as "just another way of life." Single people are likely to imply that their lives are as acceptable to them as they imagine married life is to married persons. Here again are some of their attitudes:

> "Single people live alone, that's all."

> "It don't make too much difference. Some people like to get married and some don't. You're more free when you're single; not much responsibility."

> "That's hard to answer. I've never been married. I've been perfectly satisfied. I've been independent and found my niche. I earned my living all my life and I never said, "Give me, give me!" You don't have to marry to be happy. I don't think I would marry. I made a good choice then."

> "No, I don't think so. Some of those married are in the same boat. But, I like my friends. I guess I'm selfish. You know you can't depend on children."

> "I'm very satisfied. I wouldn't know about that, not having been married. I learned a long time ago to be contented and I am."

> "I wouldn't notice any difference. If you have to work for a living, there are problems either way. I couldn't marry under the circumstances. Unfortunately, my father was an alcoholic. And my brothers had serious accidents. So there were a lot of dependents."

"I had to make a decision whether to get married or be a career woman. I had the chance to get married but the one that I would have married didn't turn out right though. I don't think the later years are different. I've led an interesting life and made the most out of my choice."

"Not to me. I was brought up very strict. I'm very much against marriage. I could never find somebody I liked. If you get married and still have to work, you might as well stay single."

"I don't know. I'm satisfied personally anyway. You're all alone of course when you get older, but it doesn't bother me too much. I've been alone all my life, so maybe it don't bother me as much as some people."

"I think that I'm just as happy as some of the married women here. They're different, but as long as you keep busy. The older people here who are married aren't very congenial. They're so indifferent to each other."

"I think that half the married people have children to keep —even when they're old. I have nobody to keep but me. I have no complaints."

"A married man—he going through the same maneuvers everyday. A single man can meet many people. A single man has a free hand. He can go and come as he pleases."

"Just as I was finishing high school, my mother got very ill and my father died. I had to be there while she was ill. I also had to care for my older aunt and grandmother. Oh yes, the later years are different [for someone who never married]. If you have a family and children, you see them. But, those things don't bother me. I learned to be alone. I kept house by myself."

It is clear from these evaluations that single elders feel that their unmarried status has a certain very important premium. They value highly the independence of being single. Being single is said to eliminate the burden of dependent relatives, especially children (even though some singles claim that the reason they never married was that they were responsible for ailing parents).

Their subjective view that being single is a different but "normal" way of life, a view that they simply take for granted, has an empirical linkage with their exasperated responses to questions on loneliness. Persons who define their lives as abnormal or deviant are likely to respond substantively to questions about their deviance; that is, they will accept the content of such questions as personally meaningful. Not so those who constitute a qualitatively different type of social personality: they personally see their behavior as "another way of life," rather than as a deviation from some more normal form. Questions that assume otherwise are likely to be construed as absurd.

The second situational condition that was examined was their social contact. To what extent do single elders maintain social relationships with their friends and kin? The following responses are typical of their answers.

"I write to cousins in England. I have cousins in New Zealand and Australia. I'm not one to make friends very easily. I never been used to going often a lot."

"I don't have any relative near here. I have cousins, but I don't wish to see them any more."

"Oh, I have dozens of friends! Years ago, I could go to them. I learned to be satisfied with what I have, I tell ya. I sit here for hours and hours, but I'm happy."

"I don't miss my relatives at all. They don't mean a thing to me."

"I have a lot of close friends. I went more often with them when I was 45. I see them enough now."

"I stopped seeing friends since I moved in this apartment. It's funny that I'm so satisfied."

Single elders often say that they associated more with friends and relatives when they were younger than they do at present. But, although they are aware that they have become more isolated from them as they have aged, they

..

do not typically say that they are lonely. A more common response is that they prefer being alone.

How do single elders use their leisure time? Respondents were asked about the nature of their leisure activity, particularly whether or not it was primarily social or nonsocial. Although the following responses show that they obviously visit others to some extent, it was also apparent that compared to elders with other marital statuses, singles engage in relatively solitary activity, and moreover, they say that they're satisfied with this.

> "Do knittin' and watch TV. Visit with my neighbors. I watch TV in the morning and in the evening."

> "I watch TV. Oh, mercy, yes!"

> "Sometimes I knit. Sometimes I play solitaire. In the morning, I straighten out my clothes. After lunch, I sometimes read or take a nap. Evenings, I watch TV and read the paper."

> "I take care of my own room. I change my bed. I fix things around here to pass the time. I've got a radio. I read some. I pass the time like that."

> "I go downtown; take a ride and look at the stores. I'm not looking for bargains. I just go down. Sometimes I rest."

> "I usually take a walk and have a glass of beer nearly every day. I do a lot of reading. I love reading. It's a good pastime when I'm home."

> "I go to bed so early—sometimes at half-past nine. I read. I walk. Sometimes I just sit and rest my eyes."

> "I read a lot and look at TV and talk on the phone to my people."

> "I might sit and mend some of my clothes. I'll wash out my stockings and things like that. I think that's about all. I listen to radio quite a bit—about half the day. It's fine."

> "I wash. I iron. I sew. I read. Oh, in the morning I sleep till nine. Then, I get up and have my devotion. I have a simple breakfast in my room. In the afternoon, I read. In the evening, I watch TV. Then I watch the eleven o'clock news."

THE SINGLE ELDER AS A SOCIAL TYPE

The preceding qualitative data have shown that single elders have a rather special attitude to old age. They are relatively isolated in later life. They typically say that they have always been isolated; but although they are isolates, they do not commonly mention that they are lonely. Rather, their daily lives are solitary ones, and they take it for granted that their daily lives are comprised of ordinary, ongoing routines.

The single elder is a special type of old person, in this sense: the set of circumstances common to elders who have remained single all their lives tend to construct a specific, personal style of dealing with the self and the everyday world. Their circumstances coalesce to give them the status of being a long-term single person. These circumstances involve personal independence, long-term continuity in life events, and relatively minimal social involvements. They produce a personal orientation to everyday life that takes for granted the normality of relative isolation in social space and the continuity of life.

There is another side to the claim that single elders constitute a social type. This is more methodological than empirical. When the elders were interviewed, several questions were put to them that had been constructed with one underlying assumption, namely, that isolation, dependence, death crisis, and loneliness were the problems common to all older persons. It was thought that even if they had not already experienced these problems, then at least they would anticipate them. In this sense, the interview items were presumed to be relevant to the situations of all elderly persons.

In the larger sample, the elders' responses to questions about isolation, dependence, death, and loneliness showed, for the most part, that their everyday worlds included thoughts about them. The exceptions to this tended to be the single elders. They were defensive when they were asked such questions. Several accused the interviewer of holding a stereotyped view of old people. Some stated frankly that they were puzzled by such questions. The problem was that these questions, since they were based on certain assumptions about the realities of elders, were perceived as forcing a social world upon these respondents (see Cicourel, 1964).

"Inappropriate" questions can serve as a channel through which to discover the separate, everyday realities that make for differences between social types. The information emerges not in the respondents' answers to these questions, but in their attitudes *toward* them (Garfinkel, 1967). When questions are answered directly, and their relevance and "normality" are implicitly acknowledged, it can be assumed that the researcher is dealing with an *a priori* known reality. But, when such questions are answered by some respondents with either direct statements or indirect inferences that such inquiries do not seem to have any meaning for them, this is a clue that a type of person qualitatively different from others may have been discovered. If such persons have certain social characteristics in common, this further corroborates the claim that they constitute a particular type of social personality.

Part IV

RETIREMENT ROLES

Introduction

In the social history of aging, retirement is a fairly recent phenomenon. It tends to emerge as societies become industrial. With increasing rationalization and bureaucratization, work is translated into a "work life." As with all lives, it begins and it ends. Retirement is an official, formal ending of a work life.

One of the problems in much of the popular and academic discussion of the retirement process and retirement roles is that it assumes them to be fairly homogeneous. The retirement process is considered to be an abrupt transition from active involvement in the world of work to active enjoyment of the world of leisure. Retirement roles are portrayed as leisure roles, either local or exotic.

The idea of homogeneous retirement is too simple. It ignores several complexities in the social patterning of work roles and their occupants. Work roles in industrial societies vary from those that are highly specific and narrow in the quality and range of tasks involved and the independence their incumbents are allowed, to those that are diffuse and broad. The first type is common in what is often called "labor," while the latter is typical of professional roles. The kinds of occupant that typically hold specific work roles also vary; for example, some are more frequently occupied by women and others by men.

The papers in this section consider some complexities of work roles that make for variations in the retirement process and in retirement roles. These studies have implications for retirement policy and retirement programs.

chapter 9

Orientation toward the Job and Retirement Adjustment among Women

ROBERT C. ATCHLEY

This paper is concerned with the causes of a positive orientation toward the job role, and the consequences of this orientation in retirement. Two sets of hypotheses were tested. The first set deals with the determinants that create a positive work orientation in women, and the second set deals with the impact on retirement adjustment of holding a positive work orientation in retirement.

The subjects in this study were 2,266 retired women. They represent a 78 per cent response rate to mail questionnaires sent to a 10 per cent random sample of retired women school teachers, and to all the retired women employees of a midwestern telephone company.

Work orientation was operationally defined by the person's responses to three questionnaire items. If the person listed the satisfaction she found in doing the work as the

This work was supported by research grant AA-4-67-012 from the Administration on Aging.

most important thing to her about her former job, if she listed being good at her work as an area of life in which failure would have bothered her the most, and if she achieved a score of four or five on the job commitment scale (Simpson, McKinney, and Back, 1966), then the respondent was said to have a high positive work orientation. If the person met two of the three criteria, she was said to have a medium degree of positive work orientation; and if she met one or none of the criteria, she was said to have a low degree of positive work orientation. This study was not concerned with changes in work orientation before and after retirement; it was concerned solely with the degree of work orientation after retirement.

In the set of hypotheses on the causes of a high positive work orientation in retirement, work orientation was obviously a dependent variable. The independent variables were those factors in the individual's current or past experience that could reasonably be expected to influence her work orientation.

Much of the literature on the relationship between the self and roles suggests that they interact strongly with one another, and that playing a role is an important prerequisite of incorporating it as an aspect of the self. As Goffman (1961) puts it:

> It is important to note that in performing a role the individual must see to it that the impressions of him that are conveyed in the situation are compatible with role-appropriate personal qualities effectively imputed to him: a judge is supposed to be deliberate and sober; a pilot, in a cockpit, to be cool; a bookkeeper to be accurate and neat in doing his work. These personal qualities, effectively imputed and effectively claimed, combine with a position's title, when there is one, to provide a basis of *self-image* for the incumbent and a basis for the image that . . . others will have of him. A self, then, virtually awaits the individual entering a position; he need only conform to the pressures on him. [p. 87]

Secord and Backman (1964) emphasize the role of social interaction and role-playing on the cognitive aspects of the self:

> As an individual moves through the social structure, he is placed in various role categories. He is first a baby, later a small boy. He is a dull pupil, John's little brother, and Tommy's best friend. As he performs these roles, he learns to see himself as various role partners see him. In each, he learns the expectations that other persons associate with the category, and he forms a subjective public entity corresponding to each. [p. 581]

If we assume that a high positive work orientation is indeed an aspect of the self, then the situation in retirement, when one is no longer playing the job role, could be expected to reduce the salience of the job role for the self, and thus to reduce the probability that the subject will hold a high degree of positive work orientation. On the basis of this logic, the following hypotheses were tested:

1. The greater the extent to which women are completely retired (neither working nor looking for work), the lower the incidence of high positive work orientation will be.
2. The longer women have been completely retired, the lower the incidence of high positive work orientation will be.

Tables 9-I and 9-II show that neither of these hypotheses received support. The fact that women are not playing the job role does not appear to influence their degree of positive orientation toward it, even over a considerable period of time. Controls for age, education, occupation, health, and a number of other variables produced no change in these findings.[1]

---

[1] The idea of using controls even in cases where the zero-order table shows that there is no apparent relationship is based on Rosenberg's (1968) concept of unmasking suppressed relationships.

Table 9-I

WORK STATUS AND WORK ORIENTATION OF RETIRED WOMEN

Work Orientation	Not in Labor Force	In Labor Force
Low	50.3%	46.5%
Medium to high	49.7%	53.5%
Numbers	1720	546

Women are generally assumed to undergo some degree of conflict between the job role and the spouse role. Accordingly, it was anticipated that working women whose commitments to the wife role compete with their work commitments would tend to have a lower degree of positive work orientation.

3. If retired women are or were married, then they will tend to have a lower degree of positive work orientation.

Table 9-III shows that there was no support for hypothesis 3. When income was controlled, however, a modest association appeared between marriage and low positive work orientation (Table 9-IV).

Table 9-II

LENGTH OF TIME RETIRED AND WORK ORIENTATION
FOR RETIRED WOMEN, BY OCCUPATIONAL CATEGORY

	Telephone Employees Time Retired						Teachers Time Retired					
	5 years and under		6 to 10 years		Over 10 years		5 years and under		6 to 10 years		Over 10 years	
	N	%	N	%	N	%	N	%	N	%	N	%
Low	117	45.3	83	55.3	50	56.8	303	41.2	163	37.4	186	48.2
Medium	115	44.6	53	35.3	29	33.0	336	45.7	199	45.6	161	41.7
High	26	10.1	14	9.3	9	10.2	97	13.2	74	17.0	39	10.1
Totals	258	100.0	150	100.0	88	100.0	736	100.0	436	100.0	386	100.0

Chi-square = 6.54; DF = 4   Chi-square = 14.13; DF = 4
$P > .10$ $P > .01$*
Lambda = 0.00   Lambda = 0.03

* In this and many of the tables that follow, a significant chi-square will be found to be unsupported by the measure of association. In this study a significant chi-square will be said to have absolutely no value, unless it can also be demonstrated that the significant difference is accompanied by an appreciable degree of association.

Table 9-III

MARITAL STATUS AND WORK ORIENTATION OF
RETIRED WOMEN, BY OCCUPATIONAL CATEGORY

| | Telephone Employees Marital Status | | | | | | Teachers Marital Status | | | | | |
| | Married | | Ever Married | | Never Married | | Married | | Ever Married | | Never Married | |
	N	%	N	%	N	%	N	%	N	%	N	%
Low	226	64.4	173	72.7	84	62.2	239	43.9	208	45.6	234	38.9
Medium	105	29.9	59	24.8	46	34.1	221	40.6	196	43.0	289	48.1
High	20	5.7	6	2.5	5	3.7	84	15.4	52	11.4	78	13.0
Totals	351	100.0	238	100.0	135	100.0	544	100.0	456	100.0	601	100.0

Chi-square = 5.91; DF = 2   Chi-square = 5.39; DF = 2
$P > .05$ $P > .05$
Lambda = 0.00   Lambda = 0.00

If an individual was obviously ineligible to play a role, this was also expected to push her away from a high positive work orientation.

4. The older the woman, the lower the incidence of high positive work orientation will be.

5. The lower the self-assessed health score, the lower the incidence of high positive work orientation will be.

No support could be found for either hypothesis. Controls produced no change in these findings.

On the basis of social class theory, respondents with high SES (socioeconomic status) were expected to show a

Table 9-IV

MARITAL STATUS AND WORK ORIENTATION OF RETIRED FEMALE
TELEPHONE COMPANY EMPLOYEES WHO REPORT HIGH INCOME

| Work Orien- tation | Ever Married | | Never Married | |
	N	%	N	%
Low	157	75.8	23	51.1
Other	50	24.2	22	48.9
Totals	207	100.0	45	100.0

Chi-square = 10.60; DF = 1
$P < .01$
Q = .50

Table 9-V

INCOME AND WORK ORIENTATION OF RETIRED WOMEN, BY OCCUPATION

Work Orientation	Telephone Employees' Incomes				Teacher's Incomes			
	High		Low		High		Low	
	N	%	N	%	N	%	N	%
Low	287	62.8	181	71.5	501	42.2	164	42.8
Medium or high	170	37.2	72	28.5	685	57.8	219	57.2
Totals	457	100.0	253	100.0	1186	100.0	383	100.0

Chi-square = 5.710; DF = 1   Chi-square = 0.000; DF = 1
$P < .025$ $P > .90$
$Q = -.20$ $Q = -.012$

high degree of positive work orientation. This led to three more hypotheses:

6. The higher the income, the higher the incidence of high positive work orientation will be.
7. The higher the education, the higher the incidence of high positive work orientation will be.
8. The higher the status of the job, the higher the incidence of high positive work orientation will be.

Table 9-V shows that there was a very slight relationship between income and work orientation, but only among the retired telephone-company women. Hypothesis 7 received no support. Hypothesis 8 received strong support, however, as Table 9-VI shows, and controls produced no

Table 9-VI

OCCUPATIONAL CATEGORY AND WORK ORIENTATION
OF RETIRED WOMEN

Work Orientation	Retired Telephone Operators and Supervisors		Retired Teachers	
	N	%	N	%
Low	487	66.6	651	41.7
Medium to high	244	33.4	912	58.3
Totals	731	100.0	1563	100.0

Chi-square = 125.5; DF = 1
$P < .001$
$Q = + .47$

significant change in the zero-order relationship. It appears that a high incidence of positive work orientation is specific to the status of the job, and is not simply a function of social class. Of course, many elements enter into the status of a job, including how demanding or enjoyable it is.

Existing theory on the relationship between the self and role thus produced poor predictions on what happens when people give up roles they have held for a considerable period of time. Of course, the crucial assumption used in constructing the foregoing hypotheses was that giving up a role would be similar to taking on a role. That perspective was more or less imposed on this research by self and role theory, which has overwhelmingly emphasized the processes whereby roles become a part of the self. Another accepted assumption in current theory on the self is that it is quite sensitive to changes in the external situation.

Most of the self and role theory we have today grew out of the work of Cooley and Mead on how children take on self-concepts. In most of the research on the self and role, adolescents (college students) have been used as subjects. Relatively little work has been done on the dynamics of the self and role among adults. Our findings lead to an alternative view of these dynamics.

To begin with, it is not merely the playing of a role as such, but rather the *quality* of the role, that produces a high positive work orientation. A high positive work orientation is not an abstract trait characteristic of a particular social class, but probably depends on the nature of the particular job held. A recent article by Kohn and Schooler (1973) found that self-direction on the job was more important than any other structural aspect of the job in producing a positive work orientation.

Second, once the individual develops a high positive work orientation, it is apparently not easily given up. The traditional lack of respect for the idea that memories can continue to reinforce a particular aspect of the self, particularly if the individual does not have to play the role, did not serve us well in this case. Selective perception as a mechanism of maintaining a given aspect of the self (Secord and Backman, 1964) is nowhere more applicable than in the case of a retired schoolteacher who wishes to remember teaching as an exciting job, and to retain an image of herself as having been good at it. In fact, according to this rationale, retirement might be expected to *increase* positive work orientation for some people. Cooley and Mead offer little that would help to explain this process. More attention will have to be devoted to the dynamics of the self and role in later life (Atchley, 1972, pp. 86–90).

But what are the consequences of carrying a high positive work orientation into retirement? Again, the theory leads to the expectation that this should create problems for the individual. A high positive work orientation in retirement would seem bound to produce dissonance; and we expected that this dissonance would be reflected in symptoms of negative adjustment in retirement. This perspective is rooted in the assumption that external reality is a crucial determinant of the individual's evaluation of the self, and that dissonance produces psychological distress unless it is reduced through change.

High positive work orientation among women in retirement was expected to be associated with high anxiety, high anomie, dislike of retirement, a need for a greater length of time to get accustomed to retirement, and a lower incidence of complete retirement.

Reasonable though these ideas may seem, not one shred of support for them could be found in our data. Perhaps the difficulty lies in the assumption that a high positive work orientation in retirement would produce dissonance. If the identity continuity theory (Atchley, 1971) had been used, little change would have been predicted in that aspect of the self as a result of retirement, and as a result we would have expected to find no personal adjustment problems. This is exactly what was found. The traditional self theory probably let us down in not alerting us to the increased salience of the desire for continuity in one's life in retirement (part of the balance theory equation).

It may be worthwhile to examine some alternative explanations for these findings. First, since men are often assumed to be more work-oriented than women, it is conceivable that our hypotheses might apply to men but not to women. Streib and Schneider (1971), however, found working women to be more work-oriented than men. In addition, in independent measures of work orientation, we found no significant difference between retired men and women with respect to the hypotheses presented here.

It could be charged that the sample is biased. This is certainly true, since the poor, the well-to-do, blacks, and various ethnic groups are not represented. For the hypotheses tested here, however, the bias of the sample may be useful. We were testing traits that are normally associated with the middle class; hence, if the hypothetical relationships did exist, they should have shown up in this sample, if nowhere else.

CONCLUSION

In this paper, a series of factors that might produce a high positive work orientation among women in retirement were examined. The kind of job the individual had was the only background variable found to be strongly related to a high positive work orientation in retirement. The consequences of holding a high positive work orientation in retirement were also examined, but no significant results were found.

The conclusions drawn from this were that the quality of the job itself is much more important than other background variables in producing and maintaining a high positive work orientation; that once an individual develops a high positive work orientation she tends to keep it; that inability to play a role does not diminish one's image of oneself as a player of that role; and that theories of how the self is created are not very good theories of how the self is maintained. The hypothesis was advanced that continuity of image occurs because memories of having played the role remain, and reinforce the image. It was also hypothesized that among older people, the desire for continuity in one's life is a salient aspect of the balance theory equation as regards the effects of retirement on dissonance and various aspects of the self. Finally, it was concluded that better theories are needed to explain the dynamics of the self and role, theories based on the situations that confront older people.

chapter 10

The Retired Scientist: The Myth of the Aging Individual

ALAN R. ROWE

INTRODUCTION

This paper deals with a myth. Like most myths, this one has a long history, and it reflects a picture of reality based upon tattered facts that are generously interwoven with extrapolation. It is largely derived from an oversimplified conception of the "life-cycle." The myth is that of the aging individual, and its structural emphasis is ubiquitous. It depicts a late stage of life, in which the social actor assumes a series of roles associated with advancing age (Breen, 1960). To be sure, the assumption of these roles is not held to be independent of the declining biological processes, but the social dimensions have long been viewed as highly important (Fisher and Birren, 1947; Linden and Courtney, 1955; Lorge, 1939; Parsons, 1942; Tibbitts and Sheldon, 1952). As Breen (1960) indicates, "The aging individual is, in effect, a responsive and responding nexus for social and sociological judgments [p. 160]." In this pattern, retirement is presented as being particularly salient (Cavan, 1952; Cumming and Henry, 1961; Donahue, Orbach, and Pollak, 1960; Havighurst, 1954; Tibbitts, 1954).

Retirement is typically viewed as creating a basic change in the individual's orientation, by "disengaging" him from one role set and resocializing him into a different one (Cumming and Henry, 1961; Donahue et al., 1960; Taylor, 1968). It is associated with the concept of the aging individual, and in American society it is viewed as profoundly altering the direction and adjustment of an individual's life (Breen, 1960). With this change new roles are assumed, which reflect the social judgments of the larger society within which the individual lives and acts. The distinction between becoming old and aging tends to be blurred, however. Too much seems to be made of general social judgments and of the individual's attitude toward retirement (Breen, 1960), as opposed to the individual's normative commitment to an occupation, and the psychological gratification he derives from "engaging" in it.

It seems plausible that people may grow old biologically, but they need not necessarily alter their primary lifestyle, especially as related to a vocation. A limited literature on retired scientists, in conjunction with recent research findings on them, lends support to this point of view.

THE RETIRED SCIENTIST

Scientists[1] are individuals who would seem likely not to follow the expected pattern of retirement (characterized by the assumption of a series of roles associated with the aging individual). This is because the concept of the aging individual links orientation too closely with roles and role change, while personal commitment in some areas of social

[1]For the purposes of this paper, a scientist is defined as an individual who has been engaged in research and/or teaching in the physical or life sciences (including mathematics, but excluding engineering and social science) in an institution of higher learning, a nonprofit research organization, or an industrial organization.

life may be more closely linked to employment than it is in other areas. Specifically, in order to understand the retired scientist, we must separate the concept of commitment from that of social position.

The social education of scientists in the "scientific ethos" (Barber, 1952; Merton, 1957; Storer, 1966) and the psychological gratification they derive from the pleasure of working in science (Eiduson, 1962) apparently tend to motivate them to search for knowledge as an end in itself. Their occupational activities are not merely means of attaining economic and status goals; instead they tend to be more akin to a "hobby" than to "work." Rather than "disengaging" from their role set as scientists after retirement, it seems likely that they would tend to continue to "engage" in this role in their search for knowledge. This would ostensibly be most true for those who found the normative commitment to science and the psychological gratification they derived from it particularly high. Rather than becoming "aging individuals," they would merely become biologically old.

Roe's (1965) findings (derived only from research on eminent scientists) lend support to the idea that scientists tend to continue to engage in science after retirement. In revisiting the scientists she had studied earlier, she found that they showed few signs of "disengagement" from science after their retirement, unless they went into administration. Beyond this, though, research findings on 142 scientists (both "ordinary" and "eminent"), retired from 11 large universities (derived from a study reported by Rowe, 1972) lend particular support to the position of this paper. Many of these retired scientists continue to engage in scientific activities directly related to research, spending time on research, discussing research, and writing, and furthermore, age and length of retirement do not affect this continued engagement (Tables 10-I and 10-II).

Beyond activities directly related to research, most of

Table 10-I

PERCENTAGES OF RETIRED SCIENTISTS WHO SPEND
TIME ON SCIENTIFIC ACTIVITIES, BY AGE

Scientific Activities	Percentages, by Age Group		
	65-70	71-75	76-94
Time spent on scientific research			
Yes	54	59	58
No	46	41	42
Time spent discussing research			
Yes	63	63	54
No	37	37	46
Time spent on scientific writing			
Yes	61	65	58
No	39	35	42
(Total number of scientists)	(46)	(46)	(50)

Table 10-II

PERCENTAGE OF RETIRED SCIENTISTS WHO SPEND
TIME ON SCIENTIFIC ACTIVITIES, BY LENGTH OF RETIREMENT

Scientific Activities	Percentages, by Number of Years Retired		
	1 or less	2-5	6-23
Time spent on scientific research			
Yes	60	49	62
No	40	51	38
Time spent discussing research			
Yes	67	55	61
No	33	45	39
Time spent on scientific writing			
Yes	67	45	64
No	33	55	36
(Total number of scientists)	(30)	(51)	(61)

Table 10-III

MEMBERSHIP OF 142 RETIRED SCIENTISTS
IN SCIENTIFIC ORGANIZATIONS

Number of Scientific Organizations	Percentage of Retired Scientists who Belong
Eight or more	25
Seven	4
Six	6
Five	8
Four	15
Three	13
Two	13
One	8
Zero	7

these retired scientists continue to belong to one or more scientific organizations (they belong to a median number of 4.6 organizations; Table 10-III). But membership does not necessarily indicate activity, and only half of the retired scientists are very active, or even somewhat active, in any of these organizations (Table 10-IV). Nevertheless, half of them do still remain somewhat or very active in these organizations after retirement, which indicates that while some may disengage from science in this respect, others do not.

Most of the retired scientists continue to subscribe to one or more scientific journals (a median number of 4.5 journals; Table 10-V), and most of them feel that they "keep up" with their scientific area by means of these journals (Table 10-VI). As with activity in membership organizations (Table 10-IV), about half of the retired scientists

Table 10-IV

DEGREE OF ACTIVITY OF 142 RETIRED
SCIENTISTS IN MEMBERSHIP ORGANIZATIONS

Amount of Activity in Membership Organizations	Percentage of Retired Scientists
Very active	20
Somewhat active	30
Hardly active	14
Not active	36

Table 10-V

PURCHASE OF SCIENTIFIC SUBSCRIPTION
JOURNALS BY 142 RETIRED SCIENTISTS

Number of Subscription Journals Purchased	Percentage of Retired Scientists
Eight or more	23
Seven	4
Six	8
Five	8
Four	12
Three	8
Two	14
One	11
None	12

perceive themselves as "keeping up" with their scientific area though scientific meetings (Table 10-VI). Contact with scientific preprints does not appear to be very common, however (Table 10-VI), which may indicate that the retired scientist becomes somewhat isolated from those of his colleagues who are not retired.

Thus, these retired scientists do not altogether sever themselves from their role set of the professional scientist after retirement; to varying degrees, they are still involved in professional activity (other than that directly related to research). This is most true with regard to journals, less so for meetings, and least true for preprints. What seems to occur is that it is easy for them to engage professionally through the things most directly under their control, such as journals. On the other hand, it undoubtedly requires more effort to participate in activities that necessitate travel

Table 10-VI

PERCENTAGE OF 142 RETIRED SCIENTISTS WHO PERCEIVE
THEMSELVES AS KEEPING UP IN THEIR SCIENTIFIC AREA
THROUGH JOURNALS, MEETINGS, AND PREPRINTS

Self-Perception as Regards Keeping Up	Means of Keeping Up		
	Journals	Meetings	Preprints
Keep up	87	55	41
Do not keep up	13	45	59

and social contact, such as meetings, and there is less professional engagement in this area. Access to preprints generally requires membership in "in-groups" and "invisible colleges" (Hirsch, 1968), and it is here that retirement may have one of the most negative effects on the scientist. Yet, it does not follow that retirement necessarily leads to "disengagement" from science; since clearly some retired scientists (at least 41% of the 142 subjects) are not affected, and as already indicated (Tables 10-I and 10-II), many are still engaged in a most active way in science, in activities directly related to research.

Although these scientists tend to continue to engage in science, this is not because they dislike retirement. Indeed, 88% of these 142 scientists find something in retirement that they like, but less than one out of every three relate this favorable comment to scientific activity. The favorable comment typically involves some dimension of "freedom" (which may or may not include scientific activity). A typical favorable comment related to science is that retirement gives "freedom to do what you please in a scientific area," while a typical favorable comment that is not particularly related to science is that one does "not have to live on a schedule." Retirement, then, is often perceived in a positive way, especially in that it gives more freedom; but this hardly implies that these individuals are necessarily disengaging from the role set of the scientist or are in the process of aging. Nor do many of these scientists perceive retirement as intruding on their desired scientific activity; only 20% of the 142 scientists state that they have suffered any personal loss of contact with their area of scientific interst. To be sure, whether or not a given scientist "enjoys" retirement is problematic. The point here, however, is that this is not necessarily relevant to continued engagement in the structure of action associated with the scientific role set (Eiduson, 1962; Storer, 1966). What seems to be especially relevant to the scientist's activity after retirement is his commitment to science as a vocation in the sense defined by Weber (1946).

Thus these scientists may grow old and retire, but they do not necessarily accept the role of the aging individual. The unavoidable concession that they do make to the "aging process" is in the biological realm. Their most commonly expressed sense of loss is the loss of health (31% of the 142 state this). Moreover, less than half of the 142 scientists express satisfaction with their current age. A typical reason expressed for this dissatisfaction is "that [an earlier age] was the age in which I felt the best and could do the best work. . . . One of the disadvantages [of that age is] you don't stay very long at that age." Nevertheless, 48% of the 142 retired scientists still derive their greatest psychological gratification from their continued engagement in science.

Personal eminence,[2] however, appears to be particularly salient to continued engagement in science. For the 142 scientists, this is true not only of their engagement in scientific research, but also of their perception of science as pleasurable. Moreover, additional findings on 281 scientists retired from 20 large state universities, 10 state colleges, 20 small private colleges, 7 "ivy league" universities, 20 nonprofit research organizations, and 4 industrial organizations (derived from a study reported by Rowe, 1973) corroborate this (Table 10-VII). Thus it appears that personal eminence may be related to continued engagement in science after retirement, and also to the psychological gratification derived from it. This is consistent with Roe's (1965) finding that apart from the minimum requirements (for example, an I.Q. of about 121) the attainment of eminence is most influenced by motivation, particularly the degree to which an individual's scientific work is important

[2]Measures of eminence were based on weighted citations in the *Science Citation Index;* they were calculated by the technique developed by Cole and Cole (1967).

Table 10-VII

TIME SPENT ON SCIENTIFIC RESEARCH, AND PERCEPTION
OF THINGS RELATED TO SCIENCE AS PLEASURABLE,
IN RELATION TO EMINENCE

Study of Scientists Retired from 11 Large Universities	Eminence		
	Low	Medium	High
Time spent on scientific research[1]			
some	42	60	69
none	58	40	31
Perception of things related to science as pleasurable[2]			
yes	29	52	62
no	71	48	38
(Number of scientists)	(45)	(52)	(45)

Study of 281 Scientists Retired from Large State and "Ivy League" Universities, Small Private Colleges, and Nonprofit Research and Industrial Organizations	Eminence		
	Low	Medium	High
Time spent on scientific research[3]			
some	18	47	64
none	82	53	36
Perception of things related to science as pleasurable[4]			
yes	28	37	49
no	72	63	51
(Number of scientists)	(139)	(70)	(72)

1. Chi square = 6.72; DF = 2; $.05 > P > 0.02$
2. Chi square = 10.51; DF = 2; $.01 > P > 0.001$
3. Chi square = 46.98; DF = 2; $P < 0.001$
4. Chi square = 8.84; DF = 2; $.02 > P > 0.01$

to him. It is of special interest here that in cases where organizational factors worked against the scientist's attainment of eminence, and he indicated that research should be done "for its own sake," he typically continued to engage in science after retirement (Rowe, 1973). Thus, it seems to be commitment to the "scientific ethos" and the psychological gratification derived from the pleasure of working in science (Fiduson, 1962) that largely account for the retired scientist's apparent deviation from the pattern of the "aging individual."

SUMMARY

It has been the contention of this paper that some mythical concepts are inherent in the overgeneralized picture of the aging individual. An examination of retired scientists indicates that it is important to make a clear distinction between becoming old (which is based on biological changes) and the "process of aging" (which is based on fundamental role alterations). Too much appears to be made of general social judgments on the matter of retirement, and of the individual's attitude toward retirement, as opposed to the individual's normative commitment to an occupation and the psychological gratification he derives from engaging in it. Barring illness, it is ostensibly the scientist who perceives science as a vocation (Weber, 1946) who is most likely to continue to engage in it after retirement, rather than "disengaging" from one role set and becoming resocialized into a different role set, associated with the "aging individual."

Thus, commitment to science as a vocation is largely independent of the possession of a distinct organizational role as a scientist, and a strict "structural" depiction of retirement does not account for the case of the retired scientist. Moreover, it is suggested that the case of the retired scientist is not epiphenomenal. For example, Benz (1958) found that the dominant attitude of the retired academic was this: "What I like best [about retirement] is the fact that I am able to continue my scientific research and with good remuneration." A particularly interesting aspect of her findings is that scientists and other academics identify with their discipline and with the continued search for knowledge through research. Perhaps when an individual has the chance and the capacity to unite devotion to his subject with creative insight, he does not age, but merely becomes old. Given this, the concept that the process of aging leads to the stereotyped "aging individual" may be more problematic and less valid than had hitherto been supposed.

chapter 11

Retirement and Perceived Status Loss: An Inquiry into Some Objective and Subjective Problems Produced by Aging

HAROLD STRAUSS
BRUCE W. ALDRICH
AARON LIPMAN

Gerontologists regard certain aspects of the aging process as critical to the physical, social, and emotional well-being of the elderly segments of our population. One of these aspects is whether older people are able to maintain their dignity while they lose some of the essential social roles they once performed (Berwick, 1967, pp. 257–260). Our society has been successful in prolonging the average life span, which ensures that an increasingly higher percentage of our population will ultimately reach old age; but we have not ensured that old age will be productive and dignified. The extent of our society's failure to provide a meaningful social situation for many of the elderly is shown by recent data on the social status of the aged; in 1968 for example, over 70 per cent of the population aged 65 or over had annual incomes of $2,500 or less, and 90 per cent received $5,000 or less annually (United States Department of Health, Education and Welfare, 1970). Given the present cost of living and rate of inflation, it is evident from these statistics that many of our elderly receive incomes that are grossly inadequate to meet their basic economic needs, and that the depth of this inadequacy merely increases as inflation erodes the buying power of largely fixed incomes.

Another recent trend, which lends even greater significance to the problems of aging, is the tendency of business and other bureaucracies to retire wage-earners from the wage force earlier. This trend is accelerating: in 1947, 47.8 per cent of men over 65 were still at work in paid employment, but by 1966 this figure had dropped dramatically to 27.0 per cent (United States Senate, Special Committee on Aging, 1969). Early retirement has some negative consequences that make adjustment to nonproductive social roles even more difficult. It is liable to result in fewer social security benefits, which compounds further the economic plight of retired persons. Moreover, many retired persons may accept early retirement simply because they feel they have no alternative, since employers show little inclination to recruit or hire persons just below retirement age (United States Senate Special Committee on Aging, 1969, p. 1183).

The trend toward early retirement and decreased participation of the aged in the labor force appears to be a concomitant of industrialization, and has been a characteristic tendency in our society for some time (Riley and Foner, 1968). Increasing specialization and automation of our economy may serve to accelerate this trend, and eventually many persons may face forced retirement in their mid- to late fifties.

Some recent studies give strong support for the contention that retirement, which involves the loss of a major social role, can have a number of negative effects on the retired person. It was found, for example, that older persons who are retired tend to show less satisfaction with life in general than do those who are still working. This remained the case even when health and socioeconomic variables were held constant for both the retired and working segments of the sample population (Riley and Foner, 1968, pp. 350–351). Additional evidence suggests that people who are retired are more likely to *feel* old than are their age-peers who are still employed (Riley and Foner, 1968, p. 305). These results seem to indicate that retired older people are likely to be less satisfied with life, less well-adjusted, and less hopeful about the future than are their working age-peers. The stigma that our youth-oriented culture attaches to old age seems to have been internalized to some extent by the older people themselves, and the maintenance of the occupational role symbolizes a more youthful orientation.

There is evidence to suggest that physiological consequences are associated with retirement, and these consequences point out the importance of the loss of productive social roles. On the basis of a recent longitudinal study of aging conducted at Duke University, Palmore (1969, pp. 103–108) found that work satisfaction was positively related to longevity, and concluded that the maintenance of health, mental abilities, and satisfying social roles are the most important factors that promote longevity.

Social science has produced considerable support for Burgess' contention (1960, pp. 3–28) that the elderly face the prospect of having to play a "roleless role" in our society. In the United States, retired persons have few, if any, really vital functions to perform. This may be especially acute for the husband, since the wife can retain the role of homemaker so long as she is physically able, and can derive considerable satisfaction from this function. The husband, however, faces the loss of his economic function, which is the major social role that adult males play in this society. Accordingly, there may be substantial differences between the ways elderly men and women perceive old age, and aging may be more problematic for men than for women.

There are a few additional social factors that make retirement and aging all the more difficult to face in our changing society. The past few decades have witnessed the passing of the extended family. Industrialization and urbanization have accelerated the emergence of the conjugal family as the dominant type; these social forces have also encouraged neolocal residence patterns and the erosion of the authority of the aged in family decision-making. In such a family system, the once favored positions of the grandfather and grandmother lose importance. Neolocal residence patterns can produce conditions under which grandparents, isolated from their relatives, are faced with an overabundance of leisure time; some of this might have been consumed in family activities had the relatives been living closer, but as things are it is left unfilled. Thus many older persons are provided with little direction or orientation, if any, for the productive use of their leisure time, and retirement may be perceived as a period of loneliness, inactivity, and even despair. As has been suggested, these problems may be particularly acute for retired men.

The reasons we have outlined make it evident why one of the problem areas of key interest in the gerontological literature is the loss of status that males feel after retirement. In particular, gerontologists focus on whether older people feel that the lack of self-maintaining work in old age is an indication of social failure, and hence is a justification for the generally inferior social status accorded the aged in our society.

The results we have reviewed suggest that retirement is a situation that can cause male retirees to experience a reduction in feelings of confidence and personal worth, because they are cut off from participation in the most important interests and activities of the society. Since the male derives his major status from his role in the occupational system, it is believed that once he disengages from this system, he feels the loss of the prestige and respect that it formerly brought him. While this construct appears plausible on the theoretical level, other behavioral factors may intrude. We endeavored to study some of the factors associated with the maintenance of feelings of self-respect and social worth among the retired, in order to determine what resources are available to help them to adjust to aging and the loss of productive social roles.

A sample of 100 retired males and 100 retired females over 60 years of age who resided in metropolitan Miami were interviewed. In order to maximize variability they were selected from almost all of the Census Tract areas of Dade County. The majority (over 80 per cent) were migrants from other states (particularly from the north and northeast). All were married; the median ages were 69 years for the males and 64 for the females. Most of the males were drawn from the upper occupational and educational levels. Our respondents were asked to agree or disagree with the statement: "People treat a man who's retired with less respect than they did while he was working." Eighty-three per cent disagreed with this statement. When the same question was more personally oriented, thus: "Now that you have retired, do you think people treat you with more respect or less respect than before you retired," 7 per cent said they received more respect, 15 per cent said they received less, and the majority, 78 per cent, felt that people had treated them with the same amount of respect before retirement as they did after retirement. In both cases, the overwhelming majority of respondents denied that they had lost status due to retirement.

This initial finding contradicted our expectations, which were based on a review of previous research, and we were forced to research this question further.

As we have noted, retirement in our society is not always voluntary. Forced retirement may involve a loss of autonomy for the male; since others initiate this action for him, it is implied that the individual who is forced to retire will lose status. These factors may help to explain why a number of other studies have found forced retirement to be associated with poor morale. The men in the sample were asked whether they felt that a man lost self-respect if he was forced to retire even though he was healthy enough to continue working. Here a larger percentage (36 per cent) agreed that there was a loss of self-respect, but 60 per cent of the respondents still maintained that self-respect was not lost, even after forced retirement.

While these figures are admittedly subject to the inaccuracies that arise when people are asked questions of this type, they are still high enough to suggest that the widely accepted contention that retirement reduces self-respect should be re-examined.

During the course of interviews with these 100 respondents (and with their spouses, who were interviewed separately), it was apparent that many of the aged people did not feel that prestige was lost as a result of retirement alone.

In a deeper investigation of these findings, we found that many of the retirees in our study maintained identification with their former occupational status, despite retirement. Few of the men viewed themselves as just "retired." They identified themselves as "retired businessmen," "retired lawyers," "retired doctors," and so on. Any titles that reflected status were also retained after retirement from the occupational system; the doctor, the professor, or the colonel did not come to be called "mister." They frequently gave proof of their former occupations by hanging diplomas and degrees on the walls of their dwellings. This attachment to occupational titles seemed particularly char acteristic of men of professional status. Although they relinquish the occupational activity, they apparently maintain the occupational title and its attendant prestige.

While former occupational status and its prestige level may serve as a resource that retired men can draw upon to deal with the problems that arise from the loss of productive roles through retirement, educational attainment may be a related factor. We found a statistically significant relationship between educational attainment and a continued sense of high status after retirement. The highly educated experienced the least perceived status loss. The association between high educational attainment and the absence of

Table 11-I

EDUCATIONAL LEVEL AND PERCEPTION OF
STATUS LOSS DUE TO RETIREMENT, BY SEX

| | Educational Level | | | |
	Less Than High School	High School	College	Total
Perception of Status Loss among Males:				
Agree	10 (35.7%)	5 (14.7%)	1 (3.0%)	16 (16.8%)
Disagree	18 (64.3%)	29 (85.3%)	32 (97.0%)	79 (83.2%)
Totals	28	34	33	95

Chi square = 10.810; DF = 2, $.01 > P > .001$ contingency coefficient* = .466

	Less Than High School	High School	College	Total
Perception of Status Loss among Females				
Agree	8 (29.7%)	2 (4.3%)	3 (14.3%)	13 (13.7%)
Disagree	19 (70.3%)	45 (95.7%)	18 (85.7%)	82 (86.3%)
Totals	27	47	21	95

Chi square = 9.339; DF = 2, $.01 > P > .001$ contingency coefficient* = .408

*These contingency coefficients have been corrected to allow for a systematic interpretation, with a maximum possible value of 1.00. Without such a correction, the maximum value the contingency coefficient could attain is .894, regardless of how radically the data are distributed. For 2 x 3 tables, contingency coefficients must be divided by a factor of .685 to achieve this correction. (Source: Champion, D. J., "Basic statistics for social research," pp. 205-206. Scranton:Chandler Publishing Co., 1970.)

feelings of status loss was more apparent among males; but the relationship was statistically significant for both males and females, and the differences between the sexes as regards perceived status loss were not significant in any educational category (Table 11-I).

Only three per cent of the college-educated males felt a loss of status upon retirement, while over a third of those who had less than a high school education felt a loss of status. Since education is closely associated with socioeconomic status, the economic resources that were available to the poorly educated worker before retirement probably decline after retirement. Thus he is faced with a real loss of ability to control the contingencies of his life. Upon retiring, a worker without much education would lose much of the sense of mastery he may once have had, since this was based on his ability to work and support his family.

We wanted to determine whether these feelings of status loss could be studied more objectively; accordingly, we focused upon indicators of another source of self-respect and self-esteem for the retired male, namely, the relative power the husband holds in decision-making. Some recent studies have indicated that the power the husband holds in family decision-making may be closely related to his self-concept, and this may be an important source of continued self-esteem in retirement. Some of Blood and Wolfe's studies (1960) confirm that resources such as occupational status, educational attainment, and income contribute strongly to the relative power held by each spouse in decision-making. Generally, the greater the relative contribution to family resources, the greater the relative power of the partner in decision-making will be. If we extrapolate their findings to later life, husbands with substantial resources such as occupational status and income may retain their relative power in decision-making even after they have retired. On the other hand, in lower-income families, the husband cannot draw upon resources such as his former occupational prestige to maintain his relative power in decision-making; hence he may experience a considerable loss of power upon retirement. Under these conditions, the drastic decline that occurs in the lower-class husband's resources upon retirement (Blood and Wolfe, 1961) can be traced to his loss of income, which was derived from low-prestige occupations. The professional worker, however, can carry over occupational prestige into retirement, and so can retain some of his occupation-related resources, despite what may be a substantial loss of income.

As we have already noted, professionals and other individuals of high occupational status often continue to identify with their former occupations after retirement. Through this continued identification, they can probably retain the prestige associated with their occupational standing long after their productive activity in those occupations has ceased. Persons in low-status occupations, however, are more likely to divorce their work from other aspects of their lives. By so doing, they make it less likely that they will be able to carry over whatever prestige their occupations may have into retirement, since their major sources of identity are less likely to be related to their employment. Since education and relative occupational status are closely related in our society, husbands who hold high relative power in decision-making might use this educational factor as a resource to replace those lost through retirement. In particular, those husbands who continue to identify with their high-status occupations after retirement may use this maintained occupational and educational prestige as a source of power in decision-making. Because education and occupational attainment are closely correlated, we were able to study whether husbands in general, and especially highly educated husbands (who had probably been employed in high-status occupations), felt that they lost power in decision-making upon retirement.

Table 11-II

EDUCATIONAL LEVEL AND PERCEIVED LOSS OF POWER
IN FAMILY RELATIONS DUE TO RETIREMENT, BY SEX

| | Educational Level | | | |
	Less Than High School	High School	College	Total
Husband's Loss of Relative Power in the Family:				
Agree	14 (51.8%)	10 (28.6%)	12 (35.3%)	36 (37.5%)
Disagree	13 (48.2%)	25 (71.4%)	22 (64.7%)	60 (62.5%)
Totals	27	35	34	96

Chi square = 3.653; $>.207$ $P>.10$; DF = 2; contingency coefficient* = .193

Wife's Loss of Relative Power in the Family:				
Agree	9 (32.1%)	16 (38.1%)	4 (18.1%)	29 (30.5%)
Disagree	19 (67.9%)	30 (61.9%)	17 (81.9%)	66 (69.5%)
Totals	28	46	21	95

Chi square = 1.695; $.50>P>.30$; DF = 2; contingency coefficient* = .151

*These are corrected contingency coefficients. See Table 11-I for explanation.

Our findings suggest that the better educated males are somewhat less likely to feel that they had lost power to their wives upon retirement. Over half of the men who had less than a high school education felt so, while just over a third of the college-educated men felt so (Table 11-II).

The relationship between lack of educational attainment and perceived loss of power in the family did not attain statistical significance among either males or females. When Table 11-II is dichotomized, and those who have high school or higher levels of education are compared with those who lack high school diplomas, the relationship approaches (but does not reach) statistical significance at the .05 level among males only. No consistent linear relationship was observed between education and the lack of perceived status loss, since college-educated males were somewhat more likely to feel they had lost power to their wives than were males with a high school education.

It is also apparent that college-educated males perceive a somewhat greater loss of power in family relations upon retirement than do males with a high school education. Although we do not have data to confirm our speculations, it is possible that the college-educated male may feel he has lost power because the wife has possessed quite a bit of power all along (gained through educational achievement, organizational participation, and/or gainful employment), and retirement produces a more diffuse division of labor in the family, and hence increases the relative power of the wife. Since college-educated males are likely to marry college-educated females, the college-educated wife may find that when her husband retires, she has more opportunity to realize her educational resources than she had while her husband was working (often in a demanding professional or business career). Also, after retirement the husband may appreciate the highly educated wife's resources more fully, particularly if both engage in self-expressive activities during their newfound leisure time.

Our findings also show that college-educated females are somewhat more likely than less well-educated females to feel a loss of power in family relations when their husbands retire. This may reflect the extent to which resources such as occupational identification, which may be maintained after retirement, serve as a power base for the husband. It may also indicate the wife's realistic perception of her husband's education as a resource, as he would most probably be highly educated.

Our findings relate directly to objective factors such as educational attainment, status loss, and power in decision-making, but these findings can perhaps also be interpreted in the light of the possibility that retirement is a multidimensional phenomenon that has distinct objective and subjective components. We may be dealing both with objective

Table 11-III

POSSIBLE COMBINATIONS OF EDUCATIONAL LEVELS WITH ACTUAL
AND PERCEIVED LOSS OF STATUS FOR RETIRED MALES

	Level of Education	Status Situation Objective Reality	Subjective Reality
A	high	loss	loss
B	low	loss	loss
C	high	loss	no loss
D	low	loss	no loss
E	high	no loss	no loss
F	low	no loss	no loss
G	high	no loss	loss
H	low	no loss	loss

social reality and with the retired person's perception of
this reality in relation to himself and those in his group—
in essence, with his definition of the situation. If we consider these two realities, objective and subjective, and relate them to the educational level, we can construct a
paradigm with eight possible combinations (Table 11-III).

If our findings are valid, the most probable combinations we would expect to find among the retired are C, E,
B or H.

If combination C is valid (a high educational level combined with an objective loss of status and a subjective denial
of this loss), the society regards the retiree as possessing a
lowered status, but he himself refuses to accept this fact
subjectively, in much the same way that some old people
refuse to think of themselves as being chronologically old
(Drake, 1958, p. 388). (It is, of course, conceivable that the
lowered self-esteem of the retired male is a function not so
much of his retirement as of his advanced age.) In this case,
as in the case of B (a low educational level combined with
an objective loss of status and a subjective acceptance of
this loss), the researchers would be correct in pointing out
that one of the stresses brought about by the loss of the
economic role is "the downgrading of status" (Donahue,
1963, p. 376). The disparity between these two possibilities

and the greater denial of reality by the upper educated than by the lower-educated would still remain to be explained. Possibly the more highly educated group has more to lose by admitting this reality; those who had lower status to begin with would presumably feel less involved in, and less threatened by, a reduction in status; since the downward movement would not be very great. This seems to be borne out by B. Since the majority of those who said that they felt a loss of status had possessed lower status to begin with, it is conceivable that the maintenance of a false self-image regarding status may be less important to men of lower educational rank than it is for those on the upper levels.

If combination H is valid (a low educational level combined with no objective loss, but with a subjective sense of loss of status), then the less well-educated male may merely be reflecting a general and continued feeling of lowered self-respect engendered by his participation over the years in an achievement-oriented society, rather than a loss specifically due to retirement. His low self-esteem is merely another reflection of the general view stated thus by Beckman, Williams, and Fisher (1958): "The greater a person's education, the better prospects he appears to have for favorable adjustment in later maturity [p. 664]." (Highly educated people possess greater resources for life adjustment in general, at all ages.)

Theoretically, the most potentially fruitful of all these combinations is E (a high education combined with no objective loss of status and no subjective sense of loss); in other words, for highly educated men, the subjective feeling that they have undergone no loss of prestige would be a reflection of true societal conditions. If this is true, we can explain the strong relation between maintained status and educational level by postulating that, although the occupation originally confers the status (since status is generally felt to inhere in the occupation, rather than in the individual), after retirement, even though he no longer actively performs the functions of his occupation, the higher-level retired person continues to hold the associated prestige. This retention of prestige may in fact be a compensatory mechanism for the disengagement from the job. Furthermore, the expertise, education, and training that were necessary for the occupational role remain intact within the individual, and will reinforce this firm and lasting identification with the occupation. The retired person can rest on the underpinnings of prestige (such as education and technical competence) that originally gained him his position, even after he relinquishes his occupational role. This agrees with and amplifies the finding that occupational identity increases with the years of professional training involved and with pride in the attendant skills (Kuhn, 1960, pp. 39–55; Becker and Carper, 1956, pp. 289–298). Cumming and Henry (1961) imply that prestige is retained when they ask, "Why is it not suggested . . . that old people may want recognition for having *been* useful, for a *history* of successful instrumentality [p. 20]?" Levin (1963) explicitly postulates that status is retained, thus: "The maintenance of equilibrium in the aged can be thought of in terms of the person's attitudes toward the past, the present and the future. Many an older person maintains his self-esteem on the basis of past performance [p. 164]."

A further possibility exists, which is not necessarily indicated by our data, however. This sense of loss of personal worth may have been a true reflection of societal conditions for retired people of both high and low educational levels when the Protestant Ethic was an important normative element in our society. In the White House Conference on Aging (1960), it was stated that "retired persons find difficulty in filling time with leisure activities and have feelings of guilt when they do because their lives have been lived in a world that made a virtue of work [p. 25]." Today, however, sociologists have found that there is a shift away from this ethic, with its emphasis on ascetic and diligent labor, toward an ethic based more on the consumption than on the production of goods. This changing ethic may be differentially diffused, and may present a more positive self-image to the retired person with a higher level of education, who is no longer actively involved in the formerly all-important occupational system. According to Neugarten (1963), this type of person "feels he has the right, after he is retired, to sit and rock and . . . does not feel guilty about it. . . . This type is probably becoming more frequent in our society, particularly among males, as we are becoming a more leisure-oriented rather than work-oriented society [p. 15]."

The above discussion and findings are admittedly suggestive rather than definitive. They seem, however, to point up a need for further research into the area, research that would lead to a critical reevaluation of the commonly accepted contention that lowered status and lowered feelings of self-worth are inevitable concomitants of the male's retirement from the occupational system.

Part V

INTERGENERATIONAL ROLES

Introduction

One of the most discussed public issues of the last decade has been the relations between generations and the changing character of the family. This is variously referred to as "the generation gap" and "the breakdown of the family."

Much of the public discussion about the generation gap and the changing family has been youth-centered. This results from such questions as: Why can't the young understand their elders? What is the source and nature of adolescent rebellion? Why are older persons "distrusted" by the young? Very little of this has delved into the meaning of the differences and similarities between generations for older people.

This last section of the book considers the meaning of generational differences and family structure for elders. First the nature of the intrafamilial "generation gap" is explored, and a way of considering it is suggested. Second, generational relations are considered in non-Western context, in a society quite different from an urban-industrial one. Third, two kinds of familial roles typical of old age are considered: those of the grandparent and the widow.

chapter 12

The "Generation Gap" and Aging Family Members: Toward a Conceptual Model

VERN L. BENGTSON
EDWARD B. OLANDER
ANEES A. HADDAD

Social scientists have paid relatively little attention to intergenerational relations among adult members of society. Yet the continuity and conflict between aging parents and their middle-aged children is quite as worthy of interest, as a subject of scientific inquiry and as a social problem, as the more often discussed relationship between the young and their elders. In this paper we will first review some current perspectives on relationships between adults and the young, and suggest ways in which these orientations are appropriate to generational relations that involve the elderly. Second, we will describe an analytical framework that may prove useful in researching and forming a

This paper was originally presented at the annual meeting of the National Council on Family Relations, Estes Park, Colorado, August 25–28, 1971. The concepts developed here stem from the University of Southern California study *Generational differences: Correlates and consequences.* The study was funded by grant MH-18158 from the National Institute of Mental Health.

concept of intergenerational relations. Third, we will present examples from the literature to illustrate how this framework illuminates the study of relations between aging family members and younger generations. Finally, an explicit model that contains formally defined propositions will be presented to illustrate the potential utility of this approach.

The Popular Concept of Intergenerational Problems

The issue of differences between generations has attracted considerable interest recently, as is manifested in current media, both popular and scholarly. In the past decade, there has been much evidence of concern, bordering on anxiety, about the extent of differences between the young and the old. Such concern probably becomes evident sooner or later in every family and every social system, given the two inevitable events of individual aging and social change. That such interest is unusually great in contemporary society is evidenced by the appearance of a new cliché, the "generation gap," to describe the flavor of the contrasting orientations of different age groups in America in the past decade.

As several writers have pointed out, the term is a misnomer, if indeed it has any meaning at all, since that to which it refers is neither "generational" nor a "gap" (see Troll, 1970, for more complete discussions of the various definitions of the term "generation"). Nevertheless, the phrase is used so often (in discussions by politicians and priests, parents and professors) that it can scarcely be avoided in any discussion of inter-age differences. It seems to reflect the experience of differences, profound or trivial, in the behavior or standards of individuals or groups of different ages (Friedenberg, 1970; Mean, 1970; Thomas, 1974). The present paper follows the current popular usage, and the term will be employed throughout. We would be less than candid, however, if we did not point out our disaffection for the term from the very beginning.

Lineages, Cohorts, and Aging

The "generation gap" (and it is felt as such) seems to impinge upon the older person in today's society mainly in two ways. First are the differences between the behaviors or standards of his own cohort and those of younger age groups. These are attributable to differences in levels of "maturation" (aging) and to historical factors (Riley, Johnson and Foner, 1972; Hill, 1970a). Since they were born during a particular period in American history and shared certain historical experiences while coming into maturity, those individuals who are over 65 today have orientations that are often felt to be quite different from those of the younger members of the society. At the risk of spawning yet another questionable phrase, one might call this a "cohort gap" (Bengtson, 1971).

Second, there is the issue of differences between generations within the family that the aging member has parented (Streib, 1965; Hill, 1971a). Here the differences are probably much more personally relevant, since they are related to the wishes and fulfillments that parents often seek from their children's and grandchildren's lives. Within the family, the aging member may see the currents of change and conflict in the broader society as impinging on him personally, and as disturbing and questioning lifelong principles that have always governed his behavior. These family differences might be characterized by the term "lineage gap." (For a discussion of lineage effects, see Jennings, 1973.)

With a few exceptions, little attention has been given to the analysis of either type of "generation gap" so far as elderly persons are concerned, nor to the implications that such a gap might have for them. A voluminous literature does exist however, that documents cohort differences in various dimensions of opinion and behavior (Riley et al., 1972; Bengtson, Furlong, and Laufer, 1974). In addition, several recently published analyses are relevant to the lineage perspective on intergenerational relations (Adams, 1968, 1970; Hill, 1970a, b; Shanas, Townsend, Wedderburn, Friis, Milhøj, and Stehouwer, 1968; Streib, 1971; Troll, 1971; Riley et al., 1968). Still, it is clear that theoretical models and conceptual focus are at a relatively early stage of development, both in terms of interlineage and intercohort relationships.

For example, one sill sees assertions that the demographic and social changes of recent years have caused the saliency of kinship ties to decrease in American families today. Sussman and Burchinal (1962), Kerckhoff (1965), Hill (1970a), and others have shown, however, that multiple-generation families continue to function in contemporary America as a kinship system. Apparently kinship ties are not merely mechanical or normative, but are also felt to be bonds of affection. Survey data suggest that subjects in all three generations tend to feel that they experience the "generation gap" much less in their own family than they perceive it in the broader society (Bengtson, 1971). Also, in the dimension of intergenerational simliarities or differences, certain values and behaviors appear to be transmitted consistently across generation lines (Aldous and Hill, 1965; Hill, 1971a; Kandell and Lesser, 1972).

In review, it appears that lineage studies tend to reveal less "gap" than do studies based upon cohorts. Most studies, however, do not distinguish clearly between the cohort and lineage aspects of generational differences. This has led to considerable confusion on the extent of generational differences, to say nothing of the theories built to account for the probable causes of such differences.

Explanations for a Generation Gap

Theories that attempt to account for generational differences (at both the cohort and lineage levels) appear in the writings of many social scientists. In general, most of such theories have been based on two sets of factors. The first set consists of sociocultural disparities between age groups, as follows: (1) Each generation is born into a different historical period, shaped by different social events; as a consequence, the personality system of each is formed in a different zeitgeist. (2) Social institutions change over time, so that the various developmental roles (as student, parent, provider, and so on) have different meanings for the members of successive generations. (3) Status in social institutions tends to increase with the years, and hence gives the older person both greater rewards in the position and a geater stake in the *status quo.* The second set concerns biological and physiological factors, as follows: (1) changes in the relative importance of various needs with advancing maturity; (2) changes in perception, cognition, and sensation with advancing age; and (3) changes in life outlook and responses to social stimuli, brought about by the idiosyncratic ways in which each person experiences life.

According to one theory on the differences between the young and their parents, the very general age-related differences outlined above lead to a second kind of explanation for generational contrasts. These six factors give each generation a different "developmental stake" in each other (Bengtson and Kuypers, 1970). Each has a mythical fear of losing something as a consequence of the other generation's behavior. The elder generation in the dyad sense their finitude and fear that their own significance may be lost (Gubrium, 1973); they therefore wish to perpetuate their own values and institutions in their offspring. To this end they tend to deny or minimize evidence of intergenerational differences. By contrast, the younger generation fear that they may lose their own identities in the projections of their elders. Their desire is to create values and institutions for themselves, and they tend to see their parents' attempts to perpetuate old values and institutions as oppression and tyranny. Their stake in their own development causes them to exaggerate or maximize intergenerational differences.

The "developmental stake" perspective, which is based on the idea that different generations have different collective perceptions, has affinities with a distinction Smelser makes in his *Theory of collective behavior:* the actors themselves within social movements take different views of social change from those of the actors who view movements within the target social institutions ("the Establishment") from outside. The "developmental stake" concept also agrees with accounts in organizational sociology on the different points of view held in the perception and consideration of organizational commitment by the superordinates and subordinates in any social organization. The first group tends to define commitment as universal, while the latter considers it limited (Gouldner, 1960).

How does the "developmental stake" theory apply to the relationship of the oldest generation to the middle generation? Would we expect more similarities than differences, because the age-status discrepancies are less between an adult generational dyad? [The "spirit of the time" into which the middle generation were born, while different from that of their parents, probably had not yet changed as radically as it has since then.] Similarly, the greatest changes in the major institutions of society (government, marriage, the university, and so on) have occurred since the middle generation came of age; this would lead one to expect greater differences between the middle and younger generations than between the middle and older. On the other hand, one might argue that the social changes we see now represent the breakthrough of pressures that have built up across several decades, and the philosophical and ideological changes that made them possible really took form in the present middle generation. Thus Aldous and Hill (1969) suggest that the greatest differences are to be found between the middle and oldest generation, not between young adults and their parents. Status in social institutions does not continue to increase with age; it drops radically upon retirement (Litwak, 1965). This loss of status, along with the physical dependencies of old age, seem to place the aging grandparent in a position analogous to that of his youthful grandchild, who is also dependent, though for different reasons (Kalish, 1970).

A third theoretical explanation for the "generation gap," an explanation especially applicable at the cohort level, comes in the form of a concept analogous to "racism," which has been adapted from the analysis of intergroup conflict and stereotyping. Several authors (Butler, 1969; Neugarten, 1970; Bengtson, 1970) have suggested that "age-ism" may lie at the heart of perceptions of the "generation gap," particularly as expressed in the mass media. Behind many mass media discussions of the "generation gap" there lies some notion of a "youth problem," which implies that young people as a class partake of common qualities (generally invidious) that cause them to be suspect as a group. On the other side of the coin there is the image of the untrustworthy generation over the age of thirty, the "command generation" (*Time,* 1967) whose unbridled selfishness endangers our polluted and war-torn world. And finally, the fear of aging may lead some to maximize the differences between themselves and older people (Bunzel, 1972). There is something of the self-fulfilling prophecy in all this: individuals of polarized age groups come to act in accord with their stereotyped images.

Such stereotyping is obviously as inadequate for one age group as for another. In all cases it tends to create artificial "cohort gaps" that do not show regard for the qualities of individuals. Perhaps one of the reasons why the "generation gap" is perceived less within families than between cohorts is that in families, persons are seen more as individuals, and stereotyping is kept at a minimum.

It seems to us obvious that any adequate frame of reference for the understanding of intergenerational relations must first distinguish between the cohort and lineage aspects of age group differences. To focus only on cohort contrasts is to slight those interactional patterns that unite age strata in the most obvious way. Furthermore, the "gap" is multidimensional; a study that focuses only on one dimension (for example, life style) may produce findings that are quite inconsistent with those of another study that focuses on some other dimension (for example, core values). There is an evident need, then, for a conceptual scheme that focuses on lineage relations, a scheme in which all phases of family interaction can be related. Such a model is suggested in the next section. (See Hill, 1970a, for a somewhat different theoretical model, which focuses more directly on generational transmission.)

A FRAMEWORK OF THE LINEAGE RELATIONSHIP

Social Solidarity

Nisbet (1970) has suggested that the basic subject matter of sociology is the problem of the "social bond": the invisible and often unconscious ties that link individuals together in all social systems, both large and small. For example, he describes "community" as consisting of "social bonds characterized by emotional cohesion, depth, continuity, and fullness [1966, p. 6]." Others have used terms such as "integration," "cohesion," or "solidarity" to describe this basic group phenomenon. For reasons both historical and definitional, we prefer the term "solidarity."

The concept of solidarity has a long history in theoretical sociology. In the fourteenth century, Kaldoun (1348; republished in 1958) used the term in his exploration of the different dimensions of social life. Five centuries later, the concept of functional integration became central in the first social theories of the modern era, which relied heavily on the comparison of societies to biological organisms (this was first posited by Auguste Comte, and was developed further by Spencer and others). Another major viewpoint, one that still has currency after nearly a century, has been termed the "sociologistic" position. Developed by authors such as Simmel in Germany and Durkheim in France, this view sees the unifying factors of society in terms of society's need for the individual, and its control over him. A third perspective, which has been characterized as "psychologistic," sees the solidarity of society in terms of the individual's need for rewards from others (Homans, 1961; Blau, 1963).

Social psychologists have attempted to develop concepts of solidarity in a variety of ways. In building theory, some have dealt with the elements of human cohesiveness, and others have dealt with its effects. In his early work, Homans (1950) posited that there are three basic processes in human interaction: similarity, sentiment, and activity. Here "similarity" refers to those elements of behavior that interacting persons carry out in similar ways, and on which they feel some consensus of opinion. "Sentiment" has to do with the expression of emotional feeling or affect; it is a measure of their liking for each other. "Activity," on the other hand, deals with associative behavior.

Merton (1957) points out that "the degree of social cohesion has been recognized as a group-property which affects a wide variety of behavior and role-performance by members of a group [p. 915]." The notion that affection, consensus, and association represent basic ways in which individuals relate to one another has been borne out in the work of other authors. For example, Thibaut and Kelley (1967) suggest that the more cohesive the group, the more the group members will agree on group norms (this represents consensus). Deutsch and Krauss (1965) found that the greater the group cohesiveness, the more the members tend to work together (associate), and to place a high value upon one another (affection). They thus conclude that "the study of conditions affecting group cohesiveness and of the effects on group functioning of variations in group cohesiveness lies at the heart of the study of group life [p. 55]."

The most formal statement of the relationships among these components is that of Fritz Heider (1958). The outcomes of his "induction or relations and equifinality" theory can be stated in a concise paradigm (P means person, and O means other):

If P is similar to O, this induces P to like O (consensus; sentiment).

If P likes O, this induces P to have contact with O (sentiment; interaction).

If P likes O, this induces P to benefit O.

In these propositions, the same three elements of consensus, affection, and association can be seen. The final proposition also suggests a possible outcome of the interaction of consensus, affection, and association (that P benefits O), which might in practical terms mean some kind of social or psychological well-being.

The social and psychological literature seems to suggest, then, that consensus, affection, and association are vital elements in human interaction. Where these elements are high, interacting persons perceive their relationship as having a high solidarity.

Solidarity and the Family

The family is a special type of small group; in fact, it is seen by many social scientists as the prototype of all small groups. According to Parsons (1968), "The family is the 'primordial' solidary unit of all human societies. Indeed, in the most primitive, kinship, which includes much more than the nuclear family, is the mode of organization of *all* solidarity [p. 40]." If consensus, affection, and association are universal indices of solidarity in groups, they would act as a similar index of solidarity in families. They could be used to obtain a measure of intragenerational ("horizontal") solidarity, and of intergenerational ("vertical") solidarity (Haddad, 1971, pp. 25–30; Black and Bengtson, 1973).

Such an index could do much more than simply measure "generation gaps"; it could show the various levels and kinds of relationship within families, and their effects upon behavior. It could show why some families seem to be "closer" than others. For example, the data of Thomas (1971b) suggest that consensus between the parent and the child on political matters is influenced more by the associational component than by the affectional. (See Haddad, 1971, for a more complete development of the concept of family intergenerational solidarity concept, and Black and Bengtson, 1973b, for a report on its operationalization and measurement.)

Family solidarity, then, can be viewed as interaction between family members in those spheres of life that involve association, consensus, and affection. It is important to elaborate the definition of these three components:

Affectional solidarity refers to the nature and extent of positive sentiment toward members of the other generations in the family. This, then, is the "sentiment" component of family cohesion. It involves the perception of being "close" to another member of the family, of trusting and being trusted, of respecting and being respected. This dimension encompasses the sensitive areas of fairness and understanding. Understanding generates acceptance (one of a person's) grestest needs, especially as a member of a small and intimate group. People are better able derive a sense of cohesiveness from their interactions if they perceive their dealings with each other as fair and just. It is difficult to conceive of a loving, affectionate relationship between two or more persons if the basic elements of trust, fairness, respect, and understanding are not present. This does not preclude differences of opinion, and even conflict, but these represent a separate dimension of solidarity.

Associational solidarity refers to the interactional patterns between members of the family. According to Homans (1950), "If the frequency of interaction between two or more persons increases, the degree of their liking will increase, and vice versa [p. 112]." Homans assumed that people who are close to each other and who like each other will do more things together. Of course, Homan's model assumes that the association is voluntary and family members sometimes do things together only because they have to (visiting a sick parent out of a sense of duty), not because they particularly like each other (inviting a parent on a vacation). In such cases, one would expect that the frequency of interaction would be quite limited.

On the other hand, if parents and children frequently engage together in recreational activities, visit together frequently, engage in religious activities together, discuss things that concern them, or give and receive help, then we can safely assume that there is a positive "social bond" between them (here characterized as associational solidarity).

Consensus solidarity is the extent of agreement or similarity in personal and social values, opinions, and beliefs between family members. Such values and opinions can be measured in one area of social life, or in a cross-section of areas (Hill, 1970a; Jennings and Nimei, 1968). It is more profitable to study interpersonal consensus in the family in a complete spectrum of fields. The construct of social institutions, including the economy, the polity, the family, the school, and religion, furnish a good framework for investigation. Perceived similarities and differences in these areas can be delineated as the indicators of consensus solidarity between the members of the family.

The assumption that family solidarity, both intragenerational (horizontal) and intergenerational (vertical), can be measured in terms of affection, association, and consensus seems to be supported by existing theories. Nye and Rushing (1969) suggest that "items entering the instruments to measure family integration must be designed to measure these basic concepts: activities, interaction, values, and sentiments [p. 137]." In our operational definition of family solidarity, affection is roughly parallel to Nye and Rushing's "sentiments"; association to their "activities and interaction"; and consensus to their "values."

Adams (1964) notes that "values, affection and interaction are related in a general postulate of interaction theory [p. 5]." He further states that "similarity of attitudes, strong emotional attachment, and frequent interaction have been assumed by Homans and other interaction theorists to be closely associated [p. 63]." Aldous and Hill (1965) present data to substantiate this proposition: the transmission of behaviors and values between generations is directly related to family cohesion.

An important question is whether support for this model can be found in existing empirical research on the family, and particularly in research on intergenerational relations within the family. The following section addresses this issue.

FACTORS THAT AFFECT LINEAGE SOLIDARITY BETWEEN MEMBERS OF THE OLDER AND MIDDLE GENERATIONS

In the foregoing sections of this chapter the concept of generational differences, both as a myth and as reality, has been explored. Then a conceptual framework was presented from which to view the quality and extent of solidarity between generations within the family, on three dimensions: association, affection, and consensus. Much research has already been done that gives empirical support to these dimensions (though not under these particular names). In the present section, research on relations between the aging parent and his middle-aged offspring will be reviewed. In the concluding section, a model built upon this review will be presented; which may be useful in subsequent studies of solidarity between the older and middle generations of the family.

Factors that Affect Associational Solidarity

One of the most conspicuous elements in family studies during the past decade has been the evidence that kinship associations are continued, despite the spatial dislocations brought about by the demands of contemporary living (Troll, 1971). Factors that contribute to associational interactions among family members have been given the most attention in these studies, possibly because of the relative objectivity of the data, possibly because of the ease with which both the independent and the dependent variables can be operationalized. Of all the factors that influence association, residential propinquity seems to be the most significant. While many studies have shown that spatial separations do not diminish family bonds (Sussman and Burchinal, 1962; Kerckhoff, 1965; Reiss, 1962; Aldous, 1965; Gibson, 1968), distance must inevitably affect the amount of personal contact that is possible. This would be especially true for the oldest generation, who tend generally to be less mobile, and whose own social education was intended for an earlier, more stable society than the one we know today. Bott (1957) sees proximity as a necessary condition of intimacy (though not a sufficient one). Reiss

(1962) found that distance overrides the degree of kinship closeness as a factor in interaction.

Several studies have focused on the relationship between social class and visiting relationships. Studies by Kerckhoff (1965), Laumann (1966), and Gans (1962) seemed to reveal an inverse relationship between social class and intergenerational visiting patterns: members of the working class visit their family elders more than do members of the middle class, and those of the lower class visit their elders even more. When Garique and Gans (1962) controlled for residential propinquity, however, they found that middle-class subjects visit their elders as much as members of the other classes studied. It seems, then, that social class has its main effect upon residential propinquity and geographic mobility (that is, middle-class persons tend to move more, and to live farther apart).

There is, however, another way in which social class may influence intergenerational visiting patterns: some studies have shown that there is relationship between social class and the variable of filial responsibility. According to Adams (1968, pp. 62–63), loyalty to parents plays an important role in the pattern of intergenerational kinship relations. Hollinshead (1950) and Muir and Weinstein (1962) found that lower-class subjects felt a stronger sense of loyalty to their elders than did middle-class subjects. Blenkner (1965) uses the term "filial maturity" to describe a relationship in which the middle generation can be "depended upon" by their elders. We hypothesize that the variable of filial responsibility, based upon the concepts cited above, would account for some of the variations in the dimension of associational solidarity, and probably in the dimension of affectional solidarity as well.

Another important finding of family studies in the past decade has been that kinship association is assymetrical, varying to the type of sex linkage. Sweetser (1963, p. 236) found that closer ties are maintained among the kin of the female family members than among the the male kin; Robins and Tomanec (1962), Reiss (1962), Komarovsky (1964), and Aldous and Hill (1965) all found that the females kept better contacts with relatives on both sides of the family than did the males. Haddad (1971) found that the same was true of his sample of Lebanese families; this gives some cross-cultural support to the generalization that sex linkage through the female line is correlated with family association.

Specifically, in terms of the model under consideration in this chapter, this would suggest that there would be greater intergenerational association when the middle-generation member is female, and perhaps a slightly lesser increase in the amount of association when the elder-generation member is female. We would expect the greatest amount of association to take place when members of both generations are female.

When there is a great geographic distance between the residences of kin, a kind of association can be maintained through communication by mail or telephone. Litwak (1965) has maintained that this kind of communication produces almost as strong a family bonding as do face-to-face associations. Some researchers might maintain that the use of a predictive variable such as communication by mail or by telephone is tautological in this model (since the amount of communication is part of the usual operational definition of association), but we agree with Adams (1968) that it does have a modifying influence upon the more direct variable of residential propinquity, by lessening the effect that a great distance between places of residences would otherwise have.

In summary, then, the following variables emerge from the research literature as reliable indicators of association between members of the middle and older generations: residential propinquity (modified, where distance between residences is great, by communication by mail or by telephone), filial responsibility, and the type of sex linkage.

Factors Related to Affectional Solidarity

The body of research literature that deals specifically with the affectional aspects of intergenerational relationships is smaller than the body that pertains to association, but enough data are available to make some generalizations possible in this area. While most of these data pertain to continuities and discontinuities between the younger and middle generations, a few authors have focused upon affectional ties between aging parents and their grown children (Aldous, 1965; Aldous and Hill, 1965; Hill, 1970a; Streib, 1965, 1971). In general, the studies indicate that ties of affection remain strong in the American family system. Feelings of affection toward kin, and especially toward aging parents, seem to override spatial distances (Adams, 1964; Robins and Tomanec, 1962; Litwak and Szelenyi, 1968; Shorr, 1968). Brown (1960) found that the majority of elderly subjects in his sample did not feel neglected by their children.

It will be seen in this section that there is a considerable overlap between the dimensions of associational and affectional solidarity. In fact, any variable that increases association is likely to increase feelings of affection (Homans, 1950; Heider, 1958).

For example, the amount of communication by mail or by telephone is probably as much an index of the strength of affectional ties as it is a measure of association. The same might be said of the principal variable to be discussed in this section: helping behavior. Exchange of assistance or aid is obviously a kind of association; nevertheless, it is probably more closely correlated with affection than with any other single variable.

Several studies have dealt with reciprocal relationships

as against unreciprocated helping behavior. For example, Robins (1962) found that in three-generation households, the sharing of household duties by members of all generations contributed to the reduction of intergenerational tensions.

Not all behavior is reciprocated, however. When the parent is of advanced age, is extremely infirm, or is financially deprived, the more able family members are bound to give more than the parent can return. Aldous and Hill (1965) found that the middle generation tends to give more to both the older and younger generations than they receive from either.

Apparently most families have norms (whether openly declared or merely understood) that govern the kinds of intergenerational interaction deemed appropriate. Kerckhoff (1965) found, however, that the expressed norms and the actual behavior did not always agree. He found that there were rather extreme differences among the norms expressed by his subjects on intergenerational responsibilities, but there were very few differences in actual intergenerational helping behavior.

The question of what part is played by reciprocity or the lack of it in affectional solidarity has been dealt with indirectly by Hill (1970a, p. 73), in his analysis of "kin activity." According to his findings, the crucial element appears to be the giving, not the reciprocating. He found that the nonreciprocating receivers had very low kin activity scores, while all the givers, both reciprocating and nonreciprocating, ranked about the same in their kin activity, and much higher than the nonreciprocating receivers. It would seen, then, that the amount of helping behavior would be the best measure of affectional solidarity, whether or not the behavior is reciprocated.

The dependency needs of elders tend to stimulate helping behavior, although the relationship is not always direct (Aldous and Hill, 1965). For example, help may be disguised as gifts and birthdays or other ceremonial occasions; in a similar way, requests for help may also be disguised (Streib, 1965). Illness, the most dramatic of all dependency needs, brings an immediate response in most families (Sussman and Burchinal, 1962). Most nonessential helping behavior, however, is probably influenced more by affection than by need. Nonessential helping behavior is probably also influenced by residential propinquity, since interchanges of all types are much more likely to occur among persons who live nearby. The type of sex linkage is also likely to influence helping behavior, for the reasons described in the discussion of associational solidarity.

In summary, the chief indicator of affectional solidarity appears to be the amount of helping behavior, especially of the nonessential kind, that occurs within the family. This is influenced, however, by dependency needs, residential propinquity, the type of sex linkage, and the degree of filial responsibility.

Factors Related to Consensus Solidarity

This area, as applied to the aged family members, has received considerably less attention to date than the areas of association and affection. However, recent studies that have focused on the transmission of values and other traits from generation to generation provide some useful suggestions (Aldous, 1965; Borke, 1963; Hill, 1970a; Jennings and Ninei, 1968; Kandel and Lesser, 1972; Thomas, 1974).

Changing cultural values, and their conflict with the elder's generalized expectations based upon earlier socialization patterns, affect consensus solidarity between the aging person and his younger family members in at least two ways. First, studies of immigrants have shown how difficulties arise between parents reared in an Old World culture and their Americanized offspring (Davis, 1940; Campisi, 1948; Senior, 1957; Gans, 1962). In many cases the model of old age that the immigrant learned in the country of his youth is regarded as strange by his American offspring; it can even lead in extreme cases to the oldster's being institutionalized (Clark, 1968). Second, within the American culture itself a radical shift of values is demanded of persons after retirement. After living for years according to the norms of competitive achievement, the retiring oldster is expected to change overnight, shifting his values to the practice of an ethic based upon the "image of limited good," which specifies the acceptance of the *status quo,* and of cooperation rather than competition. Studies cited by Clark show that the retention of the former competitive norms after retirement is highly correlated with mental illness in the aged.

To sum this up, it appears that if the older generation is of American birth (as opposed to birth in some culturally different nation), and if family traditions permit the acceptance of changed norms for the aged by both the older and younger generations, there factors would be positively correlated with consensus solidarity. Experiences not shared across generational lines, such as different forms of educational, occupational, and peer group experiences would tend to be negatively correlated with intergenerational consensus (Hill, 1970a).

The material reviewed above shows that there is already considerable empirical support for the hypothesis that association, affection, and consensus are significant dimensions in the measurement of intergenerational solidarity, particularly between the middle and older generations. It has also been shown that these dimensions are highly interrelated, so much so that they cannot truly be regarded as independent variables, but rather are aspects of a single variable: family solidarity. One good analogy might be that of a building with three entrances, any one of which gains access to the same central area. Perhaps the differences between these three dimensions are primarily qualitative, rather than quantitative, association representing the primarily behavioral, affection the primarily emotional, and consensus the primarily intellectual components of intergenerational solidarity. The task of the following section will be to organize the material presented thus far into a theoretical construct, a model for consistent further research studies in the measurement of intergenerational solidarity.

A MODEL OF THE VARIABLES THAT INFLUENCE SOLIDARITY BETWEEN THE OLDER AND MIDDLE GENERATIONS

Since association, affection, and consensus are highly interdependent aspects of a single dependent variable (intergenerational solidarity), it is axiomatic to the theory presented here that any variable that contributes to an increase in any one of these aspects contributes correspondingly to intergenerational solidarity as a whole. We represent this graphically in the theoretical scheme (Figure 12-I) by placing association, affect, and consensus in the same box, without any clear division lines between them.

Several of the predictor variables are basic to the theory presented here. These include residential propinquity, helping behavior, American birth, acceptance of changed norms for the elderly, and experiences not shared across generational lines. The remaining variables are secondary: they modify the effects of the primary variables, as their vectors and valences indicate.

In almost every major study, residential propinquity emerges as the most important single factor in intergenerational association patterns. The vector extending from residential propinquity to the associational end of the "intergenerational solidarity" box has a positive valence, indicating that the nearer the places of residence, the greater the anticipated amount of association. This vector,

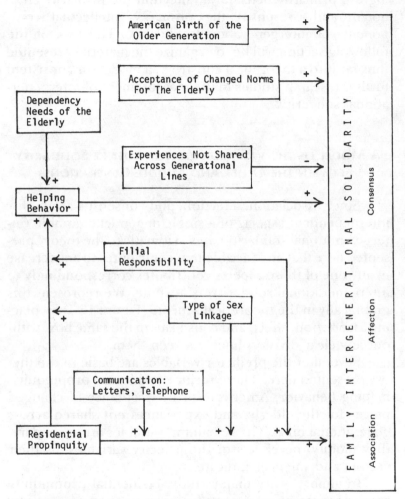

Fig. 12–I. A multivariate model of solidarity between the older and the middle generations.

however, is modified by three of the secondary variables: communication by letters or telephone, type of sex linkage,[1] and filial responsibility. These all have a positive influence on the effects of propinquity upon association, they increase the amount of expected association when residences are nearby, and mitigate the effects of distance when residences are far apart.

Residential propinquity also has a positive vector leading to helping behavior. The nearer the places of residence, the greater the probability that helping behavior will take place. This vector is modified positively by the type of sex linkage, and by filial responsibility, both of which tend to increase the effects of residential propinquity upon helping behavior.

Independently of residential propinquity and its modifiers, helping behavior is also affected positively by the dependency needs of the elderly. For example, it can be predicted that if an aging mother is seriously ill, her daughter is much more likely to fly across the country to be with her (even if this involves borrowing money) than she would be if her mother's needs were less urgent.

Helping behavior is obviously a form of association; also, more importantly, it influences the affectional component of solidarity, as the studies by Hill (1970a) suggest.

As yet, little empirical information has been gathered about the consensus dimension of family solidarity. While Black and Bengtson (1973b) have given some suggestions on the development of operational procedures to study the consensus variable, so far only three independent predictor variables have emerged from the research literature: American (or non-American) birth of the older generation, acceptance of changed norms for the elderly, and experiences not shared across generational lines. One hopes that

---

[1] In regarding the type of sex linkage as a positive factor, we assume that the amount of female contacts will be high; the highest value will be assigned where there are female members in both interacting generations.

further utilization of operational procedures by which to define consensus, along the lines begun by Hill (1970a) and Black and Bengtson (1973), will enable researchers to identify further variables that contribute to consensus. In addition, the application of recent statistical procedures such as that of canonical correlation to the present model should reveal the possible effects of other variables elaborated here upon consensus solidarity.

The theory of intergenerational solidarity presented in this chapter can be stated formally in the following propositions:[2]

PROPOSITION 1. Associational solidarity between members of the older and middle generations of a family is positively correlated with their residential propinquity.

Corollary 1a. The effect of residential propinquity upon associational solidarity is increased by the amount of communication by mail or by telephone.

Corollary 1b. The effect of residential propinquity upon associational solidarity is influenced by the type of sex linkage (that is, the effect is increased by the number of female linkages).

Corollary 1c. The effect of residential propinquity upon associational solidarity is increased by the amount of filial responsibility.

PROPOSITION 2. Helping behavior among the older and middle generations is positively correlated with residential propinquity.

Corollary 2a. The effect of residential propinquity upon helping behavior is influenced by the type of sex linkages.

Corollary 2b. The effect of residential propinquity upon helping behavior is increased by the amount of filial responsibility.

[2]These propositions are derived from the following axiom: any factor that contributes to an increase of associational, affectional, and/or consensus solidarity among intergenerational family members contributes correspondingly to an increase in intergenerational solidarity.

PROPOSITION 3. Intergenerational helping behavior is increased by the dependency needs of the elderly.

PROPOSITION 4. Affectional solidarity is positively correlated with the amount of helping behavior.

PROPOSITION 5. Consensus solidarity between the older and middle generations is increased if the older generation member was born in America, rather than in a country with different cultural values and attitudes.

PROPOSITION 6. Consensus solidarity between the older and middle generations is increased to the extent that both generations accept the changed behavioral norms upon retirement (the "image of limited good") for the older generation.

PROPOSITION 7. Consensus solidarity between the middle and older generations is negatively influenced by experiences not shared with the family (educational, occupational, and peer group experiences that differ from the family norms and traditions).

The formal statement cited above is limited to direct propositions. By axiomatic reduction (Zetterberg, 1965) further propositions could be derived from the model by the researcher, if they were germane to his research design. For example, Propositions 2 and 4 could be combined into an axiomatically derived proposition: that affectional solidarity is positively correlated with residential propinquity.

This model is limited to the prediction of lineage solidarity; it is, therefore, less inclusive than more elaborate models such as that of Hill et al. (1970a) on family development in three generations, especially as regards continuity in decision-making (Hill, 1970b), or that of Sussman (1965), who presents a functional analysis of parental aid to married children. Moreover, the model has both the advantages and the limitations of formal axiomatic theory; other factors not as yet included in the model may affect relationships in various ways. Finally, the testing of such a model involves ambitious empirical strategies, which, as

Hill (1970b) and Streib (1965) have pointed out, present many challenges to the researcher. A carefully conceptualized and formalized statement of relationships between variables can be highly useful, however, not only in summarizing previous research, but also in suggesting future avenues of inquiry on generational relations that involve aged family members.

SUMMARY AND CONCLUSIONS

The purpose of this paper has been to explore methods of analyzing the "gap" between generations, especially as it pertains to aging members of the family. Research on generational relations, spurred by the wave of popular concern that emerged in the protest-filled 1960s, has generally failed to distinguish between cohort effects (contrasts between age strata on the broader society level) and lineage effects (relations between parents and children within the family). Various explanations of intergenerational differences have been offered, applicable to both the cohort and lineage levels of analysis: sociocultural, biological, and physiological factors; the different developmental stake that each generation has in the other; and the stereotypes evident in "age-ism," directed against both the young and old.

Such highly general explanations have considerable heuristic utility; but when one is empirically assessing the relationship between generations, it seems useful to focus on either the cohort or the lineage level of analysis. Moreover, in examining aspects of the social bond between aging parents and their children, it seems necessary to define explicitly the various dimensions of the lineage relationship. We believe that the concept of solidarity, divided into components of association (interaction), affection (sentiment), and consensus (agreement) between members of the generational dyad, will be a useful conceptual tool in such exploration. A considerable body of social theory appears to support this concept.

A review of previous empirical literature suggests many possible linkages between these three components and other variables in the structural or individual attributes of the generational dyad. Reliable predictors of associational solidarity appear to be residential propinquity (or communication, where distance is great), norms of filial responsibility, and the type of sex linkage. Predictors of affectional solidarity are helping behavior (influenced by dependency needs), residential propinquity, the type of sex lineage, and filial responsibility norms. Consensus solidarity appears to be influenced by these factors, and also by cultural background and experiences not shared across generational lines, such as different educational and occupational experiences.

Such dual linkages lead to an explicit axiomatic model of the multiple predictors of solidarity between aged parents and their children. The model is presented both as a summary of the literature and as a guide for future research on factors that may predict differential "lineage gap" among families with elderly members.

chapter 13

The "Generation Gap" in an Ethiopian Society

JOHN H. HAMER

The main contention of this paper is that the basis for the so-called "generation gap" is not so much that times and values are changing (they always have been changing) as that there is a breakdown in the reciprocal social bonds between generations. There is a tendency on the part of youth to ignore their own approaching senescence, as if it could be indefinitely postponed, and to pay little heed to their own position *vis-à-vis* the following generation. Yet, as a matter of biological necessity, different social roles are a part of aging; they require changes in the patterns of reciprocal rights and obligations toward those who have preceded and those who have followed in the life cycle.

Fortes (1969) has recently suggested that the factor that distinguishes kinship from other social systems is the condition of amity between members of the kin groups. The concept of kinship amity can be extended to relationships between friends and generations, as in the friendship

---

This is a revised version of an earlier paper, read at the meetings of The Society for Applied Anthropology, Miami, Florida in 1971.

pacts and age-set systems so highly elaborated in African societies. Even in the industrial nations, amity has been a viable concept, not only within families, but between generations. Of late, however, there has developed a widespread enmity between the old and the young. Perhaps a brief examination of a society in the early stages of modernization, such as the Sidamo of southern Ethiopia who have a highly elaborated generational class system, can provide some clues as to how amity between generations was maintained in the past and, to a large extent, is maintained in the present. At the same time, we shall indicate certain features analogous to "the gap" problem, which have been brought about by the introduction of a cash economy, the Western style of schooling for youth, and the imposition of the nation-state concept on a tribal people.

The Sidamo are an eastern Cushitic-speaking people, located approximately 150 miles south of the Ethiopian capital of Addis Ababa.[1] Their settlements are scattered at various elevations in the Rift Valley, extending from the floor up the steep slopes of the valley's sides. As a consequence of the resulting ecological variation, they are a mixed horticultural and herding people, grouped in a number of patrilineal clans of considerable generational depth.

AGING AND THE LIFE CYCLE

The Sidamo place a premium on aging in terms of conceptualization, socialization, and institutional structures (Hamer, 1972). But while it is true to say that age always takes precedence in terms of prestige and privileges, it is also subject to considerable obligations, especially for

[1]The field research on which this study was based was done during 1964–65, under the auspices of the Ford Foundation, Great Lakes Colleges Association, and Ohio Wesleyan University.

the aged male. Because wisdom and circumspection are ascribed to old men, they are the makers of public policy and the source of justice; both of these roles require a considerable outlay of time and energy. There are also certain character distinctions beyond that of ego between the first and second generations, in the sense that the paternal generation is considered authoritarian and coercive, while the truly "old men" (the second ascending generation) are said to be kindly and persuasive. In line with the sexual division of labor, the warm and nurturing attributes ascribed to women are believed to increase with age. Though these admired attributes are supposed to be present after marriage, their full development is delayed by the tensions of bearing children and the hard work of laboring to enhance the prestige of a husband. For both men and women, the valued character traits are socialized as ideals early in life, but they are not expected to emerge as fully developed until old age. Thus, in contrast to Western industrialized societies, the highest qualities of humanity are expected to develop gradually, and to reach a zenith toward the end rather than near the beginning of the life cycle. The freedom and spontaneity associated with youth, and so highly valued in the West, must be repressed by Sidamo youth, who are expected instead to show deference and service to the older generations. Nevertheless, being young does not only entail obligations; it also involves the right to expect assistance from the elders in attaining culturally prescribed goals.

When a child reaches the toddler stage, he becomes subject to training in obedience and deference to his elders. Deference is initially learned through the elaborate courtesy involved in greeting adults, and through the way in which food is distributed (according to seniority) at mealtimes. Young children soon discover the importance of the custom of adoption as a means of providing service to their elders when they see that shortly after weaning, many of their peers go off to live with their paternal or maternal grandparents. The small grandchild becomes a substitute for an absent or dead son or daughter; he runs errands, fetches firewood, and performs other tasks required by an old grandparent.

On a more subtle level, the child begins to receive training in self-restraint, which in later life will blossom into the circumspect evaluation of events and people that is expected of elders. The technique used in this training by both older siblings and adults is that of teasing. Typically, the small child will be offered a tantalizing morsel of food or encouraged to act in a manner that is normally forbidden, only to have the food withdrawn or to be threatened with punishment just as he attempts to complete the act. He soon learns to be reticent and guarded when confronted by such temptations.

While much of a Sidamo youngster's early training is designed to teach him restraint, obedience, and skills, as he approaches adolescence he is encouraged to adopt a more aggressive, achievement-oriented stance. This change of attitude is deemed appropriate only between peers, and is not meant to be extended across generations. Nevertheless, the encouragement of an aggressive, competitive attitude among peers brings some conflict between the ego and the parental generation, since it is the latter who must gradually give up their wealth to support their own replacement by their children. The reason for all of this is that aging brings esteem, but leadership within a generation must be demonstrated by oratorical ability, acquisition of wealth, and (in the past) bravery in battle. Thus elders encourage the young to vie with one another in debate, in trade, and in developing large herds and gardens; and to motivate and train the young, they must give not only of their time and energy, but also of their wealth.

It is the patrimony in land and cattle given by the father at marriage that launches a young man on the road to fame and fortune. The patrimony (as well as bride wealth, which is also provided by the father) affects the relationship between generations in two ways. To begin with, parental favoritism, which is based on the quality of deference and service provided, encourages sibling rivalry, and with developing maturity, this rivalry is extended to peers. At marriage, the father must parcel out land in equal shares to all his sons except the eldest, who, because of his primacy in the birth order, is entitled to a slightly larger share than his brothers. Though he cannot show favoritism in apportioning land, there is nothing to prevent the father from giving occasional gifts to a favorite son, in the form of cattle or other favors, which give this son an advantage over his brothers. This can lead to hostility within the sibling group, as well as between generations. Secondly, while a man is supposed to be generous in the disposal of his property, especially with his sons, it is not uncommon for a Sidamo elder to risk acquiring a reputation for greed by seeking to postpone the marriage of a son. Thus favoritism and a certain amount of reluctance to part with wealth help to foster muted rebellion and aggressive competitiveness in youth.

After his marriage, a young man, in addition to creating a new generational cycle, concentrates on building his reputation as a man of wealth and oratorical ability. In the days before Pax Ethiopica, he would have sought fame as a warrior by raiding the herds of enemy tribes. Today, however, he spends most of his time in seeking to expand his patrimony in land, and engaging the coffee trade. If he has shown oratorical ability, he may also attend the elders' councils and participate actively in the debates over the settlement of disputes and the making of community policy.

When he is promoted to elderhood, a man reaches the most esteemed part of the life cycle, and his role changes for a third time. As an elder he receives deference and

service from the young, but his obligations and responsibilities are correspondingly great. Now it is his turn to
redistribute wealth amongst his sons, and to give time and
energy in settling disputes, especially those that involve
the property rights of others. In carrying out the role of
elderhood, he must replace his youthful impetuosity and
aggressiveness with fully developed self-control and circumspection.

The climax of aging comes with death, and it is perhaps not surprising to find that the most elaborate rituals
in the Sidamo calendar surround this event. In the industrial West, people seem to grieve more over the loss of a
child than of an old man or woman; but it is quite the
reverse among the Sidamo. The older the deceased, the
greater the sense of loss, the more numerous are the
mourners, and the more copious is their grief. Death also
serves to illustrate the circularity of the structure of aging.
The son now receives the authority and responsibilities of
the deceased father in family relationships and the distribution of land. In the latter stages of senescence, and in the
case of the spirit of the deceased, it is the father who
becomes dependent on the son. Whereas the father has fed
the son, in both the literal and symbolic meaning of the
term, in the early stages of the life cycle, it is now the son
who must feed the father. Still, there is the conception of
an element of reciprocity in the relationship, for the spirit
of the dead father is protective, after its appearance in a
dream, if he was fed on demand by the son, but is destructive if he was ignored.

Though the life cycle of women is distinctively different from that of men, in terms of their domestic and child-
rearing roles and in their subordination to male authority,
they are subject to the same principle of intergenerational
reciprocity. For example, prestigious marriage is a goal
shared by both a young woman and her parents, but the
parents, despite their authority in the matter, would be

reluctant to push such a marriage without the daughter's consent. Moreover, if a woman manages to acquire a wealthy husband, she will succeed in maintaining the marital bond not simply on the basis of her ability to bear children, but through her competence and efficiency in handling domestic matters, and her use of charm and poise to hold the attention of her spouse. Though she is always overtly subordinate to her husband, if she is skillful and energetic she is covertly influential. Her relationships with her sons and her daughters-in-law, (after their marriages, a mother's own daughters are usually not available to play a significant part in her life) are in many ways analogous to the reciprocity pattern between fathers and sons. In the early years the mother feeds and provides training in deportment; the son reciprocates in later life, especially after the death of the father, by taking care of her garden, shelter, and all the other material wants of her declining years. In return, the son who provides the most service will inherit the land on which the mother is living at the time of her death. A woman's daughters-in-law serve her, and her sons-in-law honor her, through elaborate avoidance taboos, the duration of which she determines. Once again this is not simply a one-way proposition, for the quality of service provided by a daughter-in-law depends on the extent to which the older woman has sought to ease the way of the young wife into her husband's village and lineage group. If the relationship becomes one of warmth and affection, the daughter-in-law will be pleased to give one of her own children to her husband's mother, to serve the latter in her old age.

Social Structure

The structural basis of intergenerational reciprocity among the Sidamo is the generational class system (Hamer,

1970). Known as the Lua, it consists of two cycles, each of which contains five named classes; each class lasts seven years, and they are arranged in sequence. A cycle may be defined as the time (a period of approximately 35 years) that it takes to induct members into each of the five classes. The names of the classes are fixed, and an individual remains for life in the one into which he is originally inducted. At any given time (with the exception of the first seven years after promotion to elderhood), the sons of two different generational cycles are present in the same class. Thus a class is composed of a junior group of initiates and a senior group of elders. A son is always initiated into the class preceding that of his father, but only after the latter's class in the older cycle has been promoted to elderhood. Within the framework of this system, the life cycle is divided into four stages: birth, initiation, circumcision and promotion to elderhood, and exalted old age. An individual goes through two cycles before his class is retired from elderhood; the cycles cover a period of approximately 63 years.[2]

Ritually and politically, the structure of the Lua institutionalizes inequality between generations and supports equality within generations. For example, during the initiation cycle young men compete with each other for prestige and fame, but they also honor and serve their elders. The relatively favored position of the eldest brother, who receives a larger patrimony and has authority over his younger siblings, is balanced by the fact that they are all initiated into the same Lua class. It is the elders who have fostered and set the limits of competition between the young; for example, when parents pick a favorite child, they

[2]There is not a complete span of 70 years, because there are only 28 years from the time of the individual's initiation until his promotion to elderhood. This is due to the fact that as a man's class completes initiation, his father's Lua, just ahead of his, finishes promotion rituals. Therefore, only three intervening classes remain before his Lua begins its seven-year promotion interval.

use as their criteria the quality of deference and service shown by the latter. This helps to promote sibling rivalry, which is ultimately extended to all one's peers in the struggle to acquire the material basis of high social prestige. Young women compete for young men (and occasionally older ones) who appear to be winning fame and fortune; hence they provide themselves with a means by which they may gauge their own success in the search for wealth and security.

Most men and women accept the competitive struggle without complaint, and some even view it with enthusiasm. Sidamo are not afraid to admire and praise the successful. Perhaps this is because the redistribution of wealth is emphasized as a means of validating the role of the "successful man," and also because of the compensation that comes with venerated old age. Regardless of their individual achievements, when a man has been promoted to elderhood, or when a woman's children have married, they are entitled to the maximum respect and service that the younger generations can provide. The woman reciprocates by becoming the affectionate confidante of both the old and young in her community. Elderhood for men entails heavy political and adjudicatory responsibilities, as part of the protection and gradual transfer to the next generation of the property they have accumulated as intiates. It is the council of elders who settle disputes and protect the property rights of all generations, regardless of kinship or territorial boundaries (Hamer, 1972).

The relationship between male generations is summarized in Figure 13–I. The deference and service demonstrated by the young supports the wealth and authority of their elders. The latter in turn have affiliative obligations to support the young generously through patrimony and bride-wealth payments. In addition, the elders contribute to the development of youth's self-interest by teaching them that planning and persistence are necessary to reach

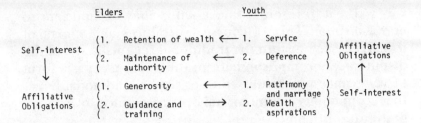

Fig. 13–I. Paradigm of intergenerational relations.

the ideal cultural goals. Thus, as the arrows indicate, there is a circular complementary relationship between the self-interest and the affiliative obligations of the different generations.

CHANGE

The development of a national court system and a cash economy has begun to produce a rift between generations, because these changes have provided the individual with options that enable him to slight his affiliative obligations in favor of self-interest (Hamer, 1972). A vicious circle has developed out of the increasing population and the desire of most people to place more land under cultivation, in order to maximize profits from the production of coffee. This in turn has led to increasing disputes over land rights and boundaries. To keep up with price changes, and to increase their wealth as rapidly as possible, men want faster decisions than can come from the laborious and conciliatory efforts of the elders' councils. Under these circumstances some men, particularly younger men, turn to the government courts or threaten to use them as a means of obtaining a conclusive settlement. The government court procedure is not faster or less costly than that of the traditional elders' council. Indeed, it is just the reverse; this is why a threat to resort to court action may be sufficient to end a dispute. This, of course, introduces an element of threat, and acts against the traditional reconciliation of the disputants. For imprisonment of the guilty party is a form of vengeance which runs counter to the traditional belief that community harmony takes precedence over self-gratification.

Western education tends to provide the young with aspirations and motivations that can only be met outside the community. This means that those who proceed very far in the educational system (so far a very small number) are not only likely to give up farming, but also to see the whole generational class system as irrelevant to their interests. If formal education has the same effect on the Sidamo as it has had in other parts of sub-Saharan Africa, it will not be long before many young migrate to urban areas, and have the opportunity to join the ranks of the disillusioned unemployed.

The elders view the threat of education and the impatient desire for money among the young with some ambivalence. Insofar as these "new ways" can be reinterpreted to fit in with traditional concepts of wealth and authority, they are welcomed as improvements. But many begin to see the changes as threats to the traditional way of life; they talk about the declining quality of deference and service, and express anxiety about the disappearance of all the "great old men." The phrase *atoteshima* (translatable as dissatisfaction) is frequently upon the lips of old men. They marvel that though there is more medicine, and material means are increasing, there seems to be more ill health and less satisfaction among the people than ever before.

Perhaps dissatisfaction will never become as pervasive as it has become in the West. For one thing, it is unlikely that the Ethiopian economy will ever be able to support the levels of affluence (and hence the options for self-indulgence without social responsibility) that have appeared in Western industrial societies. Moreover, there are some signs among the Sidamo that both elders and youth begin to see the continued need for generational interdependence, despite the process of modernization (Hamer, 1967). The old men still control the land and provide a more effective and realistic means of settling disputes than do the government courts. At the same time, the young men contribute their new linguistic and reasoning skills, and the broadened horizons, to deal with government specialists and the various levels of middlemen involved in coffee trading. Finally, there is the point (perhaps not yet self-evident to most of the youth) that a social security system lies in the very distant future for Ethiopia. This means that the young will sooner or later have to face up to the question of who will care for them in their old age.

DISCUSSION

There is just enough in the traditional and changing relationships between Sidamo generations to provide, on a comparative basis, some explanation for the existing generation gap in the West. For this Ethiopian people, the bond between generations is based not simply on calculated self-interest, but upon a genuine affection that arises out of lifelong reciprocal support. Within generations, competitiveness engenders and intensifies the pursuit of self-interest, but this is balanced by the redistribution and community responsibilities that come with aging. The less successful in the competitive struggle know they will receive largesse from the successful, and the status prestige that comes to all with age. The security of the aged rests on the obligation of the young to honor and serve the older generations. The guidance, affection, and generosity provided by the latter play an essential part in motivating and training the young, and providing them with a sense of identity.

The complementary relationships between self-interest and affiliative obligations providing a nexus between generations has been heavily eroded in Western industrial societies. The changes that are now taking place among the Sidamo give some indication of the way in which the breakdown has proceeded in the West. The impressive, but necessarily oversimplified, models of existence provided by Western-style education lead youngsters to believe that the wisdom of the elders is no longer relevant. Their greater knowledge of the new forms of government and economics has led many of them to believe that their aspirations will be fully met by these new institutions, without the assistance of the older generations. In other words, some Sidamo youths have come to look a short distance into the future—but not far enough. They have failed to consider whether the changes will be sufficiently rapid for them to do without the security that would ordinarily be provided by their own children. It is perhaps even more important that they are ignoring the problem of maintaining the honor and dignity that has traditionally given the aged a reason for having lived.

This process is, of course, much further advanced in Western industrial societies. Here it is not so much that the intense competitiveness and pursuit of self-interest among the young is intrinsically dysfunctional, but that these attributes exclude generosity and affiliative obligations toward the members of other generations. Without complementary social bonds between generations, somewhat like those in the Sidamo model, it would seem to follow that there is no need for the continued existence of either the young or the old.

In the industrial world, tangible material support of the aged by the young may no longer be as necessary as it continues to be in tribal and peasant societies. But more subtle supports, such as courtesy and the giving of one's time and interest, are the social and psychological means by which youth may serve and honor the elders. In turn, the latter can respond by providing a perspective for youth from their cumulative knowledge of human nature, and possibly, if the process can be encouraged and institutionalized at the family and neighborhood level, they could help to settle many of the petty disputes that arise out of day-to-day living. This is another way of suggesting that in any society, the deference and service of the young is important to the maintenance of the authority and dignity of the aged. Reciprocally, the guidance, affection, and generosity of the aged are necessary to establish aspirations and a sense of identity in the young.

chapter 14

The Significance of Grandparenthood

VIVIAN WOOD
JOAN F. ROBERTSON

The significance of grandparenthood has been a subject of much interest and speculation, but little verification. Grandparents are believed to assume important roles in poor families, particularly black families (Bernard, 1966; Frazier, 1939; Hays and Mindel, 1973), and crucial roles in most families during times of crisis (Hill, 1949; Lajewski, 1959; Sheldon, 1959; Sussman, 1953; von Hentig, 1946; Young, 1954). Yet we really know very little about the meaning and significance of the grandparents' role in modern society. Grandparents themselves, like mothers, seem unable to speak of the role in anything but laudatory terms. Some get somewhat defensive, which suggests they have an unsatisfactory relationship, and some are relatively neutral about the role, but most speak glowingly of the joys of grandparenthood, particularly of the fun, the enjoyment, and the lack of responsibility involved in the role. Even a late White House occupant, Lyndon B. Johnson, was quoted as saying that the grandparent role, which he described as his "link to the future," was a "role that has given me more joy than any other."

A number of social scientists, when studying the aging process and the family, have commented on grandparenthood. Clark and Anderson (1967) state that the grandparent status seems to be "a largely inactive one [p. 291]," and Atchley (1972) observes that it does not bring continuing interaction into the lives of grandparents. As for the function of grandparents, Messer (1968) has noted that the interaction of grandparents and grandchildren "does not so much meet a socialization function as it does a consummatory gratification function for both parties [p. 271]." Along the same lines, Riley, Foner, Hess, and Toby (1969) make the following statement:

> The grandparent (like the parent of an adult child) is permitted to dispense certain services and material supports, and to engage in certain expressive activities; yet is prohibited by the norm of independence from encroaching upon the parental responsibilities of his young adult offspring or interfering with their authority. It is no longer his function to socialize or control either the young adults or their little children. [p. 963]

The changing nature of grandparenthood makes this an important area of research for students of the family. In recent decades there have been major changes in the timing of events in the family cycle; as a result, grandparenthood has become a middle-age, rather than an old-age phenomenon. These changes, which result from earlier marriages and earlier and more closely spaced childbearing, have been described by Glick (1955). Grandfathers are usually still in the work force when they assume this new status; and as middle-aged, married women have returned to work in large numbers, grandmothers are increasingly likely to be working women. People now become great-grandparents in old age, and the four-generation family has become relatively commonplace (Townsend, 1966).

RESEARCH ON GRANDPARENTHOOD

In this paper the writers will review the literature on the meaning and significance of grandparenthood from three perspectives: that of the middle-aged and older individual who assumes the role of grandparent; the perspective of the other in the role, the grandchild; and the broader viewpoint of the extended family. These perspectives will be presented in reverse order, and will serve as background for a report on the investigators' current research in this area. In the final section, an attempt will be made to delineate some of the remaining issues and unanswered questions on the meaning and significance of grandparenthood in society today.

It should be clear, of course, that these three perspectives are interrelated. As Schorr (1960) points out, all three systems may benefit from the grandparents' behavior:

> Grandparents may indulge their grandchildren in a way parents cannot—in a way, in fact, that parents cannot approve. But this is a relationship from which grandparents get satisfaction, and it may serve salutary purposes for the grandchildren. Moreover, the relief that the parents, the middle generation, may find in the mediating influence of grandparents has been less adequately explored than the resentment that they express. [p. 16]

Significance Within the Family

Little attention has been given to the contributions grandparents make to the family system. It seems to have been assumed that grandparents have very little influence in the family. Troll (1971) attributes this lack of attention to the grandparents' roles in the family to the high value placed upon the independence of the nuclear family in child rearing, and to the consequent belief that a grandparent should not be involved in the socialization of a child.

Psychoanalytic writers have focused on the negative and pathological influences of grandparents (Abraham, 1955; Borden, 1946; Fried and Stern, 1948; Rappaport, 1958; Vollmer, 1937). An exception is Hader (1965), who maintains that grandparents sometimes serve an important function, acting as stabilizers in the family. It should be remembered that most of these reports are based on clinical cases, not on studies of representative samples of older people. To some extent, these writings have created an image of grandparents as meddlesome intruders in family processes. Robertson (1973) has recently attempted to discount what she refers to as "the myth of the meddlesome grandmother."

Parsons' thesis (1943) that the nuclear family is isolated from relatives denied the possibility that grandparents could play a significant contributory role in the family, and may be partially responsible for the inattention of family sociologists to the grandparental role. The results of studies of the extended family carried out in the 1950s (Dotson, 1951; Sharp and Axelrod, 1956; Sussman, 1953, 1954; Townsend, 1957) led to a re-examination of the concept that the nuclear family is socially isolated (Sussman, 1959). Litwak (1960) presented cogent arguments for a "modified" extended family: a family system with somewhat complicated networks of aid, service, and interaction, in which nuclear units are linked together both vertically and horizontally. The widespread existence of the modified extended family has been substantiated by sociological studies (Adams, 1968; Shanas, 1962; Shanas, Townsend, Wedderburn, Friis, Mihøj, and Stehouwer, 1968; Sussman and Burchinal, 1962b, 1971; Townsend, 1963), and this family type is now widely accepted as the typical family structure in Western societies.

Most of the research on intergenerational relationships in the extended family has focused on patterns of interaction and help between adult children (the second generation) and their parents (the first generation). For the most part, these studies are concerned only indirectly, if at all, with the relationship between grandparents and grandchildren (the third generation). Studies of the extended family in which the third generation is mentioned include those of Streib and Thompson (1958), Hill (1965, 1970), Shanas et al. (1968), and Boyd (1967).

Streib and Thompson (1958) found that approximately one-half of their respondents aided their adult children by baby-sitting or otherwise caring for their grandchildren. No indication was given of the frequency of such help, or of the occasions for it.

In a study conducted in several nations in 1962 (Shanas et al., 1968), one-half of the older respondents in the United States reported that they gave help to their grandchildren. In comparison, one out of three in Great Britain, and only one out of eight in Denmark, gave such help.

Hill (1965, 1970) has studied intergenerational exchanges of help in three-generation families in which the grandchild generation consisted of married adults. He found that grandparents were high receivers and meager givers; as a result, they had a quasi-dependent status. The parents in the middle generation were modest receivers and high givers; theirs was a patron-type status. Hill (1965) claimed that the youngest generation saw itself as more or less in equilibrium in terms of giving and receiving, with a status of high reciprocity and interdependence. One cannot determine from his data what proportion of the help the youngest generation received from the two older generations was given by the grandparent generation.

Boyd (1967) concluded that in the four-generation families she studied, grandchildren often saw grandparents as supplying family history and providing a liaison between generations. She also reported that grandparents were often viewed as indulgent friends and confidants, as "friendly equals." This type of relationship might be important to the family system if the proposition made by Radcliffe-Brown (1952) were substantiated. He has posited that in primitive societies, "friendly equality" between grandparents and grandchildren functioned as a relief from the tensions caused between the parents and children by parental authority and by the obligation each has toward the other. It has been suggested that modern American parents are themselves permissive, and often adopt an egalitarian and friendly relationship with their children. Hence children have no need for grandparents as mediators or allies against parental authority. Cumming and Henry (1961) used this as an explanation for their finding that the old people in their Kansas City study did not maintain feelings of closeness to their grandchildren. The grandparent role did not seem to be a focal one for most of the respondents.

Von Hentig (1946) has suggested that grandparents live on the fringe of the family group, so long as the family structure remains intact. In cases of family disruption, they assume a vital function, providing a source of rescue, refuge, and identification for their grandchildren. Indeed, a number of investigations of the family have turned up evidence that grandparents give help in emergencies. Several studies (Sheldon, 1959; Sussman, 1952; Townsend, 1957) show that grandparents, particularly grandmothers, often take on major household responsibilities when the mother is giving birth or working. They also intervene and provide assistance in times of illness, crisis, and disaster (Hill, 1949; Shanas, 1962; Young, 1954).

Moreover, numerous studies indicate that grandparents interact and exchange aid and services with the younger generations on a regular basis, not just in emergency situations. Studies of the English working-class family (Townsend, 1957; Young and Wilmott, 1957) indicate that grandparents, particularly grandmothers, often play important functions in sustaining the family by taking over a variety of household tasks, and sometimes even rearing the children. Grandparents often give this type of help while the two families maintain independent households. Also, economic help is sometimes given in the form of shared living arrangements, although neither the older parents nor the adult children usually consider this as "help" (Shanas, 1967). The old mother or old father who cannot afford to live independently may move in with the family of a married child; hence someone is in the house to look after the children, which makes it possible for both parents to work.

Although there are probably fewer day-to-day demands in middle-class extended families, there is considerable evidence that the family aid exchanged in these families is not limited to crisis and ceremonial occasions (Bell, 1968; Sussman, 1953). In fact, in a national survey (Shanas et al., 1968), a higher proportion of white-collar grandparents reported that they gave aid to both children (68 per cent) and grandchildren (58 per cent) than did working-class grandparents (57 per cent and 48 per cent respectively).

Sussman (1953) found that most middle-class parents and their married children develop a pattern of mutual aid in nursing care, house-repairing, planning vacations, and similar activities. The flow of aid, particularly financial aid, is chiefly from the parents to the children, especially in the early years of the latter's marriage. Parent's help their children to establish their homes and families; in return they expect their children to give them continued affection and personal help and attention, and to include them in some of their activities. Sussman and Burchinal (1962a) have constructed theories on the effects of parental aid to married children on the functioning of the family, but there have been no definitive studies in this area.

Both Sussman (1953) and Bell (1968) point out that young married middle-class couples find it important to avoid obligations and keep their independence. Parents, who are usually cognizant of this, find indirect ways of helping their married children; the most common method is to give gifts to their grandchildren and help with their educational expenses.[1]

Sussman (1965), in an extensive review of research on the relationships between adult children and their parents, states that the extended kin-family network is the basic social system in urban society. Parents, adult children, and grandchildren see each other frequently and help one another to meet the demands of everyday living. Additional research is needed to establish whether grandparents influence their grandchildren directly, or whether their influence is largely indirect (through their children in the middle generation).

Recently investigators have turned their attention to the study of the transmission of values, personality, and other characteristics from generation to generation within the family (Aldous, 1965; Aldous and Hill, 1965; Borke, 1963, 1967; Fengler and Wood, 1973; Fisher and Mendell, 1956; Hill, Foote, Aldous, Carlson, McDonald, 1970; Kalish and Johnson, 1972; Troll, Neugarten, and Kraines, 1969). The findings to date indicate that there is some similarity between parents and children, and perhaps even grandchildren, with regard to values and occupations. Faris (1947), focusing on the family as a central mechanism for the transmission of culture, maintained that the desire for continuity in families (that is, the passing on of family traditions and heirlooms from generation to generation) was widespread, though not universal. He discussed the intangible capital that the older members of families pass on to successive generations, a kind of folk wisdom whereby the young learn criteria of mate selection, methods of main-

---

[1]Bell (1968) has described, in detail, patterns of help and the avoidance of obligations in middle-class English families.

taining the authority necessary to rear children, and techniques for maintaining harmony and teamwork within a social group. Faris maintained that this heritage is very important to the maintenance of a successful family institution.

A study of extended families in which there are active grandparents and strong intergenerational bonds are compared with families in which intergenerational ties are weak or nonexistent may help to determine the value of these intergenerational links and the significance of the grandparent generation to the family system.

Significance of Grandparenthood to Children

Very few investigators have examined the grandparent-grandchild relationship, particularly as regards its meaning and significance for the grandchild. This lack of attention may reflect an implicit assumption that this relationship has little importance for either grandparents or grandchildren. In the past decade, however, the value of grandparents to children has been demonstrated outside the family. The Foster Grandparent Program has employed poverty-level retired persons to act as surrogate grandparents for emotionally deprived children in institutions. Such programs have been shown to alleviate some of the symptoms associated with emotional deprivation, such as social immaturity, depression, and poor intellectual functioning (Saltz, 1970).

Bekker and Taylor (1966) have explored what influence the number of generations in a young person's own family will have on his perceptions of old people. Their findings suggest that young people with grandparents and great-grandparents have fewer age prejudices than those who do not. Specifically, they found that young subjects who had living great-grandparents perceived their grandparents as having fewer characteristics of old age than did young people who had no living great-grandparents. There was no significant difference in the ages of the grandparents of the two groups.

The different meanings that grandparents have for children at different developmental ages (4–5, 8–9, 11–12) was examined by Kahana and Kahana (1970). The youngest group, they found, valued grandparents mainly for their indulgent qualities; the middle group preferred active, fun-sharing grandparents; and the oldest group appeared to have become distant from their grandparents. The authors concluded that as grandchildren grow up, they grow away from doting grandparents.

Divergent results were found in two studies that investigated the attitudes of adult grandchildren toward their grandparents. In one study (Robins and Tomanec, 1962), the respondents, who were mostly college students, reported that they felt closer to grandparents than to aunts, uncles, and cousins, while respondents in Adams' study (1968) ranked uncles and aunts slightly above grandparents and cousins. In a somewhat different vein, Looft (1971) asked respondents of different ages across the life span to name the principal source of knowledge on how to get along in the world (a) for the school-age child and (b) for the adolescent; respondents were then asked to name other important agents who help children and youth to grow into happy and competent adults. Parents were seen as the most important transmitters of information for children; peers, for adolescents. Of greatest interest in the present review is the fact that no mention at all was made of grandparents.

Gilford and Black (1972) attempted to learn whether the grandparent-grandchild relationship is based on ritual or affect. They focused on the relationship as perceived by the grandchild, in order to determine how young adult grandchildren develop positive sentiments for their grandparents. Their findings suggest that to some extent, feelings toward kin are transmitted from parent to child, and that even if the child has little opportunity to interact with grandparents, these feelings persist, even into the child's adulthood; this imparts a ritual quality to the grandchild-grandparent relationship. In contrast, if the grandparent and grandchild have an opportunity to develop an independent relationship, the transmitted feelings may be modified by their actual interpersonal interactions.

In summary, the quantity and quality of research, and the ambiguity and contradictory nature of the findings, make it impossible at this time to draw any substantive conclusions on the significance of grandparents to grandchildren. The changing status of grandparents, and the influence this will have on the grandparent-grandchild relationship, suggest that this will be an area of emerging interest in family research.

Significance of Grandparenthood to Adults

The few studies that have focused on grandparenthood itself do not give much information on what meaning and significance the role has for those adults who become grandparents.

Albrecht (1954), who studied a representative sample of old people in a small midwestern community, found that grandparents neither had nor desired responsibility toward their grandchildren. She found that they are not held responsible for the mistakes and shortcomings of their grandchildren or great-grandchildren, but they can bask in reflected glory when grandchildren achieve success.

On the basis of data from interviews with both the grandfather and the grandmother in 70 middle-class families, Neugarten and Weinstein (1964) determined the primary significance of grandparenthood for each of the 140 respondents. These were classified into five categories: (1) biological renewal and/or continuity; (2) emotional self-fulfillment; (3) service as a resource person to the child; (4) vicarious achievement through the child; and (5) remoteness—little effect on the self. Most of the grandparents were in the first, second, or fifth category. There was only one significant sex difference: a higher proportion of grandmothers than of grandfathers were in the biological renewal category. With regard to ease with which they performed the role, these investigators indicate that 60 per cent of the respondents found the grandparent role comfortable and pleasant. Nevertheless, approximately one-third experienced difficulty in the role, and expressed disappointment or referred to discomfort and strain or lack of positive rewards from the role.

Seemingly, grandparenthood is a relatively undemanding role; few, if any, clearcut demands are made on grandparents as a category. This very ambiguity may cause discomfort for some; on the other hand, Boyd (1969) suggests that the older person has an opportunity here to create a role that is valued by the family. Such a valued role must be learned, she maintains; it is not automatic and traditional, but is acquired and learned. Her advice for the person who wishes to become a valued grandparent is that he should learn to accept change, and should be able to relinquish the parent role with his children and enter into a new role with his grandchildren, a role that supplements the parental role and in no way conflicts or competes with it. Boyd's (1969) analysis of the characteristics of the valued grandparent are based on her studies of four-generation families in an urban community of 60,000 in the South.

It has been suggested that grandparenthood is one of the few "ready-made" roles available to the aging person at a point in his life cycle when his former roles are lost or decrease in significance. The question of whether the grandparent role becomes more salient when individuals retire, are widowed, or exist from other roles has been considered, but no definitive answer is available as yet.

Kahana and Coe (1969) were interested in whether grand-parenthood was an important source of gratification for older persons who lived in a home for the aged and had few opportunities to establish new role relationships. They report that 59 per cent of their institutionalized respondents derived little gratification from their grandparenthood (as compared to 21 per cent of a comparable community group that they studied). They conjecture that grandparents who live in the community use grandchildren to anchor themselves in the social structure on which they are losing hold; institutionalized grandparents, on the other hand, since they have disengaged from the social system, have little use for the social roles provided by grandparenthood (Kahana and Coe, 1969).

Lopata (1973), in a study of widows in Chicago, concluded that "grandmothers and grandchildren are not so frequently close and free of problems as idealized in the literature." Her study indicated that older widows found their relations with grandchildren significant only in cases where the social distance between the generations was decreased by frequent contacts, without interference from the middle generation. Apparently this is possible for only a minority of widows. Women who are widowed in middle age or earlier generally work, and probably have little time for grandchildren. The grandchildren of older widows, on the other hand, are apt to be adults who are involved in getting married and establishing their own families.

The situation for retired people is similar. Even if their grandchildren are not yet old enough to have children of their own, they are very likely to be at the adolescent stage, a period in which they are attempting to establish their independence from adults (among whom they presumably would include grandparents). It seems likely that teenagers would become more distant from grandparents; at any rate, the period that grandparents find most satisfying appears to be when the grandchildren are small. The role of great-grandparent is becoming increasingly available to older retired persons, but there is little indication that most older people find this any more than a symbolic role. The age gap is probably too wide to overcome, and in any case, older persons are apt to find the noise and activity of small children confusing and irritating.

In sum, research to date indicates that the grandparent role has only limited significance for most older persons. This is related to the changing family cycle, as a result of which grandparenthood has become a middle-age event and great-grandparenthood has emerged as a new old-age phenomenon. Parents of past generations, whose families were larger and more widely spaced (over a longer period of childbearing), were often actively engaged in parenting for most of their adult lives. Parents today are usually through the active phase of the role by their early fifties (Glick, 1955). According to Troll (1971), for the first time, grandparents, because they themselves have only a few, closely spaced children, "are truly grandparents in identity, and not also themselves parents of young children [p. 278]." If the latter is true, then the question arises of whether their identity shifts to that of great-grandparent as their grandchildren start families of their own, and whether they become more involved with their children's grandchildren and less with their own.

CURRENT RESEARCH

The writers have conducted a study[2] of the meaning and significance of grandparenthood to middle-aged and older adults in a predominantly stable working-class area of Madison, Wisconsin (population 173,000). The cross-sec-

[2] This study was partially supported by National Institute of Mental Health Small Grant MH 19773.

tional area probability sample consisted of 257 grandparents (125 women and 132 men). The sample of grandmothers were interviewed in their homes during the winter of 1970; the grandfathers, 42 of whom were husbands of grandmothers in the study, were interviewed in the spring and summer of 1971. The only limiting criteria for the sample were that the grandparents could not be living in the same household as their grandchildren, nor could they have acted as surrogate parents for their grandchildren.

The major characteristics of the respondents are shown in Table 14-I. In general, the average age of both grandfathers and grandmothers was approximately 65. The majority of the males were from skilled and semiskilled blue-collar occupations; over half were retired. Almost half of the grandmothers were widowed, as compared to less than eight per cent of the grandfathers. For the majority, education was limited to the high school level or less. They were predominantly Lutherans and Roman Catholics, of Germanic and Scandinavian backgrounds.

Most of the women had become grandmothers in their forties, while most of the men had become grandfathers in their late forties and early fifties. We found a few who had first become grandparents in their thirties, and a few in their sixties. But for the most part, the grandparent role is first assumed in early middle age. At the time of the study nearly two-thirds of the women and over half of the men had been grandparents for fifteen years or more. Most of the respondents had had two or three children of their own, and the average number of grandchildren was six. (While a few grandparents had 20 or more grandchildren, most had two to four.) The ages of the grandchildren ranged from infancy to adulthood; the majority were of school age. Well over a quarter of the women and a fifth of the men had great-grandchildren.

The focus of the study was on the grandparents' con-

Table 14-I

SOCIAL AND DEMOGRAPHIC CHARACTERISTICS
OF GRANDPARENTS, BY SEX

	Grandfathers (132)		Grandmothers (125)	
	N	%	N	%
Age				
40-49	5	3.8	11	8.8
50-59	36	27.3	33	26.4
60-69	47	35.6	34	27.2
70-79	32	24.2	38	30.4
80 and older	12	9.1	9	7.2
Marital status				
married	118	89.4	59	47.2
widowed	10	7.6	51	40.8
divorced/separated	4	3.0	15	12.0
Education				
college	23	17.3	11	8.8
9-12 grades	56	42.4	66	52.8
0-8 grades	52	39.5	48	38.4
not ascertained	1	0.8	0	0.0
Religion				
Roman Catholic	38	28.8	38	30.4
Protestant-Lutheran	55	41.7	53	42.4
Protestant-other	31	23.4	31	24.8
none	6	4.6	3	2.4
not ascertained	2	1.5	0	0.0
Work Status				
employed	58	43.9	54	43.2
looking for work	6	4.5	1	0.8
retired	68	51.6	22	17.6
housewife	—	—	48	38.4
Number of grandchildren				
1-3	54	40.9	44	35.2
4-6	25	19.0	24	19.2
7-9	22	16.7	24	19.2
10-12	14	10.5	17	13.6
13-15	7	5.3	6	4.8
16 or more	10	7.6	10	8.0
Number of great-grandchildren				
none	107	81.2	88	70.4
1-4	21	15.8	18	14.4
5-8	2	1.5	10	8.0
9-12	2	1.5	5	4.0
13 or more	0	0.0	4	3.2

Age became a grandparent

31-38	2	1.5	7	5.6
39-46	33	25.0	47	37.6
47-54	58	43.9	50	40.1
55-62	32	24.3	20	16.0
63 and older	6	4.6	1	0.8
not ascertained	1	0.7	—	—

ceptions[3] of their roles, which we saw as having two components: (1) the ideational, the individual's subjective evaluation and description of the role; and (2) the behavioral, the way the person actually enacts the role. The analytic framework drew upon a combination of the theory of action (Parsons and Shils, 1951) and interactionist theory (Mead, 1934); the former was used to examine role behavior, and the latter to measure the meaning of the role. It was reasoned that individuals have conceptions of the meaning of a role which are distinct from and precede behavior in that role. These orientations toward a role that the individual may expect to assume eventually are the product of anticipatory socialization.

Meaning of the Grandparent Role

The concept of the meaning of the grandparent role used in the study is based on the belief that attitudes and expectations on the role derive from two major sources: those that are determined almost exclusively by social or normative forces, and meet the needs of society, and those that stem from personal forces within the individual, and meet his needs. We therefore examined the meaning of the role within the context of two independent, but not mutually exclusive dimensions, based on these two sources: we

[3]For a more detailed description of the theoretical framework and methodology used in the study, see Robertson (1971) and Robertson and Wood (1970, 1973).

labeled one of these a social dimension, and the other a personal one.

On the basis of exploratory interviews, we devised a series of Likert-type items to tap these two dimensions, and established their independence through factor analysis. The set of items that fell within the first factor, items that indicated how the meaning of the grandparent role was conceived in normative terms, were used to measure each respondent's position on the social dimension; the items that fell within the second factor, which showed the personal meaning of the role, were used to measure the position of respondents on the personal dimension. The median score for each set of items was used as a cut-off point, to divide respondents into high and low categories on each dimension. Grandparents high on both dimensions were assigned to the apportioned type; those low on both dimensions, to the remote type. Individuals who were high on the personal but low on the social dimension were seen as being the individualized type, while the opposite—those high on the social but low on the personal dimension—were seen as the symbolic type. Use of these procedures resulted in the distribution of the grandparents among the role types shown in Figure 14–I.

The scores on the social dimension all tended to be quite high, which suggested that almost all the grandparents accepted the normative, perhaps somewhat stereotyped ideas on the meaning of grandparenthood. On the other hand, scores on the personal dimension were lower on the whole, and were spread over a wider range. In the light of the above, division of the respondents into high and low categories above and below the median of the social dimension scores may not be particularly meaningful. Consequently no major differences would be expected between the apportioned and individualized types, or between the symbolic and remote types. Rather, the major differences would be between the apportioned and individualized

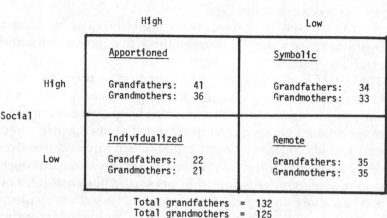

Fig. 14–I. Types of role meaning for grandparents.

types on the one hand, and the symbolic and remote types on the other. Subsequently, when respondents in the different role categories are compared, we will return to this point.

Findings

Several variables were examined in the analysis of role types: work status, marital status, education, age, the level of involvement with friends and in community organizations, the number of grandchildren, the number of activities with grandchildren, and the age at which the grandparent role was assumed. There were significant differences between the role types in four of these variables: age, education, the number of grandchildren, and the number of activities with grandchildren. These variables are interrelated to some extent, in that older persons have less education than younger ones (in line with historical trends). Furthermore, the older individuals usually had more grandchildren on the average; the younger ones probably did not yet have all the grandchildren they would eventually have. In addition, the number of activities with grandchildren was related to some degree to the number of grandchildren.

In general, grandparents from the apportioned and individualized groups were older and less well educated, had more grandchildren, and engaged in a greater number of activities with them. Another factor related to age was that a smaller proportion of grandparents from these two categories were still working (38 per cent, compared to 49 per cent). As we predicated earlier, on the basis that scores on the social dimension for all respondents were uniformly high, there were only minor differences between grandparents from the apportioned and the individualized role categories. (Respondents from both groups scored high on the personal dimension, it will be remembered.) Those in the former group were slightly younger on average than those in the individualized category, yet the average number of grandchildren for the apportioned group was the highest of all groups (but not significantly higher than the average for the individualized category).

When the two groups in which respondents scored low on the personal dimension are compared, the differences noted are that those in the symbolic group have a lower mean age and are slightly more involved in community organizations and with friends than are the remote group. The major difference, however, is that grandparents in the remote group, even though they have a higher number of grandchildren on the average, engage in significantly fewer activities with them.

The fact that respondents who place a high emphasis on the personal dimension have a greater number of activities with their grandchildren suggests there is a relationship between the two. As individuals have increased experience with the grandparent role, they may attach a

Table 14-II

SCORES ON PERSONAL DIMENSION
BY LEVEL OF GRANDPARENT ROLE ACTIVITY
(N = 257)

Number of Activities with Grandchildren	Mean Score on Personal Dimension
Low (0-4)	19.8
Medium (5-7)	21.1
High (8-13)	22.5

F ratio = 19.01 $P < .001$

more highly personal significance to the role. This is exemplified in the responses of two grandparents. A 77-year-old grandparent in the symbolic category (in which respondents place high emphasis on the social dimension but little on the personal dimension) said, "We want our grandchildren to get a good education, to be good, clean people, good workers as they grow up. . . . A good grandparent is to be a real Christian, set examples, practice what you preach." The opposite attitude of the individualized group (grandparents who emphasize the personal and have little concern for normative proscriptions) is best typified in the comments of another individual who said of the grandchildren: "They've helped me forget that I'm getting older—they keep me from getting lonesome—they help me forget my problems."

Further evidence that additional experience in the grandparent role may lead to greater emphasis on the personal significance of grandparenthood is presented in Table 14-II. It will be noted that the higher the number of grandparental activities, the higher the score is on the personal dimension.

Individuals with higher activity levels also had a greater number of grandchildren on the average; they were also older at the time of the study and had become grandparents at a younger age than had individuals with lower activity levels.

Grandparenthood and Life Satisfaction

The grandparent role is often seen as one of the few new roles available in later life, at a time when most individuals undergo major role losses (chiefly widowhood and retirement). All the respondents in our study had assumed the role, but they were involved in the role to different extents, placed different degrees of emphasis on the personal significance of grandparenthood. We wanted to find out whether these differences were related to general life satisfaction.[4] First of all, the levels of grandparent role activities and life satisfaction were not related at a statistically significant level, although the more involved grandparents did tend to have slightly higher levels of life satisfaction. The more involved grandparents also had slightly more friends and were more active in community organizations than the less involved grandparents. Moreover, there was a very definite and positive relationship between the amount of activity in friendship and organizational roles and life satisfaction. This supports Blau's contention (1973) that an older person who has a single good friend is more able to cope with old age than one who has a dozen grandchildren but no peer-group friends.

Among the role types, the average life satisfaction was somewhat lower in the remote group than in the other three groups: the mean LSI-Z scores were 9.77 for the apportioned group, 9.75 for the symbolic group, 9.57 for the individualized group, and 8.51 for the remote group. Thus life satisfaction was as high for the symbolic group, who placed little emphasis on the personal dimension of grandparenthood, as for the two groups (apportioned and individualized) who placed high emphasis on this dimension; this suggests that the degree of emphasis on the per-

[4]Life satisfaction or morale was measured by the 13-item LSI-Z (Wood, Wylie, and Sheafor, 1969).

sonal elements of grandparenthood does not account for the significantly lower general life satisfaction of grandparents in the remote group. Apart from their lower levels of life satisfaction and less involvement with grandchildren (Table 14–II), this group was quite similar to the symbolic group and differed further from the apportioned and individualized groups only in the degree of emphasis they placed on the personal dimension. It has been speculated elsewhere (Robertson, 1971) that grandparents in the remote category were somewhat different personality types, who were generally impersonal, distant, and slightly ritualistic in all their interpersonal contacts. This might account for both their distant relationship with their grandchildren and their general dissatisfaction with life.

It could be asked why activity in the grandparent role, which is so universally lauded by grandparents themselves, was generally unrelated to life satisfaction. First, grandparenthood should probably be added to motherhood and country as sacrosanct terms, concepts that one cannot criticize. Secondly, there are probably strictures on the grandparent role, the existence of which older people are reluctant to admit, perhaps even to themselves, but which interfere with their enjoyment of the role.

Blau (1973) claims that older persons are really "outsiders" in relation to their adult children's families, and try to camouflage this by pretending that intimacy exists. She describes their "outsider" status thus: "The old have neither the prerogatives nor the responsibilities of full-fledged nuclear unit membership. They cannot disturb their children's families, or offer advice, or get involved in disputes. They may, upon request, perform such services as baby-sitting [p. 53]." Like Rosow (1967), she questions whether surveys that report older persons' frequent contacts with their adult children and their families really convey anything about the actual nature of the relationships involved.

In our study, when we asked grandparents about their conception of a good grandparent, the vast majority of both grandfathers and grandmothers described a good grandparent as someone who loves and enjoys their grandchildren and helps them out when they can. Although they generally avoided discussing negative attributes, one in five of the grandmothers specifically mentioned that a good grandparent should not interfere with his or her grandchildren's lives or upbringing. This idea was expressed thus by one woman whose grandchildren lived next door:

> You have to be careful not to get too tied up in your grandchildren, as it isn't good for you or for them. We go to Florida three or four months of the year, so I guess we have a built-in protector against seeing them too much or stepping into their lives too far.

In Lopata's study (1973), a few of the older widows "bluntly stated that their own children would not let them get close to the grandchildren [p. 172]." She speculated that tension in relations with the middle generation may often prevent a satisfactory relationship from developing between grandparents and grandchildren. Studies conducted at the University of Wisconsin at Madison indicate that the parent generation acts as mediators between the first and third generations (Kennedy and Pfeifer, 1973; Robertson, 1971); we plan to investigate the significance of this in subsequent studies.

While grandparents verbally attribute a great deal of significance to the role in discussions and interviews, the behavior of most grandparents in the role is relatively limited. It is true that most of them baby-sit, take their grandchildren to the zoo, movies, and so on, read to and play with them, give them gifts, and remember their birthdays, but for most grandparents these activities occur only a few times a year. Less than half of the grandparents reported that they had told their grandchildren about family history and customs, or had taught them a special skill such as sewing, cooking, fishing, or a craft.

In summary, despite their lack of involvement in grandparent activities and the lack of effect that the role apparently had on their general morale, it is not possible to dismiss the importance of the grandparent role for most older adults. Grandchildren appear to be significant to older individuals because they provide primary group reference. If, as Rosow (1967) contends, "relations to children are by far the most emotionally charged area of life, one fraught with anxiety, subject to distortion and denial, about which [older people] constantly try to reassure themselves," older people may see the grandparent role as at least one socially acceptable avenue through which they can involve themselves in their children's families. Perhaps they are content to be without the usual parental responsibilities of child rearing, and to view their grandchildren as untapped resources, whom they can talk and boast about when they achieve, and ignore when they do not. Overall, grandparents do not seem to expect tangible commitments from their grandchildren; they appear to be content if their grandchildren give them a modicum of interest and concern, however ritualistic or superficial this may be.

CONCLUSION

Additional research is needed on the significance of grandparenthood in modern society. As we indicated earlier, when we ask about the significance of grandparenthood, we have to designate from whose perspective we are asking the question. Kahana and Kahana (1971) have delineated some of the theoretical and research issues involved in the study of grandparenthood from the grandparent's and from the grandchild's perspectives. There is the additional perspective of the family. What difference does it make whether grandparents are available in an extended family? Do families function better with or without them? The suggestion was made that comparative studies of families with and without active grandparents could be carried out.[5] Similarly, comparative studies could be made of children who do and do not have grandparents available, and of older persons who do and do not have grandchildren.

This is closely related to the relative importance of friends and the family in old age. A number of investigators (for example, Shanas et al., 1968) regard family relationships as of prime importance. On the other hand, Blau (1973) maintains that children cannot be counted on for continued emotional commitment of a steady and general nature. Instead, she says, the older person "must seek restitution for work, for marriage, and for his children among comtemporaries who share his needs, his interests, and his attitudes [p. 56]." (See also Gibson, 1972.) Rosenberg (1970), on the basis of his study of working-class families, has also raised questions about the viability of kinship networks beyond the domestic unit. Sussman (1965) seemingly laid the issue to rest with his statement that "the isolated nuclear family is a myth," a question that "does not merit any further attention of the field," but questions still remain regarding the quality of the relationship between older persons and their adult children, and the meaning of the relationship to the older person.

Another important subject (virtually ignored in family research to date) is the role that parents play as intergenerational mediators in three-generation families. Apparently their role to a large extent conditions the nature of the grandparent-grandchild relationship, but we have no

[5]The dearth of research on family functioning is probably due to the lack of (a) adequate criteria of good as compared with poor functioning, and (b) methods of studying the family as a unit.

knowledge of the degree to which parents make this influence felt, or the mechanisms by which they do it.

Finally, we urgently need to understand how the changing family cycle is influencing the grandparent. Although it is recognized that most persons now become grandparents in middle age or earlier, grandparenthood is still largely seen as an old-age role. This is partly because most research on grandparenthood has been done within the context of studies of aging *per se*. What does it mean to become a grandparent when one is young and fully involved in other social roles, particularly work? It is somewhat paradoxical that grandparenthood first comes when the individual is busy and involved, and subsequently, when he has major role losses and plenty of time for grandparenthood, this role may have lost its salience; the opportunity to develop a meaningful relationship may have long since passed.

These are only a few of the major issues that need investigation. They show that this area of research is important for developmental psychology, sociology, family research, and gerontology. One hopes that such research will not be conducted in separate compartments by these specialities; rather it appears to be a fertile field for interdisciplinary efforts.

chapter 15

Family Structure and Residential Patterns of the Widowed in Israel

ALBERT CHEVAN
J. HENRY KORSON

The conjugal family system has historically fostered fairly narrow definitions of the living arrangements favored or desired by its members. Upon marriage, blood and affinal relatives in such a system are expected to maintain separate households, at distances that vary by society, and within a given society by social background. Not that extended family living arrangements are proscribed or unheard of in a conjugal family society, but they deviate from the preferred or normative patterns, and are therefore usually considered temporary arrangements. The conjugal

This paper is part of a continuing study of the widowed population in Israel as well as the United States. Financial support was made possible by grant 10–P–57331/1–01 from the Social Security Administration of the Department of Health, Education and Welfare. The authors acknowledge with thanks the assistance of Moishe Sicron and Zvi Eisenbach, who made the Israeli data available. Thanks are also due to Eleanor Weber for her devoted technical assistance.

This paper is an expanded version of one presented at the annual meeting of the American Sociological Association in August, 1974 in Montreal.

family household usually contains both parents and their young, unmarried children.

Family formation, parenthood, aging, and the dissolution processes of divorce and/or death intervene to alter the membership of the household, so that its composition is not static for very long. In order to develop a composite theory of the conjugal family system, it is necessary to include the living arrangements of single adults, the divorced or separated (with or without children), and the widowed. Indeed, an examination of the living arrangements of these marital status groups (particularly the widowed) in the course of the family cycle form a critical test of the nature of family systems. All three groups may nominally lay claim to nuclear dyadic family bonds between parent and child or between siblings, but only when family norms support such claims. Under an extended family system, norms exist according to which these groups are incorporated into household living arrangements with close relatives. They are not expected to maintain separate households, and may be enjoined to live with specific close relatives such as parents, children, or siblings. In a conjugal family system no such attitude exists. It is the acceptance or shedding of the "responsibility" for these three marital status groups that in part marks the difference between the two systems, and the change from one family system to another.

The aging process creates widowed groups in all societies, and internal interaction processes within the family, as well as those outside the family, contribute to the establishment of their living arrangements. As a result, significant changes in the number of widowed, and especially in the living arrangements of the widowed, occurred in the United States between 1940 and 1970. In a previous study by the authors (Chevan and Korson, 1972, p. 46), it was found that within the span of one generation (1940–70), the proportion of the widowed in the United States who lived alone had increased dramatically from 19.6 per cent to 49.8 per cent. The increase was uneven, and the different living arrangements appeared to be dependent upon several demographic and social factors. Income and cultural background (in that order), among all the variables, appear most to influence the decision to live alone.

The American family system presents a limited case of the fate of the widowed, and some have argued that it presents an extreme case (Berardo, 1968; Lopata, 1973; Troll, 1971). Conclusions drawn from the American family experience may indicate the impingement of unique social and economic forces on the American family, and are not necessarily true of families in other, more traditional societies. At the very least, studies of the widowed in other societies will provide some useful comparative perspectives from which to view some aspects of the changing structure of the family. Factors that appear to operate in the American family scene may be less important under other family systems, while elsewhere other factors may be of greater consequence.

In Israel, Arab and Jewish family laws emphasize the property rights of the surviving spouse. Although the vast majority of Arab Moslem families in Israel are of the conjugal type, the tradition that the extended family of three or more generations lives in one household is still very strong. Furthermore, kin ties are undoubtedly stronger among Arab families than among Jewish families, since the latter largely originated in Western Europe, and are closer to the nuclear type in ethos. The Koran makes no statement about the residence of a widowed person, but appears to be concerned only with the *property rights* of a widowed person, and spells out very carefully the division of such property. Dawood's translation of the Koran (1956) puts it thus:

> You shall inherit the half of your wives' estate if they die childless. If they leave children, a quarter of their entire

estate shall be given after payment of their debts and any
legacies they may have bequeathed. Your wives shall inherit
one quarter of your estate if you die childless. If you leave
children, they shall inherit one-eighth, after payment of your
debts and any legacies you may have bequeathed. [p. 356]

In the same manner, various shares of an estate are
carefully spelled out under various sets of conditions, so
that disagreements among heirs are reduced to a minimum.
Also, a son will receive twice as much as a daughter. The
assumption here is that a woman will always be cared for
by her husband, brother, or other male relative. Furthermore, the extended kin group among Moslems probably
has few counterparts in Western societies. For example, the
ancient Persian term *biraderi* (broder, brotherhood), which
is much used in Moslem societies, refers to one's kin ties
based on blood relationship "as far as one recognizes a
blood relative" (Wakil, 1970). The ethos of such cognitive
feelings is almost tribal among Moslems, since theoretically
one ultimately traces one's ancestry to a tribal chief. Moslems have always felt strongly about blood ties, more so
than members of most other religious communities. Although the constraints of *purdah* vary widely in different
Moslem societies, it generally limits women's participation
in the labor force, so that their economic dependence on
male relatives continues throughout life. For this reason,
then, a widow, in particular, would expect to return to her
father's household if he is still alive, or to the household of
the oldest brother who has, in all likelihood, become the
family head. If neither of these alternatives exists, the
widow (or widower) would expect to join the household of
another male relative.[1] In such a highly patriarchal society,
the woman continues to look to her father, brother, or

[1]Although the *Koran* does not specifically state that a widowed or divorced
woman will return to the household of her father or that of her (oldest) brother,
this long-established custom in Moslem societies has been the normative pattern.

some other male blood relative in times of difficulty. For example, Goode (1963) states that a woman might go "to stay in her father's or brother's house as a result of a quarrel with her husband [p. 393]."

Although they are entitled to one-half of the share of a brother's inheritance, Arab Moslem women will in almost every instance surrender such rights to their brothers in exchange for the lifelong protection guaranteed to them in their deceased father's household. This protection includes the right of return to that household in the event of ill-treatment by her husband, divorce from him, or his death. The young widow must return to her father's house to be remarried, while the widow with unmarried sons may remain in her deceased husband's home. She may have to fend off the claims of her husband's family on his property, but this is no problem for the strong-willed woman, because the bulk of the inheritance is in her sons' names.

Jewish family law is similar to Arab family law in that it ignores the living arrangements of the widower, and assumes that in a patriarchal society he can provide for himself. A widow's rights are provided for in her *Ketubbah*, the marriage contract, which, if well written, guarantees that she will be maintained from her husband's estate. In all likelihood the agreement entitles her to continue to live in her home after her husband's death (*Jewish Encyclopedia*, 1905: XII, p. 515). "You shall dwell in my home and be maintained in it out of my estate throughout the duration of your widowhood" was a familiar insertion in the marriage contract in ancient Jerusalem and Galilee, although it was not universal. The practice of the marriage contract was continued until recently; it has receded as marriage by individual choice has supplanted marriage by family choice among Western Jews. Although some of the widowed Jewish subjects of this study may have a traditional Ketubbah (this includes Oriental Jews, among whom the practice was widespread until recently) it is highly unlikely that their children will have such a document, unless they belong to one of the orthodox communities. Israeli law recognizes the Ketubbah as a valid document in those cases where it exists, but in its absence civil law provides for the widow in the spirit of the Ketubbah.

Arab and Jewish family laws specify the *means* by which the widow should live, rather than with whom she should live. Because the Arab female is under the protection of her father's family throughout her lifetime, she may return to her father's or a brother's household. In many cases this is a short trip, because marriages are generally contracted locally and the family will be close at hand. Residential propinquity is one of the hallmarks of the Moslem extended family (Korson, 1968). Village as well as clan endogamy is widely practiced among the Arabs of Israel, and Baer (1944), in a study of five Palestinian villages, found that 73.5 per cent of all marriages were contracted between families in the same village. *Ird,* or family honor, forbids a young woman to live alone and places her under the protection of her family.

The ethnic-religious families of Israel may be placed along the traditional-modern continuum, as Bar Yosef and Shelach have indeed done (1970). Rural Arab Moslems and Western Jews represent the poles at the ends of a continuum; somewhere between them are the Oriental Jews. The placing of Arab Christians and Israeli Jews is difficult, because they have some characteristics of both the rural Arab Moslems and the Western Jews.[2]

Factors that seem to contribute to the modernization of the family (in this investigation interpreted as a situation in which the widowed can live alone) will be weighed. Urban residence, participation in the labor force, educational achievement, reduced fertility, and age at marriage have all

[2]A sample of 145 Druze is available. They are included in Table 15–I, but are not included in later discussion.

been associated with the spread of the conjugal family system. Three other factors investigated (age, sex, and the number of times married) are more representative of the internal dynamics of family living and opportunity structures for the widowed.

Several possible living arrangements are available to the widowed in this study: (1) they may continue to live in the home they were in at the death of their spouse, either alone or (2) with others; (3) they may move, to live either alone or (4) with others. There are family constraints in some situations, and children, parents, or other relatives may not be available to offer a household to the widow. Constraints are also imposed by the housing market. In a country that is hard-pressed to meet the housing demand, persons who desire to live alone may have to compete in the private and public housing sectors with families that have greater social and monetary resources. Israeli houses and apartments are usually small and overcrowded, and in some circumstances it may be considered burdensome to fit another person in. In this study, the 192 widowed who are living in a Kibbutz, or collective settlement, are part of a local housing market in which living arrangements are determined by a housing committee.

The data for this study are from the B sample of the Israeli Census of 1961. This sample included 15,759 widowed, which represented 20 per cent of the 1961 widowed population of Israel. The data are in most respects compararable to the Public Use Samples issued by the United States Bureau of the Census, and were obtained from the Israel Central Bureau of Statistics. They include data on all members of the household, as well as on the widowed members themselves.

There is an aspect of living arrangements that the cross-sectional data gathered by a census cannot capture. Families are dynamic as they go through the life cycle, and even in societies that have static family systems, this dynamism continues on into widowhood. The children of those who are widowed at a young age may eventually leave the household, perhaps to return at a later point in time. Physical capacities change with age, and adjustments made at one point in time may later prove inadequate, which will prompt changes in the living arrangements. Cross-sectional data indicate only the life-cycle changes, which are intertwined through the age variable with broader social changes.

The living arrangements of six ethnic-religious groups are presented in Table 15–I. Two important features of these arrangements differ considerably among the six ethnic-religious groups: the percentage who are living in households, and the position of the widowed within the households. Western and Israeli Jews utilize institutional and Kibbutz living arrangements to a greater extent than the other four ethnic-religious groups. Less than one per cent of the non-Jews are found in institutions, and, as might be expected, there are none in a Kibbutz. Individuals in traditionally oriented societies, either from choice or necessity, have no alternative to living in a family situation. In such societies, the family serves as a nursing home and/or old-age home.

Among the household population, the widowed preponderantly have the position either of household head or of a parent. The widowed who are living as a son or daughter, other relative, or an unrelated individual constitute no more than 11.1 per cent of the widowed population in any group, and only 6.4 per cent of the widowed in all groups combined. Among Arab Christians, 95.7 per cent are either a household head or a parent, and in no group does this combination represent less than 85 per cent of the widowed population. Some Arab widowed may return home to live with a brother's family. The percentage of widowed who are living as "another" relative (which includes the relationship of sister) is not dominant, however. Thus, the

Table 15-I
LIVING ARRANGEMENTS AND RELATIONSHIPS OF WIDOWED
Percentage per Ethnic-Religious Group*

Living Arrangement and Relationship	Total	Oriental Jew	Western Jew	Israeli Jew	Arab Moslem	Arab Christian	Druze
Total	100.0	100.0	100.0	100.0	100.0	100.0	100.0
In household	93.6	97.3	90.3	91.9	99.0	99.4	100.0
Head	48.2	40.8	52.1	62.8	49.6	53.1	45.5
alone	23.4	12.9	30.3	28.0	21.4	17.3	26.2
not alone	24.8	27.9	21.8	34.8	28.2	35.8	19.3
Others	45.4	56.5	38.2	29.1	49.4	46.3	55.5
parent	39.1	48.8	32.8	25.0	40.9	42.6	43.7
of Head	25.5	36.9	16.1	16.9	38.4	38.9	39.3
of Wife	13.6	11.9	16.7	8.1	2.5	3.7	4.4
son or daughter	1.3	1.5	1.0	3.0	2.3	0.0	2.8
other relative	4.5	5.9	3.5	1.0	5.9	3.1	8.3
unrelated	0.6	0.3	0.8	0.0	0.3	0.6	0.0
Institutional residence	5.2	2.4	7.7	6.4	0.9	0.6	0.0
Kibbutz	1.2	0.3	2.0	1.7	0.0	0.0	0.0
Average household size	3.6	4.5	2.7	3.0	4.5	4.5	4.5
Numbers	15,759	5,446	8,528	296	1,020	324	145

* Adapted from the "B" sample of the Census of Israel (1961).

return of the Arab widow to the patriarchal household, while it may occasionally occur, is far from being the rule.

The division of parents into two groups, parents of the household head or parents of the wife of the household head, reveals patterns that are not unexpected on the basis of our knowledge of the Arab and Western family. The Western Jew follows more closely the egalitarian Western family ideal, which does not favor children of one sex over those of the other. The Western Jew is about as frequently an in-law in the household of a daughter and son-in-law as a parent in a household headed by a son or daughter. The Arab and Druze widowed try to avoid the in-law situation, (although not completely); they generally live with a son or, less frequently, a daughter. This is not surprising, because residence is patrilocal and the Arab wife is considered an outsider by the husband's family. Under most circumstances, it would be thought inappropriate for the wife to invite her mother or father to join the household. The Israeli Jew tends to follow the Western model, and the Oriental Jew the Arab model.

Data on all members of the household are available in the sample; they provide the opportunity to observe the characteristics of the household as a whole. In those households in which the widowed person lives as a parent, the percentages in which daughter is present as household head or wife of the household head are as follows: Western Jew, 55.8; Israeli Jew, 41.9; Oriental Jew, 28.7; Arab Christian, 12.3; Druze, 9.5; Arab Moslem, 6.9. Family norms clearly reach into widowhood and direct the choice of living arrangements, including the choice of the child with whom the widowed person may dwell. Furthermore, a household in which a widow is living as a parent raises the image of a traditional three-generation extended family household. In three-quarters of all such households, the image is correct. In such households, the characteristics of other household members deeply affect the activities, opportunities, and social relations of the widowed person. It is impossible to say to what extent the prospects of living in a three-generation household and fulfilling a grandparent role enter into the decision to live as a parent, but it is undoubtedly a factor in some decisions.

In a similar vein, 86.0 per cent of all household heads who are not living alone have one or more children in the household. It is of interest to note that the more traditional the ethnic-religious group, the larger the average size of the household. The Arab Moslems, Arab Christians, Druze, and Oriental Jews have an average of 4.5 persons per household, while the average for the Israeli Jews is 3.0 and the Western Jews have the lowest average, 2.7. The presence and ages of children are elements of the situation that are taken into account when a separate household is maintained. The age of the other persons in the household appears important only in those few households in which the widowed person is not related to the head. In only 8.0 per cent of the households in which the widowed are not alone is there at least one other person within ten years of the widowed person's age; this contrasts with 63.0 per cent of the "unrelated" households, and 39.0 per cent of the "other-related" households. Households in which such an age relationship exists may well be companionate households, in which individuals of similar interests, circumstances, and characteristics are found. Further support for this idea is provided by the presence of two or more widowed persons in a household. One out of ten of the widowed is in a household that contains two or more widowed, but the concentration increases sharply in households of the "unrelated" and "other-related" types (to levels of 53 and 30 per cent respectively). Companionate households are surrogates for family living, and are rarely found in Israel. They do, however, illustrate one basis for the living arrangements of the widowed.

In Table 15–I, household heads have been divided

according to the absence or presence of other persons in the household. The division of the widowed into those who live alone and those who live with others, whatever their position in the household, is the major concern of this study. Clearcut differences are evident between the various ethnic religious groups with regard to the "alone" status. Western Jews are least likely to live with others present in a household, while Oriental Jews are most likely. About 17 percentage points separate the two groups. These differences are also reflected in the average size of the household for each group, also shown in Table 15–I. The tendency of the Western Jew to live alone is not unexpected, but the relatively large number of Arab Moslems who also do so is not in keeping with our conception of the traditional Arab family. As Bastuni has observed (1973, p. 415), the Palestinian Arab Moslem family may be a transitional family.

MULTIPLE CLASSIFICATION ANALYSIS

Having shown that one factor, the ethnic-religious factor, influences the living arrangements of the widowed, we must now introduce other factors into this analysis, and narrow the focus to one living arrangement—that of living alone. In this analysis we wish to establish the effects of several factors, some of which may be labeled demographic, and others as emerging from the modernization of the family. By including the ethnic-religious variable among our factors, we will be able to place it in proper perspective, and ascertain its meaning in the context of family modernization.

Theoretical considerations and previous research indicate that family modernization is dependent upon several interrelated factors. By itself, any one of these factors may be a weak predictor of living arrangements among the widowed. When added together or combined, however, they may reveal much about living arrangements. The statistical

Table 15-II

MULTIPLE CLASSIFICATION ANALYSIS
OF THE PERCENTAGE OF WIDOWS WHO LIVE ALONE*

Variable	Number	Percentage who Live Alone Unadjusted	Adjusted	Beta Coefficient
Children ever born:				.235
0	906	60.7	56.2	
1	1567	33.3	29.0	
2 or 3	3768	25.1	22.4	
4 or more	5828	14.3	18.0	
Ethnic-religious group:				.141
Oriental Jew	4494	12.2	16.0	
Western Jew	6251	32.4	28.7	
Israeli Jew	228	30.3	28.9	
Arab Moslem	835	20.6	26.4	
Arab Christian	261	16.5	20.5	
Age:				.136
Under 60	4505	20.0	17.5	
60-74	5446	29.2	29.9	
75 or more	2118	17.3	20.5	
Participation in labor force:				.071
In labor force	2059	34.6	30.3	
Not in labor force	10010	21.4	22.3	
Residence:				.062
Large city	4898	30.2	26.9	
Small city	5245	19.9	21.4	
Rural	1926	17.3	21.6	
Years of education:				.059
0	5667	16.4	23.1	
1-8	4061	25.3	21.6	
9 or more	2341	38.4	28.5	
Times married:				.055
1	10801	22.7	22.9	
2 or more	1268	31.5	30.4	
Age at first marriage:				.032
Under 20	3816	19.0	25.5	
20-24	3870	23.9	22.2	
25 or more	4383	27.5	23.3	
Multiple correlation coefficient		.372		

* Adapted from the "B" sample of the Census of Israel (1961).

technique chosen for this investigation, multiple classification analysis (MCA), is designed to examine the relationship between several independent variables and a
dependent variable. It has several features that are useful

for the purposes of this study: (1) the model is additive in the sense of the classical regression model; (2) the technique uses predictors with nominal measurement, such as the ethnicity-religion or sex; (3) interrelationships between various predictors, and between predictors and dependent variables, may take any form—this is crucial for the age variable, which has a curvilinear relationship to living alone; (4) the technique yields useful statistics through which to interpret the effects of predictor variables, singly and together, and of categories within the predictor variables; and (5) the dependent variable may be in dichotomous form (for example, living alone or not living alone).

Several variables considered in this study are interrelated. By statistically controlling for the effects of copredictors, MCA has the capacity to assess the contribution of each variable to the levels of the dependent variable.

The major analyses are contained in Tables 15–II and 15–III. Rather than presenting the effects of the various categories of a variable as deviations from the mean percentage who are living alone, we have chosen to present the percentage who are living alone both before adjusting for the effects of other variables, and after adjustment. The percentage referred to throughout the analysis will be the adjusted figure. The partial beta coefficient is included in the tables. It permits one to assess the relative influence of each predictor (Andrews, Morgan, and Sonquist, 1967). Beta squared is a measure of the number of standard deviation units that the dependent variable moves when the predictor changes by one standard deviation. The Druze are omitted from Tables 15–II and 15–III, because the Druze sample was small, and only the household population was considered. In a census, the number of children ever born is a concept usually applied to females, and the figures are not available for males. The figures in Tables 15–II and 15–III, therefore, apply only to the children of the female population.[3] Tests of significance indicate the ability of a factor to contribute significantly to the prediction of the numbers living alone, after the effects of other factors have been taken into account. In Table 15–III the ethnic-religious factor is dropped from the prediction scheme and five analyses are presented, one for each ethnic-religious group. The logic of this analytic design will become apparent. The eight variables of Table 15–II have been ordered according to their relative ability to influence the numbers living alone.

The outstanding influence on whether a widow lives alone is the number of children born to her. There is a strong inverse association between the number of children ever born and whether a widow lives alone. Among childless women, 56.2 per cent live alone, while among widows who have borne children, 29.0 per cent of those with one child live alone, 22.4 per cent of those with two or three children live alone, and 18.0 per cent of those with four or more children live alone. The traditional family view that children are a source of support has usually been stated with old age in mind. By their very existence, children would seem to lend social support to the widowed, and probably emotional support as well. The majority of the widowed (66 per cent) had one or more children present in the household. When we note that for all but the Western Jew, the median number of children ever borne was 5.0 or more, the traditional view of the function of children appears to be fulfilled. Among Western Jews the median was 2.8 children per woman; hence they had fewer opportunities to live with children by reason of their smaller families.

[3]An MCA analysis in which sex is used as a predictor variable in addition to all the other variables in Table 15–II (except number of children) indicates that sex is a poor and statistically insignificant predictor of living alone.

Table 15-III

MULTIPLE CLASSIFICATION ANALYSIS OF THE PERCENTAGE
OF WIDOWS WHO LIVE ALONE, BY ETHNIC-RELIGIOUS GROUP†

Variable	Oriental Jew				Western Jew				Israeli Jew				Arab Moslem				Arab Christian			
	N	U	A	B	N	U	A	B	N	U	A	B	N	U	A	B	N	U	A	B
Children ever born				.186				.252				.193*				.236				.419
0	182	40.7	39.7		648	66.7	64.5		14	64.3	63.4		43	51.2	54.1		19	68.4	69.0	
1	307	17.3	17.1		1201	38.0	36.7		17	23.5	25.9		26	15.4	15.6		16	31.3	29.8	
2 or 3	878	13.7	13.7		2648	28.7	28.3		63	31.7	32.3		125	31.2	31.7		54	16.7	15.2	
4 or more	3127	9.6	9.7		1754	21.5	23.7		134	26.9	26.4		641	16.7	16.4		172	9.3	9.8	
Age				.075				.161				.195*				.229				.254
Under 60	1880	10.5	9.5		2100	30.4	24.1		84	22.6	19.6		346	12.1	11.2		95	3.2	4.4	
60-74	1959	14.2	14.8		2915	38.9	40.3		119	37.0	38.6		328	30.8	31.6		125	25.6	25.0	
75 or over	655	11.0	12.2		1236	20.4	27.6		25	24.0	26.3		161	18.0	18.4		41	19.5	18.7	
Participation in labor force				.066				.083				.024**				.016**				.026**
In labor force	484	17.6	18.3		1463	41.4	39.4		37	27.0	27.7		58	19.0	23.0		17	5.9	12.8	
Not in labor force	4010	11.5	11.4		4788	29.6	30.2		191	30.9	30.8		777	20.7	20.4		244	17.2	16.7	
Residence:				.096				.046				.154**				.087*				.053**
Large city	1397	17.2	16.8		3262	35.6	34.4		173	33.5	34.3		24	45.8	40.9		42	14.3	14.5	
Small city	2276	9.6	9.8		2533	29.2	30.3		48	20.8	17.8		272	21.0	19.5		116	16.4	15.1	
Rural	821	10.7	10.9		456	27.0	29.0		7	14.3	17.4		539	19.3	20.3		103	17.5	18.9	

	N	U	A	N	U	A	N	U	A	N	U	A	N	U	A
Years of education:	B = .032**			B = .071			B = .110**			B = .024**			B = .100**		
0	3649	12.3	12.6	943	27.0	30.3	88	33.0	27.9	807	20.7	20.8	180	15.6	14.7
1-8	681	10.6	9.8	3182	28.8	29.9	98	25.5	27.9	27	18.5	15.3	73	16.4	22.0
9 or more	164	16.5	13.7	2126	40.2	37.0	42	35.9	40.9	1	0.0	18.5	8	37.5	6.6
Times married:	B = .033*			B = .062			B = .140*			B = .065*			B = .010**		
1	4016	11.6	11.8	5666	31.2	31.4	193	27.5	27.5	681	18.9	19.4	245	16.3	16.6
2 or more	478	16.7	15.3	585	44.1	41.5	35	45.7	45.3	154	27.9	26.1	16	18.8	15.1
Age at first marriage	B = .024**			B = .039			B = .042**			B = .093*			B = .105**		
Under 20	2205	12.0	12.6	1055	32.6	36.4	79	26.6	29.5	372	22.6	24.7	105	11.4	16.3
20-24	999	10.6	10.7	2501	29.8	31.4	81	29.6	28.5	217	18.4	18.2	72	11.1	11.2
25 or over	1290	13.7	12.6	2695	34.7	31.8	68	35.3	33.2	246	19.5	16.4	84	27.4	21.3
Multiple correlation coefficient	.232			.335			.250			.322			.474		

† Adapted from the "B" sample of the Census of Israel (1961).

Key: N = number; U = unadjusted percentage; A = adjusted percentage; B = beta coefficient; * = no significant contribution to prediction at the .01 level; ** = no significant contribution to prediction at the .05 level.

The ethnic-religious factor wields the second strongest influence on living alone. Cultural background has meaning beyond that of the other seven variables. The particular ethnic-religious group to which a widow belongs determines the sets of norms and role definitions for the widow and her family. The family living arrangements are defined by these expectations. As Lopata (1973; p. 16) and others have shown, these norms are reinforced by appropriate attitudes and personality structures.

The difference between the percentages who live alone in the various ethnic-religious groups is reduced when the effects of all the other variables are controlled. The figures for Arab Moslem widows become closer to the Western Jews when this adjustment is made. The cultural influence of the ethnic-religious factor is more clearly seen if the effects of this variable are removed by conducting an MCA that excludes it. Under these circumstances, the multiple correlation coefficient is reduced from .372 to .356. This is a loss of about 10 per cent in the predictive power, since the multiple correlation coefficient squared, or the amount of total variance explained, is reduced from .139 to .127.

The widowed most likely to live alone are those aged between 60 and 74. At these ages their physical capacities are not yet the decisive factors that they become in later years, and most children who desire to leave the household will have left. When the widowed are under 60 years of age, unmarried children are still likely to be found in the home. Age is a demographic variable, for all widowed go through the aging process. Increased life expectancy is associated with modernization, however; as a result, in the future many more widowed can expect to complete the processes of household contraction and expansion implied by this cross-sectional analysis.

The remaining five variables (labor force status, residence, education, the number of times married, and the age at first marriage) are less important than the previous three. Widows in the labor force are more likely to live alone than widows who are not working. No question was asked about income in the Israeli Census of 1961, but it seems likely that those widows who work have higher incomes at their disposal. Financially, they can sustain an independent household. In conjunction with the independence that comes with holding a job, a widow may need to work if she has no family members who are willing to support her or live with her. Here it is difficult to know whether living alone or working has causal priority. More of the widowed in the three large cities of Jerusalem, Tel-Aviv, and Haifa live alone than in the rural areas and small cities of Israel. There are several possible reasons for this: urban areas may attract those widowed who desire to live alone; family norms and community and social services in large urban areas may more readily permit the widowed to live alone; and housing of the one- and two-room type, in which a person can easily live alone, may also be more readily available in urban areas than elsewhere.

The adjustment procedure of a multiple classification analysis reduces a substantial unadjusted relationship between education and living alone. The education of females is customarily associated with family modernization, as it introduces new and broadened opportunities outside the family and affects family roles and relationships within the family. The median age of females in the 1961 sample was 64, so that more than half were born before the turn of the century, when it was rare for a female to receive any education in the countries of Asia, North Africa, and Eastern Europe. A woman who attended even the first grade could be considered "modern." *Prima facie* evidence demonstrates that education is only weakly related to the form of family modernization represented by living alone. There may be several routes to family modernization. Factors that influence one aspect of modernization may be of little consequence for others, and may have a stronger influence in one group than in another.

As we have suggested elsewhere (Chevan and Korson, 1972), the relationship between the number of times a widow has been married and whether she lives alone would appear to be a matter of the strength and tone of interpersonal relations with other family members. A second marriage probably lends some distance to the relationship between the widowed person and the children of the first marriage, if there were any children. Family norms may be ambiguous as regards the living arrangements of the twice-married person.

Before adjustment, age at first marriage has only a weak relationship to whether the widow lives alone. After adjustment the relationship is weakened further, and its direction is reversed. This factor is usually associated with family modernization, but as with education, it is found to add little to our understanding of living alone. A later age at marriage may be related to reduced fertility, educational achievement, and participation in the labor force, but by itself age at marriage does little to distinguish between those who live alone and those who live with others.

The theme of the factors that contribute to family modernization in each ethnic-religious group is pursued more fully in Table 15-III. In no group is the order of importance of the variables the same as the order for the total population, but there is a close relationship between the order of importance in Table 15-II and in Table 15-III. Western Jews, who constitute half of the sample, exhibit the highest consistency with the results shown for the total population in Table 15-III. For the Oriental Jews, the direction of the relationship between living alone and each variable is consistent with the findings for the total population, but these relationships are weaker and the proportion of the widowed who live alone is lower. As a consequence of this weakness, the Oriental Jews have the lowest multiple correlation coefficient of the five groups. Among the small sample of Israeli Jews, only three variables (the number of children ever born, current age, and the number of marriages) contribute significantly (at the .05 level) to living alone, although the betas for residence and education are the largest for any group. In both Arab populations, the labor force status has no bearing on living alone. The major determinants among the Arabs are age and the number of children, and in the Arab Christian population these are the only statistically significant influences. Although a decrease in fertility is associated with family modernization during widowhood, only 7.5 per cent of the Arab Moslem women and 13.5 per cent of the Arab Christian women have borne fewer than two children. It would seem that the existence of widows who live alone in the Arab Moslem, Arab Christian, and Israeli Jewish groups can be accounted for mostly by low fecundity in some couples and by aging processes.

It should be pointed out, however, that age itself need not be construed as a straightforward demographic variable. Age as a personal characteristic to which family members respond takes its cue from its ethnic-religious context. At each age, the proportion who live alone differs greatly according to cultural background. Living alone during widowhood, after all other variables are controlled, seems to be viewed differently by Oriental Jews, Western Jews, and the Arab population. The widow at age 60–74 is granted, and probably expects, more independence in the Western Jewish family than in other families. Physical capacities at age 75 and over are probably no greater in Western Jews than in widows in other groups. Yet the Western Jewish widow lives alone more than others. Nor do children have the same effect in all ethnic-religious groups. For widows without children, the proportion of Oriental and Western Jews who live alone differ by 25 per cent, and there are large differences at other levels of fertility.

CONCLUSION

Family modernization during the last stage of the family life cycle is not uniform among the ethnic-religious groups of this study. It appears furthest advanced among Western Jews, and least advanced among Oriental Jews and Arab Christians. Israeli Jews incline toward the Western model, and Arab Moslems toward the traditional family model. Oriental Jews, Israeli Jews, and Arab Moslems have some characteristics of a modernizing population. The major influences on living alone in each group stem more from natural biological processes (aging and childbearing) than from any social process. A more comprehensive comparative viewpoint reveals that there are strong cultural determinants and some weaker social determinants of whether a widow lives alone.

Several changes could eventually bring about an increase in the proportion who live alone, including decreased fertility, shifts in the age structure of the population, increased urbanization, increased remarriage of the widowed, and increased participation in the labor force. Whatever changes may occur in the future, the pace of family modernization will be interpreted in a social and cultural ethnic-religious setting. Family change is unlikely to occur in a similar manner in any two groups.

In any effort to predict the future trend of residential patterns among the widowed in Israel, it seems unlikely that the two extreme forms shown in the data above will converge. With the continued modernization of Israeli society, it is more likely that the social structures of the families of the most traditional ethnic-religious groups (Arab

Moslems and Oriental Jews) will incorporate some attributes of the more "modern" Western Jews, namely fewer children, a continued decline in the importance of the extended family, and a concomitant trend toward a more nuclear family; as the result, the widowed among these traditional groups will increasingly come to live alone, so matching the pattern of the "modern" groups.

As has been demonstrated above, the more traditional the family, the larger the average size of the household, and the more "modern" the family, the smaller the household will be. Should the average size of the traditional family decline in the future to approximate that of the "modern" family, the status of the widowed is likely to change accordingly.

Bibliography

Chapter 1

Anderson, J. E. The use of time and energy. In J. E. Birren, (Ed.), *Handbook of aging and the individual: Psychological and biological aspects.* Chicago: University of Chicago Press, 1959.

Aristotle. *Physics.* Translated by R. Hope. Lincoln: University of Nebraska Press, 1961.

Augustine. *Confessions.* Translated by V. J. Bourke. New York: Fathers of the Church, 1953.

Benjamin, H. Biologic versus chronologic age. *J. Gerontol.,* 1947, *2,* 217–227.

Berger, P. L., and Luckmann, T. *The social construction of reality.* New York: Anchor Books, Doubleday & Company, Inc., 1967.

Berger, P. L. and Pullberg, S. Reification and the sociological critique of consciousness. *History and theory,* 1965, *iv,* 196–211.

Bergson, H. *Duration and simultaneity.* Translated by L. Jacobsen. Indianapolis: the Bobbs-Merrill Co., Inc., 1965.

Bindra, D. and Waksberg, H. Methods and terminology in studies of time estimation. *Psychol. Bull.,* 1956, *53,* 155–159.

Binswanger, L. Symptom and time: a casuistic contribution. *Existential Inquiries,* 1960, *1,* 14–18.

Birren, J. E. Principles of research on aging. In J. E. Birren (Ed.), *Handbook of aging and the individual: psychological and biological aspects.* Chicago: University of Chicago Press, 1959

Blumer, H. *Symbolic interactionism.* Englewood Cliffs: Prentice-Hall, 1969.

Bongers, L. S. A developmental study of time perception and time perspective in three cultural groups: Anglo American, Indian American and Mexican American. Unpublished Ph.D. dissertation. Los Angeles: University of California at Los Angeles, 1971.

Burgess, E. W. *Aging in western societies.* Chicago: University of Chicago Press, 1960.

Callahan, J. F. *Four views of time in ancient philosophy.* Cambridge: Harvard University Press, 1960.

Cameron, P. The generation gap: time orientation. *Gerontologist,* 1972, *12,* 117–119.

Carrell, A. Physiological time. *Science,* 1929, *71,* 618–621.

Cavan, R. S., Burgess, E. W., Havighurst, R. I., & Goldhammer, H. *Personal adjustment in old age.* Chicago: Science Research Associates, 1949.

Coser, L. A. *Masters of sociological thought: ideas in historical context.* New York: Harcourt, Brace, Jovanovich, Inc., 1971.

de Beauvoir, S. *The coming of age.* Translated by P. O'Brian. New York: Warner Books, Inc., 1973.

de Grazia, S. *Of time, work and leisure.* Garden City: Anchor Books, Doubleday & Company, Inc., 1964.

Denbigh, K. G. In defense of the direction of time. In J. T. Fraser, F. C. Haber, and G. H. Muller, (Eds.), *The study of time.* Berlin: Springer-Verlag, 1972.

Descartes, R. *The philosophical works of Descartes.* Translated by E. S. Haldane and G. R. E. Ross. Volume I. New York: Dover Publications, 1956.

Durkheim, E. *The division of labor in society.* Translated by G. Simpson. New York: The Free Press, 1933.

Durkheim, E. *The elementary forms of religious life: a study in religious sociology.* Translated by J. W. Swain. New York: The Macmillan Company, 1915.

El-Meligi, A. M. A technique for exploring time experiences in mental disorders. In H. Yaker, H. Osmond, and F. Cheek (Eds.), *The future of time.* New York: Doubleday & Company, Inc., 1972.

Ennis, W. D. Letter. *Science,* 1943, *98,* 301–302.

Eson, M. E., and Greenfield, N. Life space: its content and temporal dimensions. *J. Genetic Psychol.,* 1962, *100,* 113–120.

Feifel, H. Judgment of time in younger and older persons. *J. Gerontol.,* 1957, *12,* 71–74.

Fink, H. H. The relationship of time perspective to age, institutionalization, and activity. *J. Gerontol.,* 1957, *12,* 414–417.

Frank, L. K. Time perspectives. *J. Social Phil.,* 1970, *4,* 239–312.

Fraser, J. T. The study of time. In J. T. Fraser, F. C. Haber, and G. H. Muller (Eds.), *The study of time.* Berlin: Springer-Verlag, 1972.

Fraser, J. T., Haber, F. C., and Muller, G. H. (Eds.). *The study of time: proceedings of the first conference of the international society for the study of time.* Berlin: Springer-Verlag, 1972.

Friedrichs, R. W. *A sociology of sociology.* New York: The Free Press, 1970.

Gioscia, V. On social time. In H. Yaker, H. Osmond, and F. Cheek (Eds.), *The future of time: man's temporal environment.* Garden City: Doubleday & Company, 1972.

Goldstone, S., Boardman, W. K., and Lhamon, W. T. Kinesthetic cues in the development of time concepts. *J. Genetic Psychol.,* 1958, *93,* 185–190.

Grünbaum, A. *Modern science and Zeno's paradoxes.* Middletown: Wesleyan University Press, 1967.

Gulliksen, H. The influence of occupation upon the perception of time. *J. Exp. Psychol.,* 1927, *10,* 52–59.

Gurvitch, G. *The spectrum of social time.* Dordrecht, Holland: D. Reidel Publishing Company, 1964.

Gurvitch, G. Social structure and the multiplicity of times. In E. Tiryakian (Ed.), *Sociological theory, values and sociocultural change.* Glencoe: The Free Press, 1963.

Heath, L. R. *The concept of time.* Chicago: University of Chicago Press, 1936.

Heidegger, M. *Being and time.* Translated by J. Macquarrie and E. Robinson. London: SCM Press, 1962.

Husserl, E. *The phenomenology of internal time-consciousness.* Translated by J. S. Churchill. Bloomington: Indiana University Press, 1966.

Hutcheon, P. D. Sociology and the objectivity problem. *Sociol. Social Res.* 1970, *54,* 153–171.

Kant, I. *Critique of pure reason.* Translated by N. K. Smith. London: Macmillan & Co., Ltd., 1956.

Kastenbaum, R. Cognitive and personal futurity in later life. *J. Individual Psychol.,* 1963, *19,* 216–222.

Kastenbaum, R. On the meaning of time in later life. *J. Genetic Psychol.,* 1966, *109,* 9–25.

Kuhlen, R. G., and Monge, R. H. Correlates of estimated rate of time passage in the adult years. *J. Gerontol.,* 1968, *23,* 427–433.

Kuhn, T. *The structure of scientific revolutions.* Chicago: University of Chicago Press, 1962.

Lauer, Q. *Phenomenology: its genesis and prospect.* New York: Harper & Row, Publishers, 1965.

Mann, H., Siegler, M., and Osmond, H. The psychotypology of time. In H. Yaker, H. Osmond, and F. Cheek (Eds.), *The future of time.* New York: Doubleday & Company, Inc., 1972.

Mannheim, K. *Essays on the sociology of knowledge.* Edited by P. Kecskemeti. London: Routledge & Kegan Paul, 1952.

Mannheim, K. *Ideology and Utopia.* New York: Harcourt, Brace and Company, 1936.

Martindale, D. *The nature and types of sociological theory.* Boston: Houghton Mifflin Company, 1960.

Matson, F. W. *The broken image: man, science and society.* New York: Anchor Books, Doubleday & Company, Inc., 1966.

Merleau-Ponty, M. *Phenomenology of perception.* Translated by C. Smith. London: Routledge & Kegan Paul, 1962.

Meerloo, J. A. *Along the fourth dimension: man's sense of time and history.* New York: The John Day Company, Inc., 1970.

Mumford, L. *The myth of the machine: technics and human development.* New York: Harcourt, Brace & World, Inc., 1962.

Murray, I. M. Assessment of physiologic age by combination of several criteria—vision, hearing, blood pressure, and muscle force. *J. Gerontol.,* 1951, *6,* 120–126.

Neuringer, C., Levenoon, M., and Kaplan, J. M. Phenomenological time flow in suicidal, geriatric and normal individuals. *Omega,* 1971, *2,* 247–252.

Nitardy, F. W. Letter. *Science,* 1943, *98,* 110.

Pittendrigh, C. S. On temporal organization in living systems. In H. Yaker, H. Osmond, and F. Cheek (Eds.), *The future of time.* New York: Doubleday & Company, Inc., 1972.

Plato. *Timaeus.* Translated by F. Cornford. London: Routledge & Kegan Paul, 1937.

Pollock, G. H. On time, death, and immortality. *Psychoanalytic Quart.* 1971, *XL,* 435–445.

Pöppel, E. Oscillations as possible basis for time perception. In J. T. Fraser, F. C. Haber, and G. H. Muller (Eds.), *The study of time.* Berlin: Springer-Verlag, 1972.

Reichenbach, H. *The philosophy of space and time.* Translated by M. Reichenbach and J. Freund. New York: Dover Publications, 1958.

Reichenbach, M. and Mathers, R. A. The place of time and aging in the natural sciences and scientific philosophy. In J. Birren, (Ed.), *Handbook of aging and the individual.* Chicago: University of Chicago Press, 1959.

Rezsohazy, R. The concept of social time: its role in development. *Intern. Social Sci. J.,* 1972, *24,* 26–36.

Rioux, M. Critical versus aseptic sociology. *Berkeley J. Sociol.,* 1970, *XV,* 33–47.

Sartre, J. *Search for a method.* New York: Alfred A. Knopf, Inc., 1963.

Schutz, A. *Collected papers I. The problem of social reality.* Edited by M. Natanson. The Hague: Martinus Nijhoff, 1967.

Shakespeare, W. *As you like it.* Edited by A. Quiller-Couch and J. D. Wilson. London: Cambridge University Press, 1957.

Sherover, C. M. *Heidegger, Kant and time.* Bloomington: Indiana University Press, 1971.

Siegman, A. W. Future-time perspective and the perception of duration. *Perceptual and Motor Skills,* 1962, *15,* 609–610.

Simmons, L. W. *The role of the aged in primitive society.* New Haven: Yale University Press, 1945.

Sokolowski, R. *The formation of Husserl's concept of constitution.* The Hague: Martinus Nijhoff, 1964.

Sorokin, P. A. *Sociocultural causality, space, time: a study of referential principles of sociology and social science.* New York: Russell & Russell Publishers, 1964.

Strehler, B. L. *Time, cells and aging.* New York: Academic Press, Inc., 1962.

Surwillo, W. Age and the perception of short intervals of time. *J. Gerontol.,* 1964, *19,* 322–324.

Swift, E. J. and McGeoch, J. A. An experimental study of the perception of filled and empty time. *J. Exp. Psychol.,* 1925, *8,* 240–249.

Tejmar, J. Age differences in cyclic motor reaction. *Nature,* 1962, *195,* 813–814.

Tiryakian, E. A. (Ed.) *Sociological theory, values, and sociocultural change.* Glencoe: The Free Press, 1963.

Triplett, D. The relation between the physical pattern and the reproduction of short temporal intervals: A study in the perception of filled and unfilled time. *Psychol. Mon.,* 1931, *XLI,* 201–265.

Wallace, M., and Rabin, A. Temporal experience. *Psychol. Bull.,* 1960, *57,* 213–236.

Wallach, M. A. and Green, L. R. On age and the subjective speed of time. *J. Gerontol.,* 1961, *16,* 71–74.

Wallis, R. *Time: fourth dimension of the mind.* Translated by B. B. and D. S. Montgomery. New York: Harcourt, Brace & World, Inc., 1966.

Watanabe, S. Creative time. In J. T. Fraser, F. C. Haber, and G. H. Muller (Eds.), *The study of time.* Berlin: Springer-Verlag, 1972.

Weber, M. *The methodology of social sciences.* Translated and edited by E. Shils and H. Finch. New York: The Free Press, 1949.

Whitrow, G. J. *The natural philosophy of time.* London: Thomas Nelson & Sons Ltd., 1961.

Whorf, B. L. *Language, thought, and reality.* Edited by J. B. Carroll. Cambridge: The M.I.T. Press, 1956.

Wild, J. The Cartesian deformation of the structure of change and its influence on modern thought. *Philosoph. Rev.,* 1941, *L,* 36–59.

Wilen, F. Letter. *Science,* 1943, *98,* 301.

Wilkerson, T. E. Time and time again. *Philosophy,* 1973, *48,* 173–177.

Woodcock, G. The tyranny of the clock. *Politics,* 1944, *3,* 265–267.

Yaker, H., Osmond, H., and Cheek, F. (Eds.) *The future of time: man's temporal environment.* Garden City: Doubleday & Company, Inc., 1972.

Zibbell, R. A. Activity level, future time perspective, and life satisfaction in old age. Unpublished Ph.D. dissertation. Boston: Boston University, 1971.

Zimbardo, P. G., Marshall, G., and Maslach, C. Liberating behavior from time-bound control: expanding the present through hypnosis. *J. App. Social Psychol.,* 1971, *1,* 305–323.

Chapter 2

Atchley, R. C. Disengagement among professors. *J. Gerontol.* 1971, *26*, 476–480.

Birren, J. E., Butler, R. N., Greenhouse, S. W., and Yarrow, M. R. (Eds.), *Human aging: A biological and behavioral study.* Washington: Public Health Service Publication No. 986, 1963.

Blau, Z. S. Structural constraints on friendship in old age. *Amer. Sociol. Rev.*, 1961; *26*, 429–439.

Blumer, H. *Symbolic interactionism: Perspective and method.* New York: Prentice-Hall, Inc. 1969.

Bott, E. *Family and social network.* London: Tavistock, 1957.

Brehm, H. P. Sociology and aging: Orientation and research. *Gerontologist*, 1968; *8*, 24–31.

Carp, F. C. *A future for the aged: Victoria plaza and its residents.* Austin: University of Texas Press, 1966.

Carp, F. C. Compound criteria in gerontological research. *J. Gerontol.*, 1969, *24*, 341–347.

Chellam, G. *The disengagement theory: Awareness of death and self-engagement.* Ph.D. dissertation. Cleveland: Department of Social Work, Western Reserve University, 1964.

Crawford, M. P. Retirement and disengagement. *Human Relations*, 1971, *24*, 255–278.

Cumming, E., Dean, L. R., Newell, D. S., and McCaffrey, I. Disengagement: A tentative theory of aging. *Sociometry*, 1960, *23*, 23–25.

Cumming, E., and Henry, W. *Growing old.* New York: Basic Books, Inc., 1961.

Cumming, E. Further thoughts on the theory of disengagement. *Intern. Social Sci. J.*, 1963, *XV*, 377–393.

Desroches, H. F., and Kaiman, B. D. Stability of activity participation in an aged population. *J. Gerontol.*, 1964, *19*, 211–214.

Dreitzel, H. P. (Ed.). *Recent sociology, no. 2: Patterns of communicative behavior.* London: Macmillan & Co., Ltd., 1970.

Eisenstadt, S. N. *From generation to generation: Age groups and social structure.* New York: The Free Press, 1956.

Frankel, J. J. *The conflict between older workers and younger age groups.* Ph.D. dissertation. New York: Sociology Department, New York University. 1962.

Goode, W. *World revolution and family patterns.* New York and London: The Free Press, 1970.

Gutmann, D. The country of old men: Cultural studies in the psychology of later life. *Occasional papers in gerontology, no. 5.* Ann Arbor, Michigan: Institute of Gerontology, University of Michigan-Wayne State University, 1969.

Havinghurst, R. J., Neugarten, B. L., and Tobin, S. S. Disengagement and patterns of aging. In B. L. Neugarten (Ed.), *Middle age and aging.* Chicago: University of Chicago Press, 1968.

Henry, W. The theory of intrinsic disengagement. In P. F. Hansen, (Ed.), *Age with a future.* Philadelphia: F. A. Davis Co., 1964.

Henry, W. Engagement and disengagement: Toward a theory of adult development. In R. Kastenbaum (Ed.), *Contributions to the psycho-biology of aging.* New York: Springer Publishing Co., Inc., 1965.

Hochschild, A. R. *The unexpected community.* Englewood Cliffs: Prentice-Hall, Inc., 1973.

Koller, M. Review of *Growing Old* by E. Cumming and W. Henry. *Sociol. Symp.,* 1969, *2,* 153–53.

Kutner, B. The social nature of aging. *Gerontologist,* 1962, *2,* 5–8.

Lazarsfeld, P. F. An unemployed village. In *Character and Personality,* 1932, *I,* 147–151.

Lewin, K. *Resolving social conflicts.* New York: Harper & Row, Publishers, 1948.

Lieberman, M. A., and Coplan, A. S. Distance from death as a variable in the study of aging. *Developmental Psychol.,* 1970, *2,* 71–84.

Lipman, A., and Smith, K. J. Functionality of disengagement in old age. *J. Gerontol.,* 1968, *23,* 517–521.

Lowenthal, M. F., and Boler, D. Voluntary vs. involuntary social withdrawal. *J. Gerontol.,* 1965, *20,* 363–371.

Lowenthal, M. F., and Haven, C. Interaction and adaptation: Intimacy as a critical variable. *Amer. Sociol. Rev.* 1968, *33,* 20–30.

Maddox, G. Disengagement theory: A critical evaluation. *Gerontologist,* 1964, *4,* 80–83.

Messer, M. *The effects of age groupings on organizational and normative systems of the elderly.* Ph.D. dissertation. Evanston: Sociology Department, Northwestern University, 1966.

Morse, N., and Weiss, R. The function and meaning of work and the job. *Amer. Sociol. Rev.* 1955, *20,* 191–198.

Neugarten, B. L. (Ed.). *Personality in middle and later life,* New York: Atherton Press, 1964.

Neugarten, B. L. (Ed.). *Middle age and aging.* Chicago: University of Chicago Press, 1968.

Neugarten, B. and D. L. Gutmann (1958) Age-sex roles and personality in middle age: A Thematic apperception study. *Psychological Monographes,* *72:*17-1–13.

Presad, S. B. The retirement postulate of the disengagement theory. *Gerontologist,* 1964, *4,* 20–23.

Rabin, A. K. Review of Bernice Neugarten *et al., Personality in middle and later life. J. Gerontol.,* 1965, *20,* 257–259.

Reichard, S., Livson, F., and Peterson, P. G. *Aging and personality.* New York: John Wiley & Sons, Inc., 1962.

Roman, P., and Taietz, P. Organizational structure and disengagement: The emeritus professor. *Gerontologist,* 1967, *7,* 147–152.

Rose, A. M., and Peterson, W. A. (Eds.). *Older people and their social world.* Philadelphia: F. A. Davis Co., 1965.

Rosow, I. *The social integration of the aged.* New York: The Free Press, 1967.

Sartre, J. P. *The emotions: Outline of a theory.* New York: Philosophical Library, Inc., 1948.

Shanas, E., and Streib, G. (eds.). *Social structure and the family: Generational relations.* Englewood Cliffs: Prentice-Hall, Inc., 1965.

Shanas, E., Townsend, P., Wedderburn, D., Friis, H., Milhøj, P., and Stehouwer, J. *Old people in three industrial societies.* New York: Atherton Press, 1968.

Streib, G. Disengagement theory in socio-cultural perspective. *Intern. J. Psychiatry,* 1968, *6,* 69–76.

Tallmer, M. *Social, economic and health factors in disengagement in the aging.* Ph.D. dissertation. New York: Yeshiva University, 1967.

Tallmer, M., and Kutner, B. Disengagement and the stresses of aging. *J. Gerontol.,* 1969, *24,* 70–75.

Tobin, S. S., and Neugarten, B. L. Life satisfaction and social interaction in the aging. *J. Gerontol.,* 1961, *16,* 344–346.

Tunstall, J. *Old and alone: A sociological study of old people.* London: Routledge & Kegan Paul, 1965.

Videbeck, R., and Knox, A. B. Alternative participatory responses to aging. In A. M. Rose and W. A. Peterson (Eds.), *Older people and their social world.* Philadelphia: F. A. Davis Co., 1965.

Weber, M. *The theory of social economic organization.* Edited by Talcott Parsons. New York: The Free Press, 1966.

Williams, R. H., and Wirths, C. *Lives through the years.* New York: Atherton Press, 1965.

Youmans, E. G. Some perspectives on disengagement theory. *Gerontologist,* 1968, *9,* 254–258.

Youmans, E. G. Disengagement among older rural and urban men. In E. Grant Youmans (Ed.), *Older rural americans.* Lexington: University of Kentucky Press, 1967.

Zawadski, B., and Lazarsfeld,, P. F. The psychological consequences of unemployment. *J. Social Psychol.,* 1935, *6,* 224–251.

Zborowski, M. Aging and recreation. *J. Gerontol.,* 1962, *17,* 32–39.

Chapter 3

Cumming, E., and Henry, W. E. *Growing old: The process of disengagement.* New York: Basic Books, Inc., 1961.

Goldstine, T., and Gutmann, D. A TAT study of Navajo aging. *Psychiatry,* 1972, *35,* 373.

Gutmann, D. An exploration of ego configurations in middle and later life. In B. Neugarten (Ed.), *Personality in middle and later life.* New York: Atherton Press, 1964.

Gutmann, D. Mayan aging—a comparative TAT study. *Psychiatry,* 1966, *29,* 246.

Gutmann, D. Aging among the Highland Maya: A comparative study. *J. Personality Social Psychol.* 1967, *7,* 28.

Gutmann, D. The country of old men: Cross-cultural studies in the psychology of later life. In W. Donahue (Ed.), *Occasional Papers in Gerontology.* Ann Arbor: Institute of Gerontology, University of Michigan, 1969.

Krohn, A., and Gutmann, D. Changes in mastery style with age: A study of Navajo dreams. *Psychiatry,* 1971, *34,* 289.

Roheim, G. *Animism, magic and the divine king.* London: Kegan Paul, 1930.

Simmons, L. W. *The role of the aged in primitive society.* New Haven: Yale University Press, 1945.

Chapter 4

Cain, L., Jr. Life course and social structure. In R. Faris (Ed.)., *Handbook of modern sociology.* Chicago: Rand-McNally & Co., 1964.

Cain, L., Jr. Age status and generational phenomena: The new old people in contemporary America. *Gerontologist,* 1967, *7,* 83–92.

Cain, L., Jr. Age and the character of our times. *Gerontologist,* 1968, *8,* 250–258.

Cottrell, W. Of time and the railroader. *Bobbs-Merrill Reprint Series in Social Science,* 1939, *54.*

Gioscia, V. On social time. In H. Yaker, H. Osmond, and F. Cheek (Eds.), *The future of time.* Garden City: Anchor Books, Doubleday & Company, Inc., 1972.

Glick, P. C., and Parke, R., Jr. New approaches in studying the life cycle of the family. *Demography,* 1965, *2,* 187–202.

Haug, M. R., and Sussman, M. B. The second career: Varient of a sociological concept. In H. L. Sheppard (Ed.), *Toward an industrial gerontology.* Cambridge, Mass.: Schenkman Publishing Co. Inc., 1970.

Hendricks, J., and Hendricks, C. The role of the actor in the determination of time perception: Alternative explanations. Paper presented at the 25th annual meeting of the Gerontological Society, San Juan, Puerto Rico, 1972.

Huyck, M. Career timing, age and career attitudes among army officers. Paper presented at the 23rd annual meeting of the Gerontological Society, Toronto, 1970.

Likert, J. G. (Ed.) *Conversations with returning women students.* Ann Arbor: Center for Continuing Education of Women, University of Michigan, 1967.

Merton, R. Social structure and anomie. In L. Wilson, and W. Kolb (Eds.), *Sociological analysis.* New York: Harcourt, Brace and Co., 1949.

Neugarten, B., Moore, J., and Lowe, J. Age norms, age constraints, and adult socialization. In B. Neugarten, (Ed.), *Middle age and aging.* Chicago: University of Chicago Press, 1968.

Reichenbach, M., and Mathers, A. The place of time and aging in the natural sciences and scientific philosophy. In J. Birren (Ed.), *Handbook of aging and the individual.* Chicago: University of Chicago Press, 1959.

Riegel, L. Development psychology and society: Some historical and ethical considerations. In J. Nesselroade, and H. Reese, (Eds.), *Lifespan developmental psychology.* New York: Academic Press Inc., 1973.

Roth, J. A. *Timetables: Structuring the passage of time in hospital treatment and other careers.* Indianapolis: The Bobbs-Merrill Co., Inc., 1963.

United States Senate. *Cancelled careers: The impact of reduction-in-force policies on middle-aged federal employees.* Washington, D.C.: Government Printing Office, May, 1972.

Zatlin, C. E., M. Storandt, and J. Botwinick. Personality and values of women continuing their education after thirty-five years of age. *J. Gerontol.,* 1973, *28,* 216–222.

Chapter 5

Adams, S. Status congruency as a variable in small group performance. *Social Forces,* 1953, *32,* 16.

Barron, M. L. Minority group characteristics of the aged in American society. *J. Gerontol.,* 1953, *8,* 477.

Bell, D. *The end of ideology.* New York: Collier Books, 1962.

Benoit-Smullyan, E. Status, status types, and status interrelationships. *Amer. Sociol. Rev.* 9:151, 1944.

Blau, Z. S. Changes in status and age identification. *Amer. Sociol. Rev.*, 1956, *21*, 198.

Brinton, C. *The anatomy of revolution.* New York: Random House, Inc., 1960.

Bultena, G. L. Age-grading in the social interaction of an elderly male population. *J. Gerontol.*, 1968, *23*, 539.

Campbell, A. Social and psychological determinants of voting behavior. In W. Donahue and C. Tibbitts (Eds.), *Politics of age.* Ann Arbor: The University of Michigan Press, 1962.

Campbell, A., Curin, G., and Miller, W. E. *The voter decides.* Evanston: Row, Peterson and Co., 1954.

Claque, E. The aging population and programs of security. *Milbank Memorial Fund Quart.* 1940, *18*, 345.

Cottrell, F. Governmental functions and the politics of age. In C. Tibbitts (Ed.), *Handbook of social gerontology.* Chicago: The University of Chicago Press, 1960.

Cumming, M. E. and Henry, W. E. *Growing old: The process of disengagement.* New York: Basic Books Inc., 1961.

Cumming, M. E., and Schneider, D. Sibling solidarity: A property of American kinship. *Amer. Anthropol.*, 1961, *63*, 498.

Fenchel, G. H. Subjective status and the equilibration hypothesis. *J. Abnormal and Social Psychiatry*, 1951, *46:* 476.

Frazier, F. E. *Black Bourgeoisie.* Glencoe: The Free Press, 1959.

Goffman, I. Status consistency and preference for change in power distribution. *Amer. Sociol. Rev.*, 1957, *22*, 275.

Havighurst, R. J. Old age—an American problem. *J. Gerontol.*, 1949, *4*, 298.

Hoar, J. A study of free-time activities of 200 aged persons. *Sociol. Social Res.*, 1961, *45*, 157.

Holtzman, A. Analysis of old age politics in the United States. *J. Gerontol.*, 1954, *9*, 56.

Hughes, E. C. Dilemmas and contradictions of status. *Amer. J. Sociol.*, 1944–45, *L*, 353.

Jackson, E. Status consistency and symptoms of stress. *Amer. Sociol. Rev.*, 1962, *27*, 469.

Knupfer, G. Portrait of the underdog. In R. Bendix and S. M. Lipset (Eds.), *Class, status, and power: A reader in social stratification.* Glencoe: The Free Press, 1953.

Kogan, N. Attitudes toward old people in an older sample. *J. Abnormal Psychol.*, 1961, *62*, 616.

Kogan, N., and Wallach, M. Age changes in values and attitudes. *J. Gerontol.*, 1961, *16*, 272.

Lane, R. E. *Political life.* New York: The Free Press, 1959.

Lenski, G. Status crystallization: A non-vertical dimension of social status. *Amer. Sociol. Rev.,* 1954, *19,* 405.

Lenski, G. Social participation and status crystallization. *Amer. Sociol. Rev.,* 1956, *21,* 458.

Linden, M. E. The meaning of elder rejection, studies in gerontologic human relations VI. Paper read at the National Conference of Jewish Communical Service, Philadelphia, 1954.

Lipset, S. M. *Political man.* Garden City: Anchor Books, Doubleday & Company, Inc., 1963.

Loether, H. J. *Problems of aging.* Belmont, Cal.: Dickenson Pub. Co., Inc., 1967.

Michels, R. *Political parties.* Translated by E. and C. Paul. New York: Dover Publications, 1959.

Olsen, M. E., and Tully, J. C. Socioeconomic-ethnic status inconsistency and preference for political change. *Amer. Sociol. Rev.,* 1972, *37,* 560.

Pinard, M. Poverty and political movements. *Social Problems,* 1967, *15,* 250.

Pinner, F. A., Jacobs, P., and Selznick, P. *Old age and political behavior.* Los Angeles: University of California Press, 1959.

Rose, A. M. The subculture of the aging: A framework for research in social gerontology. *Gerontologist,* 1962, *2,* 123.

Rosow, I. *Social integration of the aged.* New York: The Free Press, 1967.

Roucek, J. S. Age as a prestige factor. *Sociol. Social Res.,* 1957, *42,* 349.

Schramm, W., and White, D. M. Age, education, and economic status as factors in newspaper reading: Conclusions. In W. Schramm (Ed.), *The process and effects of mass communications,* Urbana: University of Illinois Press, 1954.

Simmons, L. *The role of the aged in primitive society.* New Haven: Yale University Press, 1945.

Smith, J. The group status of the aged in an urban social structure. In I. H. Simpson and J. C. McKinney (Eds.), *Social aspects of aging.* Durham: Duke University Press, 1966.

Trela, J. E. Some political consequences of senior center and other old age group memberships. *Gerontologist,* 1971, *11,* 118.

Trela, J. E. Age structure of voluntary associations and activist self-interest among the aged. *Sociol. Quart.,* 1972, *13,* 244.

Weber, M. *From Max Weber: Essays in sociology.* Translated by H. H. Gerth and C. Wright Mills. New York: Oxford University Press, 1946.

Zaleznik, A., Christensen, C. R., and Roethlisberger, F. J. *The motivation, productivity and satisfaction of workers: A prediction study.* Boston: Harvard University Press, 1958.

Chapter 6

Anderson, N. The significance of age categories for older persons. *Gerontologist,* 1967, *7,* 164–167.

Back, K., and Guptill, C. Retirement and self-ratings. In I. Simpson and J. McKinney (Eds.), *Social aspects of aging.* Durham: Duke University Press, 1966.

Baker, H. *Retirement procedures under compulsory and flexible retirement policies.* Princeton: Princeton University Press, 1953.

Bell, B. D. *Life satisfaction among the occupationally retired: A tritheoretical inquiry.* Unpublished doctoral dissertation, University of Missouri, Columbia, 1973.

Biddle, B. J., and Thomas, J. *Role theory.* New York: John Wiley & Sons, Inc., 1966.

Breen, L. Z. Retirement—norms, behavior, and functional aspects of normative behavior. In R. H. Williams, C. Tibbitts, and W. Donahue (Eds.), *Processes of aging.* Vol. II. New York: Atherton Press, 1963.

Brotman, H. Who are the aged: A demographic view. In *Occasional papers in gerontology.* University of Michigan-Wayne State University, November, 1968.

Brotman, H. A profile of the older American. Address read before the *Conference on consumer problems of older people.* New York: Administration on Aging, No. 208, 1968.

Bultena, G. Life continuity and morale in old age. *Gerontologist,* 1969, *9,* 251–253.

Busse, E. W., Barnes, R., Silverman, A., Thaler, M., and Frost, L. Studies of the process of aging: Ten strengths and weaknesses of psychic functioning in the aged. *Amer. J. Psychiatry.* 1955 *111,* 896–901.

Busse, E. W., and Kreps, J. M. Criteria for retirement: A re-examination. *Gerontologist,* 1955, *4,* 115–20.

Carp, F. M. The impact of environment on old people. *Gerontologist,* 1967, *7,* 106–108.

Carp, F. M. *Retirement.* New York: Behavioral Publications, 1972.

Cavan, R. Old age in a city of 100,000. *Illinois Acad. Sci. Trans.,* 1947, *40,* 156–159.

Donahue, W., Orbach, H. L., and Pollak, O. Retirement: The emerging social pattern. In C. Tibbitts (Ed.), *Handbook of social gerontology.* Chicago: University of Chicago Press, 1960.

Friedmann, E. A., and Havighurst, R. J. *The meaning of work and retirement.* Chicago: University of Chicago Press, 1954.

Goodstein, L. D. Personal adjustment factors and retirement. *Geriatrics,* 1962, 17, 41–45.

Gordon, M. Changing patterns of retirement. *J. Gerontol.*, *15*, 300–304.

Lipman, A. Role conceptions and morale of couples in retirement. *J. Gerontol.*, 1961, *16*, 267–271.

Maddox, G. L. Persistence of life style among the elderly: A longitudinal study of patterns of social activity in relation to life satisfaction. In B. L. Neugarten (Ed.), *Middle age and aging: A reader in social psychology.* Chicago: University of Chicago Press, 1968.

McKee, J. B. *Introduction to sociology.* New York: Holt, Rinehart & Winston, Inc., 1969.

Merton, R. K. *Social theory and social structure.* Glencoe: The Free Press, 1957.

Neugarten, B. L. (Ed.) *Middle age and aging: A reader in social psychology.* Chicago: University of Chicago Press, 1968.

Neugarten, B. L., Havighurst, R. J., and Tobin, S. S. The measurement of life satisfaction. *J. Gerontol.*, 1961, *16*, 134–143.

Orbach, H. L. Social values and the institutionalization of retirement. In R. H. Tibbitts (Ed.), *Processes of aging.* Vol. II. New York: Atherton Press, 1963.

Orbach, H. L., and Shaw, D. M. Social participation and the role of the aging. *Geriatrics,* 1957, *12*, 241–246.

Peck, R. Psychological developments in the second half of life. In J. E. Anderson (Ed.), *Psychological aspects of aging.* Washington, D.C.: American Psychological Association, 1956.

Preston, C. E. Self-reporting among older retired and non-retired subjects. *J. Gerontol.*, 1967, *22*, 415–420.

Rosow, I. *Social integration of the aged.* New York: The Free Press, 1967.

Sheldon, H. *The older population of the United States.* New York: John Wiley & Sons, Inc., 1958.

Streib, G. F., and Schneider, S. J. *Retirement in American society: Impact and process.* Ithaca: Cornell University Press, 1971.

Thompson, W. E. Pre-retirement anticipation and adjustment in retirement. *J. Soc. Issues,* 1958, *2*, 35–63.

Thompson, W. E., and Streib, G. F. Personal and social adjustment in retirement. In W. Donahue and C. Tibbitts (Eds.), *The new frontiers of aging.* Ann Arbor: University of Michigan Press, 1957.

Zborowski, M., and Eyde, L. D. Aging and social participation. *J. Gerontol.*, 1962, *17*, 424–430.

Chapter 7

Adams, D. L. Correlates of satisfaction among the elderly. *Gerontologist,* 1971, *2*, 64–68.

Blumer, H. *Symbolic interactionism.* Englewood Cliffs: Prentice-Hall, Inc., 1969.

Kelley, H.: Two functions of reference groups. In H. Hyman and E. Singer (Eds.), *Readings in reference group theory and research.* New York: The Free Press, 1968.

McTavish, D. G. Perceptions of old people: A review of research methodologies and findings. *Gerontologist,* 1971, *2,* 90–101.

Meier, D. and Bell, W. Anomia and the achievement of life goals. *Amer. Sociol. Rev.,* 1959, *24,* 189–202.

Merton, R. Social structure and anomie. In Merton, R. (Ed.), *Social theory and social structure.* Glencoe: The Free Press, 1957.

Neugarten, B. Adaptation and the life cycle. *J. Geriatric Psychiatry,* Spring, 1970.

Neugarten, B., Havighurst, R., and Tobin, S. The measurement of life satisfaction. *J. Gerontol.,* 1961, *16,* 135–143.

Palmore, E., and Whittington, F. Trends in the relative status of the aged. *Soc. Forces,* 1971, *50,* 84–91.

Peters, G. Self-conception of the aged, age identification, and aging. *Gerontologist,* 1971, *11,* 69–73.

Riley, M. W., and Foner, A. *Aging and society.* New York: Russell Sage Foundation, 1968.

Romeis, J., Albert, R., and Acuff, F. G. Reference group theory: A synthesizing concept for the disengagement and interactionist theories. *Intern. Rev. Sociol.,* 1971, *1,* 66–70.

Rose, A. M. The subculture of the aging: A framework for research in social gerontology. In A. Rose and W. Peterson (Ed.), *Older people and their social world.* Philadelphia: F. A. Davis Co., 1965.

Townsend, P. Isolation, desolation, and loneliness. In E. Shanas, P. Townsend, D. Wedderburn, H. Friis, P. Milhøj, and J. Stehourver (Eds.), *Old people in three industrial societies.* New York: Atherton Press, 1968.

Wood, V. Age-appropriate behavior for older persons. *Gerontologist,* 1971, *2,* 74–78.

Wood, V., Wylie, M., and Sheafor, B. An analysis of a short self-report measure of life satisfaction: correlation with rater judgments. *J. Gerontol.,* 1969, *24,* 465–469.

Chapter 8

Berardo, F. M. *Social adaptation to widowhood among a rural-urban aged population.* Washington Agricultural Experiment Station Bulletin 689.

Pullman: Washington State University, College of Agriculture, 1967.

Berardo, F. M. Widowhood status in the United States: Perspectives on a neglected aspect of the family life-cycle. *Family Coordinator,* 1968, *17,* 191–203.

Berardo, F. M. Survivorship and social isolation: The case of the aged widower. *Family Coordinator,* 1970, *19,* 11–25.

Blau, Z. S. Changes in status and age identification. *Amer. Sociol. Rev.,* 1956, *21,* 198–203.

Blau, Z. S. Structural constraints on friendship in old age. *Amer. Sociol. Rev.,* 1961, *26,* 429–439.

Bock, E. W., and Webber, I. L. Suicide among the elderly: Isolating widowhood and mitigating alternatives. *J. Marriage and Family,* 1972, *34,* 24–31.

Cicourel, A. V. *Method and measurement in sociology.* New York: The Free Press, 1964.

Clark, M., and Anderson, B. G. *Culture and aging.* Springfield: Charles C. Thomas, 1967.

Garfinkel, H. *Studies in ethnomethodology.* Englewood Cliffs: Prentice-Hall, Inc., 1967.

Gubrium, J. Marital desolation and the evaluation of everyday life in old age. *J. Marriage and Family,* 1974, *35,* 107–113.

Thomas, W. I. *On social organization and social personality.* M. Janowitz, Ed. Chicago: University of Chicago Press, 1966.

Townsend, P. *The family life of old people.* London: Routledge & Kegan Paul, 1957.

Townsend, P. Isolation, desolation, and loneliness. In Shanas, E., Townsend, P., Wedderburn, D., Friis, H., Milhøj, P., & Stehouwer, J. (Eds.), *Old people in three industrial societies.* New York: Atherton Press, 1968.

Tunstall, J. *Old and alone: A sociological study of old people.* London: Routledge & Kegan Paul, 1966

U.S. Bureau of the Census. *Census of population.* Vol. 1, part 1. Washington, D.C.: U.S. Government Printing Office, 1960.

Willmott, P., and Young, M. *Family and class in a London suburb.* London: Routledge & Kegan Paul, 1960.

Chapter 9

Atchley, R. C. Retirement and leisure participation: continuity or crisis? *Gerontologist,* 1971, *11,* 13–17.

Atchley, R. C. *The social forces in later life.* Belmont: Wadsworth Publishing Co., Inc., 1972.

Biddle, B. J., and Thomas, E. J. *Role theory*, part 10. New York: John Wiley & Sons, Inc., 1966.

Glaser, B. G., and Straus, A. *The discovery of grounded theory*. Chicago: Aldine Publishing Co., 1967.

Goffman, E. *Encounters*. Indianapolis: The Bobbs-Merrill Co., Inc., 1961.

Kohn, M. L., and Schooler, C. Occupational experience and psychological functioning: An assessment of reciprocal effects. *Amer. Sociol. Rev.*, 1973, *38*, 97–118.

Rosenberg, M. *Society and the adolescent self-image*. Princeton: Princeton University Press, 1965.

Rosenberg, M. *The logic of survey analysis*. New York: Basic Books, Inc., 1968.

Secord, P. F., and Backman, C. W. *Social psychology*, part 4. New York: McGraw-Hill Book Company, 1964.

Simpson, I. H., McKinney, J. C., and Back, K. W. (Eds.), *Social aspects of aging*, p. 78. Durham: Ducke University Press, 1966.

Streib, G. F., and Schneider, C. J. *Retirement in American society*. Ithaca: Cornell University Press, 1971.

Chapter 10

Barber, B. *Science and the social order*. Glencoe: The Free Press, 1952.

Benz, M. A study of the faculty and administrative staff who have retired from New York University, 1945–1956. *J. Educ. Sociol.* 1958, *32*, 282–293.

Breen, L. Z. The aging individual. In C. Tibbitts (Ed.), *Handbook of social gerontology*. Chicago: University of Chicago Press, 1960.

Cavan, R. S. Adjustment problems of the older woman. *Marriage and Family Living*, 1952, *14*, 16–18.

Cole, S., and Cole, J. R. Scientific output and recognition: A study in the operation of the reward system in science. *Amer. Sociol. Rev.* 1967, *32*, 377–390.

Cumming, E., and Henry, W. E. *Growing old: The process of disengagement*. New York: Basic Books, Inc., 1961.

Donahue, W., Orbach, H. L., and Pollak, O. Retirement: The emerging social pattern. In C. Tibbitts (Ed.), *Handbook of social gerontology*. Chicago: University of Chicago Press, 1960.

Eiduson, B. T. *Scientists: Their psychological world*. New York: Basic Books, Inc., 1962.

Fisher, M. B., and Birren, J. E. Age and strength. *J. Applied Psychol.* 1947, *31*, 490–497.

Havighurst, R. J. Flexibility and the social roles of the retired. *Amer. J. Sociol.* 1954, *59*, 309–311.

Hirsch, W. *Scientists in American society.* New York: Random House, Inc., 1968.

Linden, M. E., and Courtney, D. The human life cycle and its interruptions: A psychologic hypothesis. In A. Rose (Ed.), *Mental health and mental disorder.* New York: W. W. Norton & Company, 1955.

Lorge, I. The Thurstone attitude scales. *J. Soc. Psychol.* 1939, *10*, 199–208.

Merton, R. K. *Social theory and social structure.* (Rev. ed.) New York: The Free Press, 1957.

Parsons, T. Age and sex in the social structure of the United States. *Amer. Sociol. Rev.* 1942, *7*, 604–616.

Roe, A. Changes in scientific activities with age. *Science,* 1965, *150*, 313–318.

Rowe, A. R. Scientists in retirement. *J. Gerontol.* 1973, *28*, 345–350.

Rowe, A. R. The retirement of academic scientists. *J. Gerontol.* 1972, *27*, 113–118.

Storer, N. *The social system of science.* New York: Holt, Rinehart and Winston, Inc., 1966.

Taylor, L. *Occupational sociology.* New York: Oxford University Press, 1968.

Tibbitts, C. A sociological view of aging. *Proc. Amer. Philosoph. Soc.,* 1954, *98*, 144–148.

Tibbitts, C., and Sheldon, H. D. A philosophy of aging. *Ann. Amer. Acad. Polit. Soc. Sci.,* 1952, *279*, 1–10.

Weber, M. Science as a vocation. In H. H. Gerth and C. W. Mills (Eds.), *From Max Weber.* New York: Oxford University Press, 1946.

Chapter 11

Becker, H. S., and Carper, J. W. The development of identification with an occupation. *Amer. J. Sociol.* 1956, *61*, 289–298.

Beckman, R. O., Williams, C. D., and Fisher, G. Adjustment to life in later maturity. *Geriatrics,* 1958, *13*, 664.

Berwick, K. The "senior citizen" in America: A study in unplanned obsolescence. *Gerontologist,* 1967, *7*, 257–260.

Blood, R. O., and Wolfe, D. W. *Husbands and wives.* New York: The Free Press, 1961.

Burgess, E. W. Aging in Western culture. In E. W. Burgess (Ed.), *Aging in Western societies,* pp. 3–28. Chicago: University of Chicago Press, 1960.

Cumming, E., and Henry, W. E. *Growing old.* New York: Basic Books, Inc., 1961.

Donahue, W. Introduction to part three: Psychopathology of aging. In R. H. Williams, C. Tibbitts, and W. Donahue (Eds.), *Processes of aging.* Vol. I, pp. 375–382. New York: Atherton Press, 1963.

Drake, J. T. *The aged in American society.* New York: The Ronald Press Company, 1958.

Kuhn, M. H. Self-attitudes by age, sex, and professional training. *Sociol. Quart.,* 1960, *1,* 39–55.

Levin, S. Libido equilibrium. In N. E. Zinberg and I. Kaufman (Eds.) *Normal psychology of the aging process.* New York: International Universities Press, 1963.

Neugarten, B. L. *Biological aspects of aging.* Paper presented at a religion and science colloquy at Meadville Theological School, University of Chicago, March 5, 1963.

Palmore, E. B. Physical, mental, and social factors in predicting longevity. *Gerontologist,* 1969, *9,* 103–108.

Riley, M. W., and Foner, A. *Aging and society.* Vol. 1. *An inventory of research findings.* New York: Russell Sage Foundation, 1968.

United States Department of Health, Education, and Welfare, Administration on Aging. Facts on aging. Reprint from *Aging.* AOA Publication *126,* 1970.

United States Senate Special Committee on Aging. *Economics of aging: Toward a full share in abundance.* Part 9. *Employment aspects.* Hearings before the subcommittee on employment and retirement income, December 18–19, 1969. Washington: United States Government Printing Office, 1970.

White House Conference on Aging. *Background paper on research in gerontology and social sciences.* Washington: United States Government Printing Office, 1960.

Chapter 12

Adams, B. Structural factors affecting parental aid to married children. *J. Marriage and Family,* 1964, *26,* 327–331.

Adams, B. *Kinship in an urban setting.* Chicago: Markham, 1968.

Adams, B. Isolation, function, and beyond: American kinship in the 1960's. *J. Marriage and Family,* 1970, *32,* 575–597.

Aldous, J. The consequences of intergenerational continuity. *J. Marriage and Family,* 1965, *27,* 462–468.

Aldous, J., and Hill, R. Social cohesion, lineage type, and intergenerational transmission. *Soc. Forces,* 1965, *43,* 471–482.

Bengtson, V. The generation gap: A review and typology of socialpsychological perspectives. *Youth and Society,* 1970, *2,* 7–32.

Bengtson, V. Inter-age differences in perception and the generation gap. *Gerontologist,* 1971, *11,* 85–90.

Bengtson, V. L., Furlong, M. J., and Laufer, R. S. The problem of generations: Time, aging, and the continuity of social structure. *J. Soc. Issues,* 1974, *30,* (2), 116–143.

Bengtson, V. L., and Kuypers, J. A. Generational differences and the "developmental stake." *Aging and Human Development,* 1970, *2,* 249–260.

Bengtson, V. L., and Black, K. D. Inter-generational relations and continuities in socialization. In P. Baltes and W. Schaie (Eds.), *Life-span developmental psychology: Personality and socialization.* New York: Academic Press, Inc., 1973.

Black, K. D., and Bengtson, V. L. *The measurement of solidarity: An intergenerational analysis.* Paper presented at the annual meeting of the American Psychological Association, Montreal, Canada, 1973.

Blau, P. M. *Exchange and power in social life.* New York: John Wiley & Sons, Inc., 1963.

Blenkner, M. Social work and family relationships in later life with some thoughts on filial maturity. In E. Shanas and G. F. Streib, (Eds.), *Social structure and the family: Generational relations.* Englewood Cliffs: Prentice-Hall, Inc., 1965.

Borke, H. Continuity and change in the transmission of adaptive patterns over two generations. *Marriage and Family Living,* 1963, *25,* 294–299.

Bott, E. *Family and social network.* London: Tavistock Publications Ltd., 1957.

Brown, R. G. Family structure and social isolation of older persons. *J. Gerontol.,* 1960, *15,* 170–174.

Bunzel, H. Note on the history of a concept—Gerontophobia. *Gerontology,* 1972, *12,* 116–117.

Butler, R. N. Age-ism: Another form of bigotry. *Gerontologist,* 1969, *9,* 243–246.

Campisi, P. Ethnic family patterns: The Italian family in the United States. *Amer. J. Sociol.,* 1948, *53,* 443–449.

Clark, M. The anthropology of aging. *Gerontologist,* 1967, *7,* 48–64.

Davis, K. The sociology of parent-youth conflict. *Amer. Sociol. Rev.,* 1940, *5,* 523–535.

Deutsch, M., and Krauss, R. M. *Theories in social psychology.* New York: Basic Books, Inc., 1965.

Friedenberg, E. Current patterns of generational conflict. *J. Soc. Issues,* 1969, *25,* 21–38.

Gans, H. J. *The urban villagers: Group and class life of Italian-Americans.* New York: The Free Press, 1962.

Gibson, G., and Ludwig, E. Family structure in a disabled population. *J. Marriage and Family,* 1968, *30,* 54–63.

Gouldner, A. Reciprocity and autonomy in functional theory. *Amer. Sociol. Rev.,* 1960, *24,* 146–173.

Gubrium, J. F. Apprehensions of coping incompetence and responses to fear in old age. *Intern. J. Aging and Human Development,* 1973, *4,* 111–125.

Heider, F. *The psychology of interpersonal relations.* New York: John Wiley & Sons, Inc., 1958.

Hill, R., Foote, N., Aldous, J., Carlson, R., and MacDonald, R. *Family development in three generations.* Cambridge: Schenkman Publishing Co., Inc., 1970a.

Hill, R. The three-generation research design: Method for studying family and social change. In R. Hill and R. Konig (Eds.), *Families in east and west: Socialization process and kinship ties.* Paris: Moulton, 1970b.

Haddad, A. *Family solidarity and mental health in Lebanon.* Unpublished doctoral dissertation, University of Southern California, 1971.

Hollingshead, A. B. Class differences in family stability. *Annals,* 1950, *272,* 39–46.

Homans, G. C. *The human group.* New York: Harcourt Brace and Company, 1950.

Homans, G. C. *Human behavior: Its elementary forms.* New York: Harcourt, Brace and Company, 1961.

Jennings, M. *The variable nature of generational conflict.* Paper presented at the International Political Science Association Congress, Montreal, August, 1973.

Jennings, M., and Nimei, R. The transmission of political values from parent to child. *Amer. Political Sci. Rev.,* 1968, *42,* 169–184.

Kaldoun, I. *The muqaddinah: An introduction to history.* Translated by F. Rosenthal. New York: Pantheon Books, Inc., 1958.

Kalish, R. The old and the new as generation gap allies. *Gerontologist,* 1969, *9,* 83–89.

Kandel, D., and Lesser, G. *Youth in two worlds.* San Francisco: Jossey-Bass, 1972.

Kerckhoff, A. C. Nuclear and extended family relationships: Normative and behavioral analysis. In E. Shanas and G. Streib (Eds.), *Social structure and the family: Generational relations.* Englewood Cliffs: Prentice-Hall, Inc., 1965.

Komarovsky, M. *Blue-collar marriage.* New York: Random House, Inc., 1964.

Laumann, E. *Prestige and association in an urban community.* New York: The Bobbs-Merrill Co., Inc., 1966.

Litwak, E. Extended kin relations in an industrial democratic society. In E. Shanas and G. Streib (Eds.), *Social structure and the family: Generational relations.* Englewood Cliffs: Prentice-Hall, Inc., 1965.

Litwak, E., and Szelenyi, I. Primary group structures and their functions: Kin, neighbors, and friends. *Amer. Sociol. Rev.,* 1969, *34,* 465–481.

Mead, M. *Culture and commitment. A study of the generation gap.* Published for The American Museum of Natural History. Garden City: Natural History Press, Doubleday and Company, Inc., 1970.

Merton, R. K. *Social theory and social structure.* New York: The Free Press, 1957.

Muir, D. E., and Weinstein, E. A. The social debt: An investigation of lower-class and middle-class norms of social obligation. *Amer. Sociol. Rev.,* 1962, *27,* 532.

Neugarten, B. Old and young in modern societies. *Amer. Behavioral Scientist,* 1970, *14,* 13–24.

Nisbet, R. A. *The social bond.* New York: Alfred A. Knopf, Inc., 1970.

Nye, F., and Rushing, W. Toward family measurement research. In J. Hadden and E. Borgatta (Eds.), *Marriage and family.* Itasca: F. E. Peacock, Publishers, Inc., 1969.

Parsons, T. The normal American family. In M. Sussman (Ed.), *Sourcebook in marriage and the family.* Boston: Houghton Mifflin Company, 1968.

Reiss, P. J. Extended kinship system: Correlates of and attitudes to frequency of interaction. *Marriage and Family Living,* 1962, *24,* 333–339.

Riley, M. W., and Foner, A., Moore, M. E., Hess, B., and Roth, *Aging and society.* Vol. 1. New York: The Russell Sage Foundation, 1968.

Riley, M. W., Johnson, A., and Foner, A. *Aging and society: A sociology of age stratification.* New York: Russell Sage Foundation, 1972.

Robins, A. J. Family relations of the aging in three-generation households. In C. Tibbitts and Wilma Donahue (Eds.), *Aging in today's society,* Englewood Cliffs: Prentice-Hall, Inc., 1962.

Robins, L. N., and Tomanec, M. Closeness to blood relatives outside the immediate family. *Marriage and Family Living,* 1962, *24,* 340–346.

Senior, C. Research on the Puerto Rican family in the United States. *Marriage and Family Living,* 1957, *19,* 284–291.

Shenas, E., Townsend, P., Wedderburn, D., Friis, H., Milhouj, P., and Stehower, J. *Older people in three industrial societies.* New York: Atherton Press, 1968.

Smelser, N. *Theory of collective behavior.* Glencoe: Free Press, 1962.

Smelser, N. (Ed.), *Sociology.* New York: John Wiley & Sons, Inc., 1967.

Streib, G. F. Intergenerational relations: Perspectives of the two generations on the older parent. *J. Marriage and Family*, 1965, *27*, 469–476.

Streib, G. F. Relations between older family members and younger generations. *Family coordinator*, 1971, *20*, 121–132.

Sussman, M. Relationships of adult children with their parents in the United States. In E. Shanas and G. Streib (Eds.), *Social structure and the family: Generational relations*. Englewood Cliffs: Prentice-Hall, Inc., 1965.

Sussman, M., and Burchinal, L. Family kin network: Unheralded structure in current conceptualizations of family functioning. *Marriage and Family Living*, 1962, *24*, 231–240.

Sweetser, D. A. Assymetry in intergenerational family relationships. *Soc. Forces*, 1963, *41*, 346–354.

Thibaut, J., and Kelley, H. *The social psychology of groups*. New York: John Wiley & Sons, Inc., 1967.

Thomas, L. E. Studying the generation gap: The case of the blind men and the elephant. Paper presented at the Annual Meeting of The National Council on Family Relations, Estes Park, Colorado, 1971b.

Thomas, L. E. Political attitude congruence between politically active parents and college-age children. *J. Marriage and Family*, 1971, *33*, 375–386.

Time. *The Command Generation*. Cover story, June 24, 1967.

Troll, L. E. The generation gap: Conceptual models. *Aging and Human Development*, 1970, *1*, 199–218.

Troll, L. E. The family of later life: A decade review. *J. Marriage and Family*, 1971, *33*, 263–290.

Zetterberg, H. *On theory and verification in sociology*. Totowa: The Bedminster Press, Inc., 1965.

Chapter 13

Fortes, M. W. *Kinship and the social order*. Chicago: University of Chicago Press, 1969.

Hamer, J. H. Aging in a gerontocratic society: The Sidamo of southwest Ethiopia. In D. A. Cowgill (Ed.), *Aging and modernization*. New York: Appleton-Century Crofts, 1972.

Hamer, J. H. Dispute settlement and sanctity: An Ethiopian example. *Anthropol. Quart.*, 1972, *45*, 232–247.

Hamer, J. H. Sidamo generational class cycles: A political gerontocracy. *Africa*, 1970, *XL*, 50–70.

Hamer, J. H. Voluntary associations as structures of change among the Sidamo of southwestern Ethiopia. *Anthropol. Quart.*, 1967, *40*, 73–91.

Chapter 14

Abraham, K. Some remarks on the role of grandparents in the psychology of neurosis. In H. C. Abraham (Ed.), *Selected papers and essays in psychoanalysis.* Vol. 2. New York: Basic Books, Inc., 1955.

Adams, B. N. *Kinship in an urban setting.* Chicago: Markham Publishing Co., 1968.

Albrecht, R. The parental responsibilities of grandparents. *Marriage and Family Living,* 1954, *XVI* (no. 3), 201–204.

Aldous, J. The consequences of intergenerational continuity. *J. Marriage and Family,* 1965, *27,* 462–468.

Aldous, J., Hill, R. Social cohesion, lineage type, and intergenerational transmission. *Soc. Forces,* 1965, *43,* 471–482.

Atchley, R. C. *The social forces in later life.* Belmont: Wadsworth Publishing Co., Inc., 1972.

Bekker, L. D., and Taylor, C. Attitudes toward the aged in a multigenerational sample. *J. Gerontol.,* 1966, *21* (1), 115–118.

Bell, C. *Middle-class families.* London: Routledge & Kegan Paul, 1968.

Bernard, J. *Marriage and family among Negroes.* Englewood Cliffs: Prentice-Hall, Inc., 1966.

Blau, Z. S. *Old age in a changing society.* New York: Franklin Watts, Inc., 1973.

Bordon, B. The role of grandparents in children's behavior problems. *Smith Coll. Studies in Social Work* 1946, *17,* 115–116.

Borke, H. Continuity and change in the transmission of adaptive patterns over two generations. *Marriage and Family Living,* 1963, *25,* 294–297.

Borke, H. A family over three generations: The transmission of interacting and relating patterns. *J. Marriage and Family,* 1967, *29*(4): 639–655.

Boyd, R. The emerging social roles of the four-generation family. In C. G. Oakes (Ed.), *Our elderly Americans: Challenge and response.* Spartanburg: Converse College, 1967.

Boyd, R. The valued grandparent: A changing social role. In W. Donahue, J. Kornbluh, and L. Power (Eds.), *Living in the multigeneration family.* Ann Arbor: Institute of Gerontology, University of Michigan, 1969.

Clark, M. and Anderson, B. G. *Culture and aging.* Springfield: Charles C. Thomas, 1967.

Cumming, E., and Henry, W. E. *Growing old: The process of disengagement.* New York: Basic Books, Inc., 1961.

Dotson, F. Patterns of voluntary association among urban working class families. *Amer. Sociol. Rev.*, *1951, 16, 689–693.*

Faris, R. Interaction of generations and family stability. *Amer. Sociol. Rev.*, 1947, *12,* 159–164.

Fengler, A. P., Wood, V. Continuity between the generations: Differential influence of mothers and fathers. *Youth & Society,* 1973, *4,* 359–372.

Fisher, S. and Mendell, D. The communication of neurotic patterns over two and three generations. *Psychiatry,* 1956, *10,* 41–46.

Frazier, E. F. *The Negro family in the United States.* Chicago: University of Chicago Press, 1939.

Fried, E. G., and Stern, K. The situation of the aged within the family. *Amer. J. Orthopsychiatry,* 1948, *18,* 31–54.

Gibson, G. Kin family network: Overheralded structure in past conceptualizations of family functioning. *J. Marriage and Family,* 1972, *34,* 13–23.

Gilford, R. and Black, D. *The grandchild-grandparent dyad. Ritual or relationship?* Paper presented at the 25th annual meeting of the Gerontological Society, San Juan, Puerto Rico, December, 1972.

Glick, P. C. The life cycle of the family. *Marriage and Family Living,* 1955, *17,* 3–9.

Hader, M. The importance of grandparents in family life. *Family Process,* 1965, *4,* 228–240.

Hays, W. C., and Mindell, C. H. Extended kinship relations in black and white families. *J. Marriage and Family,* 1973, *35,* 51–57.

Hill, R. *Families under stress.* New York: Harper & Brothers, Inc., 1949.

Hill, R. Decision making and the family life cycle. In E. Shanas and G. F. Streib (Eds.), *Social structure and the family: Generational relations.* Englewood Cliffs: Prentice-Hall, Inc., 1965.

Hill, R, Foote, N., Aldous, J., Carlson, R., and McDonald, R. *Family development in three generations.* Cambridge: Schenkman Publishing Co., Inc., 1970.

Kahana, E., and Coe, R. M. Perceptions of grandparenthood by community and institutionalized aged. *Proc. 77th Ann. Convention Amer. Psychol. Assoc.,* 1969, *4,* 735–736.

Kahana, E. Grandparenthood from the perspective of the developing grandchild. *Developmental Psychol.,* 1970, *3,* 98–105.

Kahana, E., and Kahana, B. Theoretical and research perspectives on grandparenthood. *Aging and Human Development,* 1971, *2,*(4): 261–268.

Kalish, R., and Johnson, A. I. Value similarities and differences in three generations of women. *J. Marriage and Family,* 1972, *34,* 49–54.

Kennedy, P., and Pfeifer, J. *Parents as intergenerational mediators: A conceptual framework and preliminary interview schedule for studying the three-generation family.* Unpublished M.S.S.W. thesis. Madison: University of Wisconsin, 1973.

Lajewski, H. C. Working mothers and their arrangements for the care of their children. *Soc. Security Bull.* August, 1959.

Litwak, E. Geographic mobility and extended family cohesion. *Amer. Sociol. Rev.,* 1960, *25,* 385–394.

Looft, W. R. Perceptions across the life span of important informational sources for children and adolescents. *J. Psychol.,* 1971, *78,* 207–216.

Lopata, H. Z. *Widowhood in an American city.* Cambridge: Schenkman Publishing Co., Inc., 1973.

Mead, G. H. *Mind, self and society.* Chicago: University of Chicago Press, 1934.

Messer, M. Age grouping and the family status of the elderly. *Sociol. Social Res.,* 1968, *52,* 271–279.

Neugarten, B., and Weinstein, K. The changing American grandparent. *J. Marriage and Family,* 1964, *26,* 199–204.

Parsons, T. The kinship system of the contemporary United States. *Amer. Anthropol.,* 1943, *XLV,* 32–38.

Parsons, T. and Shils, E. A. (Eds.). *Toward a general theory of action.* Cambridge: Harvard University Press, 1951.

Radcliffe-Brown, A. R. *Structure and function in primitive society.* London: Cohen and West, 1952.

Rappaport, E. A. The grandparent syndrome. *Psychoanalytic Quart.,* 1958, *27,* 518–538.

Riley, M. W., Foner, A., Hess, B., and Toby, M. Socialization for the middle and later years. In D. Goslin (Ed.), *Handbook of socialization theory and research.* Chicago: Rand-McNally Co., 1969.

Robertson, J. *Grandparenthood: A study of role conceptions of grandmothers.* Unpublished doctoral thesis. Madison: University of Wisconsin, 1971.

Robertson, J. The myth of the meddlesome grandmother. Unpublished paper. Madison: University of Wisconsin, 1973.

Robertson, J., and Wood, V. *Activity patterns of older adults in the community.* Paper presented at 24th Annual Meeting of the Gerontological Society, Houston, October, 1971.

Robertson, J., and Wood, V. *Grandparenthood: A theoretical perspective.* Unpublished paper. Madison, University of Wisconsin, 1973.

Robertson, J., and Wood, V. *Grandparenthood: A study of role conceptions.* Paper presented at the 23rd Annual Meeting of the Gerontological Society, Toronto, October, 1970.

Robins, L. N., and Tomanec, M. Closeness to blood relatives outside the immediate family. *Marriage and Family Living,* 1962, *24,* 340–346.

Rosenberg, G. S. *The worker grows old.* San Francisco: Jossey-Bass, Inc. 1970.

Rosow, I. *Social integration of the aged.* New York: The Free Press, 1967.

Saltz, R. Evaluation of a foster grandparent program. In A. Kadushin (Ed.), *Child welfare services: A sourcebook.* New York: The Macmillan Company, 1970.

Schorr, A. *Filial responsibility in the modern American family.* Washington: United States Department of Health, Education and Welfare, 1960.

Shanas, E. *The health of older people.* Cambridge: Harvard University Press, 1962.

Shanas, E. Family help patterns and social class in three countries. *J. Marriage and Family,* 1967, *29*(2), 257–266.

Shanas, E., Townsend, P., Wedderburn, D., Friis, H., Milhøj, P., and Stehower, J. J. *Old people in three industrial societies.* New York: Atherton Press, 1968.

Sharp, H., and Axelrod, M. Mutual aid among relatives in an urban population. In R. Freedman et al. (Eds.), *Principles of sociology,* pp. 433–439. New York: Holt, Rinehart & Winston, Inc., 1956.

Sheldon, J. H. Old age problems in the family. *Milbank Mem. Fund Quart.,* April, 1959.

Streib, G. F., and Thompson, W. E. Adjustment in retirement. *J. Social Issues,* 1958, *XIV*(no. 2).

Sussman, M. B. The help pattern in the middle-class family. *Amer. Sociol. Rev.,* 1953, *18*, 22–28.

Sussman, M. B. Family continuity: Selective factors which affect relationships between families at generational levels. *Marriage and Family Living,* 1954, *16*, 112–120.

Sussman, M. B. The isolated nuclear family: Fact or fiction. *Social Problems,* 1959, *6*, 333–340.

Sussman, M. B. Kin family network: Unheralded structure in current conceptualizations of family functioning. *Marriage and Family Living,* 1962, *24*, 231–240.

Sussman, M. B. Relationships of adult children with their parents in the United States. In E. Shanas and G. F. Streib (Eds.), *Social structure and the family: Generational relations.* Englewood Cliffs: Prentice-Hall, Inc., 1965.

Sussman, M. B., and Burchinal, L. Parental aid to married children: Implications for family functioning. *Marriage and Family Living,* 1962, *24*, 320–332.

Townsend, P. *The family life of old people.* London: Routledge & Kegan Paul, 1957.

Townsend, P. Postscript 1963: Moving towards a general theory of family structure. In *The Family life of old people,* pp. 235–255. Baltimore: Penguin Books, 1963.

Townsend, P. The emergence of the four-generation family in industrial society. In *Proceedings of the 7th International Congress of Gerontology,* Vienna, 1966. Vienna, Verlag der Wiener Medizinischen Akademic, 1966.

Troll, L. The family of later life: A decade review. *J. Marriage and Family,* 1971, *33,* 263–290.

Troll, L., Neugarten, B., and Kraines, R. Similarities on values and other personality characteristics in college students and their parents. *Merrill-Palmer Quart.,* 1969, *15,* 323–337.

Vollmer, H. The grandmother: A problem in child rearing. *Amer. J. Orthopsychiatry,* 1937, *7,* 378–382.

Von Hentig, H. The sociological function of the grandmother. *Social Forces,* 1945–46, *24,* 389–392.

Wood, V., Wylie, M., and Shaefor, B. An analysis of a short self-report measure of life satisfaction: Correlation with rater judgments. *J. Gerontol.,* 1969, *24,* 465–469.

Young, M. The role of the extended family in a disaster. *Human Relations,* 1954, *7,* 383–391.

Young, M. and Willmott, P. *Kinship and family in East London.* Glencoe: The Free Press, 1957.

Chapter 15

Andrews, F., Morgan, J., and Sonquist, J. *Multiple classification analysis: A report on a computer program for multiple regression using categorical predictors.* Ann Arbor: University of Michigan Institute for Social Research, 1967.

Baer, G. *Population and society in the Arab East.* New York: Praeger Publishers, Inc., 1964.

Bar Yosef, R., and Shelach, I. E. The position of women in Israel. In S. N. Eisenstadt, R. Bar Yosef, and C. Adler (Eds.), *Integration and development in Israel.* New York: Praeger Publishers, Inc., 1970.

Bastuni, R. The Arab Israelis. In M. Curtis and M. Chertoff (Eds.), *Israel: Social structure and change.* New Brunswick: Transaction Books, 1973.

Berardo, F. Widowhood status in the United States: Perspectives on a neglected aspect of the family life cycle. *Family Coordinator,* 1968, *17,* 191–203.

Chevan, A. and Korson, J. H. The widowed who live alone: An examination of social and demographic factors. *Soc. Forces,* 1972, *51,* 45–53.

Goode, W. J. *World revolution and family patterns.* New York: The Free Press, 1963.

Israeli Central Bureau of Statistics. *Procedures and definitions.* Jerusalem: Population and Housing Census (1961); 1965.

Jewish Encyclopedia. Vol. XII. New York: Funk & Wagnalls Co., Inc., 1905.

The Koran. Translated by N. J. Dawood. London: Penguin Books, 1956.

Korson, J. H. Residential propinquity as a factor in mate selection in an urban Muslim society. *J. Marriage and Family,* 1968, *30,* 518–527.

Lopata, H. Z. *Widowhood in an American city.* Cambridge: Schenkman Publishing Co., Inc., 1973.

Rosenfeld, H. An analysis of marriage and marriage statistics for a Moslem and Christian Arab Village. *Internat. Arch. Ethnography,* 1958, *II,* 48.

Troll, L. E. The family in later life: A decade review. *J. Marriage and Family,* 1971, *33,* 263–290.

Wakil, P. Explorations into the kin-networks of the Punjabi society: A preliminary statement. *J. Marriage and Family,* 1970, *32*(4), 700–707.

INDEX

359